THESE Beautiful PEOPLE

REAL STORIES.
RELENTLESS HOPE.

BY TWILA ERB

FriesenPress

Suite 300 - 990 Fort St
Victoria, BC, V8V 3K2
Canada

www.friesenpress.com

Scripture quotations are from the New Living Translation, unless stated otherwise.

This book is intended for mature audiences due to occasional violence, drug use, and sexual content. Parental discretion is advised.

Books can be purchased in bulk for educational, commercial, promotional, and fundraising uses. For more information, contact Twila Erb.
Phone: +1 (519) 880-4543
Email: **thesebeautifulpeople@gmail.com**
Website: **http://thesebeautifulpeople.com**
Instagram and Facebook: **@thesebeautifulpeoplebook**

Cover design: Sherrie Martin   **https://www.smart-inkdesign.com**
Interior design: Sherrie Martin   **https://www.smart-inkdesign.com**
Logo design: Karrie Miller   **http://www.schlabachprinters.com**

All photos were taken by the author or these beautiful people themselves, unless stated otherwise.

Story photos: Brad Baker   **https://www.facebook.com/BradbakerPhotograhy/**
Arm Up Media   **https://www.facebook.com/armupmedia/**
RGfondo   **www.kwetudesign.com**
Author photos: Amberly Freeman   **http://www.unfrozenphotography.com**
https://www.facebook.com/unfrozenphotography/

Editor: Alexandra Hunter   **https://alexandrahunterediting.ca**

ISBN
978-1-5255-2877-4 (Hardcover)
978-1-5255-2878-1 (Paperback)
978-1-5255-2879-8 (eBook)

1. YOUNG ADULT NONFICTION, PEOPLE & PLACES, AFRICA

Distributed to the trade by The Ingram Book Company

This book is dedicated to
you, beautiful.

And to coffee.

Because without both,
this book would have been
pointless and probably
unfinished.

Itinerary

THE HANDS

Whenever I'm asked to introduce myself, I pause.

I don't have a cut-and-dried description of what I do, no degrees or best-selling titles to wow you with.

But what I do have is a story. A beautiful, complicated, messy story that's still being written.

Several years ago I wouldn't have said that.

I had experienced so much in life that didn't make sense, but slowly I learned it was OK to not be OK. We've all been broken, no exceptions.

In 2011 I returned from Botswana, Africa, and I was struggling being at home. After almost a year, God nudged my heart. I started planning and preparing for my second trip. What started as a six-month discipleship school in Uganda turned into a two-year adventure through 10 countries in East and Southern Africa.

When I asked God what I would be doing, He replied, "You don't get to know that. You just take your story and yourself and do whatever I put on your heart."

Wait—my story? *What* story?

≪ Photograph from Unfrozen Photography

THE HANDS

THESE BEAUTIFUL PEOPLE

From that moment, God impressed on me the power of stories as one of our greatest weapons. They have the ability to tear down and to build up. To destroy the lie that says, "No one understands," and to plant the truth that whispers, "You are never ever alone."

Sharing your own story is the best way to learn this. So I did. Grudgingly.

Every secret, every heartache, every fear.

My shaking fingers gripped the edges of the tear-stained paper as I shared for the first time with my peers.

That's the moment I finally understood. Something happens when you're the one in the crowd listening, or the one baring your soul, and someone looks at you and says, "Me too."

Suddenly you're not alone.
Suddenly you're not isolated.
Suddenly there's hope for healing.

Not every story you're about to read is a gospel truth to follow. But within every story is a point that connects us and draws us toward the one *perfect* example: the Way, the Truth, and Author of life.

By now I've shared my story so many times it's like second nature. I've shared in open-air assembly halls packed with hundreds of high school students. In living rooms filled with teenage mothers. At churches, conferences, and correctional centres. On coffee dates with friends.

This is my passion: Using words and stories to break down barriers and destroy stereotypes. Tearing down the walls that keep us from each other. Setting the captives free from their prisons of silence.

But I would never have learned if I hadn't been willing to take the hard road. To take those painful first steps toward the greater thing for which I was called.

Our pain becomes our purpose.
Our greatest fears, our deepest joy.

––––––––

Here's a taste of who I am:

I work in construction and love it!
I sing and dance when people aren't watching.
I'd rather be outside and barefoot.
Laughter is my favourite, and writing and running help me process things.
Coffee is a necessity and it's possible I'm addicted to bacon.
I make lists just so I can stroke them off.
Cooking and cleaning aren't my thing, but eating and organizing are.
I'm generally clumsy, fairly obnoxious, and hopelessly awkward.
I'm an extroverted introvert, which is terribly confusing, and I struggle with technology.
Sometimes I'm awesome and sometimes I couldn't find awesome if it landed on my nose.

But I'm willing to bet I'm not so different from you. And that's the point.

No letters behind your name? No problem. Clumsy, broke, and more than a little awkward? Excellent. Believe it or not, you were never meant to be perfect. You were meant to be yourself.

You just need to be willing and ready.
You just need to hear the call and be brave enough to go.

I know this was supposed to be a "meet the author" kind of thing, but I'm not the author of these stories. Not really. I'm just the one who had the honour of writing them down.

He's the One you should meet. The author and creator of *all* our stories. He's the One who takes clumsy and crazy and nowhere near perfect and makes it work. The One who looks at this hot mess square in the eyes and says, "You. Yeah, you. I want to use all that."

He's the real deal.

And while it's an honour to meet you, I am simply the hands.

Want to know more about my story?
Read my blog: https://putdownthemask.wordpress.com/?s=the+big+picture

THE HANDS

THESE BEAUTIFUL PEOPLE

THE HEART

"How was Africa?"

The most frequently asked question upon my homecoming, and the most difficult to answer.

How does one distill two years, 10 countries, and countless experiences into one sentence? How does one express the brilliance of each sunrise, the sounds and smells of each city street, into words? How does one sum up a thousand life lessons, a million tears, and faces beyond number?

But when people ask me for my favourite part… Ah, now that's easy. Don't even have to think twice.

The people.

Sure, the food bursts with flavour, the music and dances with life, the streets with history. And yeah, the languages, cultural nuances, wildlife, and scenery have taken my breath away more times than I can count.

But Africa's real beauty—her greatest treasure—is her people.

⩽ *Photograph from RGfondo*

THE HEART

THESE BEAUTIFUL PEOPLE

The relationships I made have changed me forever.

Stories challenge our perspective, open our mind, and shape the way we see the world and the people around us. The problem? Many of us operate out of a single story—one experience, encounter, or belief—through which we view everything. This isn't wrong— it's merely incomplete. Stories have equal potential for hope and for harm, and the power of a single story lies within that tension.

Chimamanda Adichie said in her TED talk "The Danger of a Single Story" (Adichie 2009), "How impressionable we are to a single story…The consequence of the single story is that it [often] robs people of dignity."

When we see the world through a single story, we come to conclusions that aren't exactly false, but aren't entirely true. How the media portrays Africa not only misrepresents what's happening on the ground, but also robs her people of dignity. This distortion promotes a stereotype of African countries as poor, helpless, disease-ridden, war-torn wastelands.

Although a heartbreaking reality in many parts, this is not a complete picture. This is just a single story, one that has been told for years, and one that is detrimental to the development of the places and people who are misrepresented.

As a result, the single story tells us that Africa is a continent without cars, paved roads, or technology. It paints a picture of people living in the bush, sleeping in trees, sporting animal skins, and playing with elephants and lions in their backyard. It supports a notion that Africa and her people are helpless, hopeless, and "less than."

Dear friends, nothing could be farther from the truth.

I don't negate or dismiss the dire conditions of many of the places I've seen, nor the struggle, hardship, and pain so many of my friends have lived through.

But I refuse to let that be my only story. I refuse to be satisfied with the single story that speaks only to what Africa has endured and not to who she is capable of becoming.

She is so much more than her headlines, and it only takes one story to begin restoring the narrative.

THE HEART

Every time you connect with someone, you add another story. By listening, you validate that person. By entering their pain and celebrating their joy, you restore dignity and repair your own worldview.

As I travelled from country to country, lived in people's homes, ate at their tables, laughed and cried and shared life with them, I realized something: while we're different in so many ways, we're even more the same.

Pain is universal. So is joy.

Deep inside each of us—regardless of age, sex, race, religion, or birthplace—is a desire to be heard, understood, known, and accepted.

Each of us has a chance at redemption.
Each of us has the opportunity to choose life.

We're all passing through something, painful or joyous. Some are climbing the mountain; some have been in the valley for years. No matter where we are on the journey, we're all on one.

But as long as we're breathing, the story isn't over.

This book was born from a place in my heart that identifies with the journey to healing. A place that acknowledges the bravery it takes to share your story.

The people you're about to meet are some of the bravest I know.

Most had never shared their story before, but they all made a choice.

Where they could have shrunk back in fear, they stepped forward in faith.
Where they could have given up, they pressed in with perseverance.
Where they could have run away, they moved forward with courage.

They chose to trust you with their stories. To trust the power of their words to heal, both themselves and you. To point you toward the real author of their stories, the giver of their relentless hope.

I hope you understand the heart behind this book.
I hope you're ready to embrace these beautiful people.

THE HEART

THESE BEAUTIFUL PEOPLE

UGANDA

Uganda was once ranked number 13 on Buzzfeed's list of the most beautiful countries on earth (2015).

I'm not surprised! Uganda is breathtaking.

That's all I could think when I stepped out of my guesthouse that first morning. Copper-coloured roofs speckled the lush, green hills against a bright, blue sky.

Unless you're caught for two hours under a leaky gas station roof in a torrential downpour during one of Uganda's two rainy seasons. On days like that, the colours all blend together, along with your mascara. But you never have to worry because after a few hours, or even a few minutes, it will look as if it had never rained.

The second thing I noticed was the hospitality. There are two reasons Uganda is proudly known as "the pearl of Africa": her many natural resources and her culture of hospitality.

I've tested this last quality and found it to be true. I've shown up at the last minute, I've scrambled for visas, I've been lost in the chaotic perma–rush hour that is Kampala, and people have been nothing but welcoming and helpful to this confused *mzungu* (an East African term for white foreigner). Whether you're in a busy market or crowded taxi, or dodging traffic jams on the back of a *boda boda* (dangerous motorcycle-style public transportation fondly known as "the fastest way from point A to point B, if you make it"), people will notice you, talk to you, or sell you something.

I know that when I go to Uganda at a moment's notice, I'll have a place to sleep, a place to eat, a place to call home. And my Ugandan hosts won't even think twice. There's no such thing as an inconvenience in Ugandan culture—there's always time. People have gone so far as to call Uganda the number one place to be a refugee today, and I believe it's because of this unguarded hospitality.

≤ *Downtown Kampala. Photograph from Arm Up Media*

UGANDA

THESE BEAUTIFUL PEOPLE

Also, there's an abundance of children at any given time or place. With 49.9 percent of her population under 15 years of age, Uganda is the second youngest country in the world. Average life expectancy is about 53 years, so only 2.1 percent of the more than 41.5 million population is older than 65 years. Uganda is slightly smaller in surface area than the state of Oregon, which has a population of 3.9 million. That's less than three times the population of Kampala, Uganda's capital. Only 3.8 percent of Ugandans are unemployed; however, the average monthly income is about 303,700 Ugandan shillings per month (about CAD$112.00) and 19.7 percent live below the poverty line. Uganda is ranked the world's most entrepreneurial country, with 28.1 percent owning or co-owning a business.

Luckily for me and my lack of language skills, English is widely spoken in Uganda. It's one of her national languages, the other being Luganda.

Uganda became independent on October 9, 1962. In 1971 Colonel Idi Amin deposed the president and began expelling Asian residents. He began torturing and killing anyone opposed to his self-proclaimed role as "President for Life." It's estimated that 300,000 people were killed under his dictatorship. In 1986 Yoweri Museveni became president, which he has remained to this day. He managed to clean up the mess left behind by Idi Amin and turn the country's economy around. Despite the aid flooding in from Western countries to support his self-sufficient, anti-corruption plan, Uganda remains one of the poorest countries in the world today.

But unthinkable things were still coming. From 1988 to 2006, 8,000 to 10,000 children were abducted in the night by Joseph Kony and the Lord's Resistance Army (LRA) and forced to become soldiers and sex slaves. More than 1.7 million people were displaced in northern Uganda and a new generation of Acholi people were born into fear and chaos. From 2006 to 2008, the government tried to hold peace talks but Kony wouldn't show up. In 2008, with no plan for peace, the government launched Operation Lightening Thunder. Kony found out and foiled the attack; in return, the LRA attacked villages in the Democratic Republic of Congo on December 24, 2008, killing 865 people and abducting another 160. The rebels sought a ceasefire in January 2009 after their bases were attacked.

Eleven months later, however, they re-enacted the Christmas massacres in the Congo, killing 321 people and abducting another 250. The outside world knew nothing of this until months later, mostly due to the Congo's rural location. By the time news of the massacre, widely known as KONY 2012, reached North American media, it was over and Kony was in hiding.

These and other events have caused a flood of refugees across Ugandan borders, making Uganda the world's most ethnically diverse country (2013). In 2016 Uganda welcomed nearly half a million refugees from South Sudan, not including Congo, Eritrea, Ethiopia, and Somalia, among others. This cultural diversity extends to her cuisine. Besides the staples of *matooke* (smashed green bananas cooked in banana leaves), grasshoppers, *chapatti* (flat dense pancake-shaped fried pastry), *rolex* (fried egg rolled in *chapatti*), purple porridge, and the best mangoes, pineapples, and meat on a stick you'll ever eat, she's home to some of the best Ethiopian and ethnic food I've ever tasted.

You'll also find sparkling new malls and high-end coffee shops and restaurants, which attract ex-pats and locals. On any given night of the week, you can hear live music at some of the coolest locations in Kampala.

Uganda hosts a diverse group of wildlife. Of the 880 mountain gorillas in the world, half are found here. Because Uganda boasts land and water safaris, you can encounter species like lions, zebras, buffalo, elephants, giraffes, leopards, cheetahs, hippos, crocodiles, and more. She's also home to 11 percent of the world's population of birds, including the crested crane. This bird adorns the national flag and is the namesake of Uganda's beloved football (soccer) team, the Uganda Cranes.

And they're beloved for a reason! The Cranes have taken the Council for East and Central Africa Football Associations (CECAFA) Cup 13 times. This cup is the oldest football tournament in all Africa. And when the lights come on at the stadium for a home game, it's a sea of yellow, red, and black support, and eardrum-bursting *vuvuzela* (a loud plastic horn) enthusiasm.

If you need a quiet getaway, you can visit the source of the Nile River or climb snow-covered Mount Rwenzori, the fourth highest mountain in Africa at 16,761 feet. Mind you, with the equator bisecting Uganda, that's most definitely the only snow you'll find!

Besides hospitality, Uganda also hosts a culture of laughter and fun. To the untrained ear, you might think a boisterous conversation in the local language is a heated argument, only to discover it was a series of jokes. If it's your birthday, bring a change of clothes because you *will* be doused with water all day in honour of your birth. And no one gets angry or upset. It's just fun.

Each region—North, South, East, West, and Central—has its own tribes and traditional dances. And Ugandans love to dance. I promise you, when "their song" comes on, they're drawn to their feet, unable to stop themselves. No party, gathering, or ordinary day is complete without dancing—with or without music.

ABAYITA ABABIRI
BAJJUKANYA.
UNITY IS STRENGTH.

— UGANDAN PROVERB

But Ugandans aren't limited to tradition: salsa is one of the country's most widely enjoyed dance forms.

Ugandans love their country and with good cause. In a world of media that only shows the Amins and Konys of Uganda, so many other achievements deserve airtime, like the movie *Queen of Katwe*. Released in 2016, it was directed and filmed in Uganda with mainly Ugandan actors.

Uganda is home to Watoto, an organization you'll hear a lot about in this book. What started as a church planted by a vibrant Canadian couple has turned into something more: the rescuing, raising, and restoring of thousands of vulnerable children and women who are growing up to change their nation.

Uganda is among the top 10 coffee growers in the world.

Caesarian sections were being performed in Uganda way before 1879, when R.W. Felkin observed the first successful operation performed by indigenous healers in Kahura.

Uganda is sitting on as many as 300 million tonnes of rare minerals, many of which have not been mined or refined.

Uganda is one of the few countries in Africa with her own car, the Kiira. The prototype was designed by students at Makerere University in 2011.

Uganda has dramatically reduced the rate of new infections through an incredibly successful HIV/AIDS health and education campaign.

A Ugandan developed the five-minute Ebola test kit. Misaki Weyengera's breakthrough is assisting in quicker diagnosis, leading to a reduced Ebola death rate.

Now go on, read these beautiful stories. Meet some of the beautiful people of Uganda.
I dare you not to fall in love with this breathtaking country.

≪ *Top: Muyenga, Kampala*
≪ *Middle: Kampala at night; crowd at a Uganda Cranes game*
≪ *Bottom: Murchison Falls National Park; Muyenga, Kampala*

UGANDA

THESE BEAUTIFUL PEOPLE

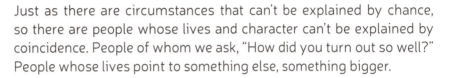

MIRACLE CHILD
≪ Fred's Story | Kampala, Uganda

Just as there are circumstances that can't be explained by chance, so there are people whose lives and character can't be explained by coincidence. People of whom we ask, "How did you turn out so well?" People whose lives point to something else, something bigger.

My Ugandan brother Fred is one of those people.

When I met Fred, we were seated next to each other in a Sunday morning service at Watoto Church South in Kampala, Uganda. Our six-month discipleship course had just begun and, like all first days, things were awkward and strange.

That day I didn't even know his name. I barely said hello, after my previous awkward attempt to introduce myself to every single one of our 60 classmates on the first day of class.

It was one of those moments where you take a deep breath and tell yourself, "Just do it. Just get up and do it."

So you do. You muster up your courage, stand up, walk across the room to meet the stares of the people lining its edges. One by one, you shake each person's hand and introduce yourself. Judging by the twisted faces and timid hellos (sometimes even blank stares), it doesn't take you long to realize this might have been a mistake, but you've started and can't stop now.

So you continue. You're just about five shy of greeting everyone when the classroom doors finally swing open and you're saved as they all hustle inside.

≪ *Photograph from Brad Baker Photography*

UGANDA: MIRACLE CHILD

THESE BEAUTIFUL PEOPLE

15

That Sunday morning, I couldn't remember if I had met him already. I wasn't willing to risk the potential embarrassment.

We stood for the opening song. He towered above me. I couldn't have even introduced myself if I'd tried. He probably wouldn't have heard me.

The song started and I was lost in it. Not just in the song, but in his *voice*. His worship. I thanked God for his height because maybe he couldn't hear me from way up there.

But he could. As we walked out of the church, I told him he had an amazing voice.

He stretched out his hand and said, "I'm Fred. And you are?"

Months later he told me, "I went home that Sunday and told my sister about you. I couldn't even remember your name, but I said, 'That girl can sing!' I just knew we would be friends."

That was how I met my brother Fred. Unofficially adopted, of course. Bonding over music and practical jokes and tears and prayer and life.

I watched him stand up for the weak, encourage the discouraged, speak life to the faint of heart, and impart wisdom to the lost and confused. I saw him lead worship with rare passion and heart. I sat with him in the hard moments and when he shed tears while listening to my story. I saw him bring smiles to the faces of others when I knew he didn't feel like it. I watched him protect and love his family, biological or not.

I was on the receiving end of his hugs when I had had the worst day. I always knew he was praying for me, rooting for me. On my side. He was a big brother to everyone. He's still mine.

One day as we sat in the back of our stuffy classroom, I asked Fred, "How did you turn out so good?"

I was sure he must have had a more stable upbringing than others.

His response was simply, "Let me tell you my story."

"I grew up in a family of four. Two older brothers and one younger sister. When I was two years old, my dad passed away. I don't even remember him. I grew up with my mom."

In his voice, such longing; yet in his eyes, peace. I was intrigued.

"My mom was one of the most hardworking ladies I've ever known. She was the person who introduced me to Christ. She was my everything. Anything without Mommy was nothing. I was always right there with her."

Things were hard for Fred's family after the passing of his father. Instead of being supported by extended family, they were worse than abandoned.

"After my dad died, his family came and took our cars, all our furniture. Everything in the house was empty. All they left was a mat. My mom covered us with her clothes."

My heart ached for his mother, coming home to an empty house. Nothing to feed your children, not even a place for them to sleep. Nothing. Already she had endured the searing pain of learning to live without her husband; now she was forced to start over with four mouths to feed. Alone.

"She would do everything she could to survive so we would have something to eat. She would wear the same dress three times a week. It was more for us and less for her. She's my hero and I love her."

But things weren't always terrible. He shared numerous stories of the mischief only a band of brothers could concoct. Eating the neighbour's chickens, sneaking out during nap time… You name it, they did it. He remembered these times fondly, usually with laughter in his voice. But these happy memories are always shadowed by reality—the reality of growing up in the midst of constant loss, struggle, and heartache.

"I was not a healthy child." He spent a lot of time in hospitals.

"That's why I hate hospitals today," he explained with a smile. I smiled, knowingly. We had been in hospital ministry together; I was well aware of his feelings toward them!

In 2000 he contracted cholera. Only three patients in the entire ward at Mulago Hospital survived. It was a miracle he did.

"We were in the news," he laughed. "And my mom was always there. She sold the little she had so I could get medication."

The more he spoke of his mother, the more my soul longed to meet her. What a mother, what a selfless sacrifice. Fred found himself in and out of school. He had survived cholera, but he still wasn't as healthy as a young boy should be.

"I remember one of my aunts coming to be with us. She had tuberculosis (TB) and was living with HIV/AIDS."

UGANDA: MIRACLE CHILD

THESE BEAUTIFUL PEOPLE

At first he thought she was favouring him. She would cook food and send all the other children away except for him. But he was wrong.

"There was something between her and Mommy, I guess. One day she spat in my food. When my brother asked why she did that, she beat him. I ate the food and contracted TB."

Just like that, at seven years old, he was bedridden in the hospital for three months. He missed almost a year of school and was completely malnourished.

"It's hard to believe I could lose so much weight. When I was a baby, I was obese. I weighed six kilograms!"

He laughed at the shock on my face. Fred? Obese? This tall, string bean of a guy sitting in front of me? I couldn't picture it.

Again, his mother was always there. And again, she sacrificed everything, including her own health.

"She and my brothers would sometimes go many days without food. She had contracted HIV/AIDS from my dad, and now she had gotten TB from looking after me. But she would never tell us. She hid it. She was sick but still did everything she could to look after us. Her immunity was low and the anti-retrovirals weren't working, but she kept going."

She had to keep going. What other option was there?

As she got more and more sick, Fred got better.

"People always wonder how I am alive." He grinned from ear to ear. "I'm like a cockroach that never dies. I refer to myself as 'Miracle Child.'"

Unfortunately, one miracle he wouldn't get. In January 2001, his mother became ill and entered the hospital. She had lost a lot of weight and her body was covered in sores.

"I saw all of that. But she was still the greatest to me. I always hoped that tomorrow would be a better day and we would walk out of that place."

He would skip school to be at the hospital with her. He didn't want to leave her side. She had to force him to leave so he wouldn't fall behind in class.

"One day someone came to pick us up from school. They never said why, just that we had to go. When we arrived home, my mom was in the living room lying on a mattress. She looked like she was just sleeping, taking a nap, but she was dead. I shook her. Then these people tell me that she is dead. I didn't take in the message—it was too much for me. I passed out and was out of it for a few days. When I woke up, it was the day of her burial."

Eight years old, an orphan.

"We buried my mom and I had many questions to ask God. We were rejected by our families. Who is going to take care of my brothers and sister? It would have been a fair exchange that I die instead of her! I blamed myself for her death because she was taking care of me and she was already ill. She did what any other mother would have done for her child. Just be there.

"I wanted to be buried with her. I jumped into the grave but they pulled me out with ropes."

Fred became angry. Angry at God, angry at his father's family, angry at life for taking something so precious from him.

"Not one of my father's relatives came to help us during our time of need. I just kept remembering all the awful things they had done. One time they pretended to have a family party. They brought food and my mom served them."

Even though they had taken everything from her instead of helping her raise her family, she served them anyway.

"I remember I was small, and I crawled up to one of my aunties and gave her a big smile. She began to cry and gave me back to my mom. As she handed me to her, she whispered, 'Don't eat anything they give you because it's poisoned.' They wanted her dead so they could get the rest of my father's stuff." Why did these people get to live while this woman of love and grace had to die? Why did this evil seem to go unpunished? It simply wasn't fair. Fred was angry.

After his mother's death, her brother came and moved in with Fred and his siblings. His older brothers took care of themselves. They didn't go far in their education because they couldn't afford the school fees. Instead, they began working at the ages of 12 and 14. Even today they are hard-working and still live at home. I've met them and they are incredible young men.

"But me and my sister were too young and my uncle needed to find a place for us. He did everything he could to make sure we were taken care of. That's when we moved to Watoto. I was 10 and my sister was eight."

UGANDA: MIRACLE CHILD

THESE BEAUTIFUL PEOPLE

Fred, me, and Mamma Robina outside their home, Suubi village

The first years in his new house mother's home, with his sister and six unrelated children, weren't easy. Breaking into a close-knit community and making new friends at the age of 10 isn't ideal, but even then God was looking out for him.

"My first day in the village, I didn't have any friends or anyone to play with. That's when Albert came. He brought me a shirt and a truck. He became my friend."

Fred was rebellious, though, and refused to call his house mom Mother.

"I'm not dumb. I just buried my mother and you are *not* my mother!" he shouted at her.

He would get into trouble, stealing fruit from the trees in other people's yards.

"One day I got so angry at my house mom, I ran away. As I was running, I got hungry. I asked the mamma

UGANDA: MIRACLE CHILD
THESE BEAUTIFUL PEOPLE

if I could have starfruit from her tree and she obliged. But as I was leaving, I saw her guava tree." A mischievous smile spread across his face.

"I just *had* to have some of those guavas! They looked so delicious! I snuck up the tree and was content for a long time, eating one guava after the other. Until my sister found me.

"She threw rocks at me in the tree until I fell out. I still have a scar to prove it, but the worst thing was when I looked up. There stood that mamma who had given me the starfruit. All she said to me was, 'You thief, you deserve it!' It was all she could get out between fits of laughter. I ran home so fast, praying all the way that I would never see that mamma again!"

We laughed, but we knew the house he ran back to wasn't home. He didn't have a real mamma waiting for him.

Fred and his house mom fought and argued until he no longer wanted to live.

"That's when I was nominated to go on choir."

His musical ability was apparent to the leaders of the Watoto Children's Choir, who discovered potential in youth at risk. Fred joined the choir and toured the United States and Canada at 12 years old.

"Seeing how big and different the world was opened up my mind and made me believe I could make something out of my life. It encouraged me to become a pilot."

Arriving back in Uganda, all the moms were at the airport waiting to greet them. His house mom was nowhere to be seen. Little did he know, he had been switched to a new home.

"One by one, the kids walked off with their moms. In the end, I couldn't believe my eyes. There, standing in front of me, was my new mom—*that* mamma! The one I had stolen the guavas from. She just stood there and opened her arms wide and said, 'Welcome home, my prodigal.'" Fred grinned.

I grinned, too, because I have met this mamma. Mamma Robina. She was one of my Ugandan mammas. I could picture the look of forgiveness on her face, her arms stretched wide, her eyes sparkling as she remembered the first time she had met Fred.

"And she has been my mamma ever since." Fred smiled. "Even my biological brothers call her Mommy. She has been there for me. She has disciplined me many times. She didn't give up on me. All those things I did,

Watoto Children's Choir, Canada, 2004; the moment Fred decided to become a pilot

Flight school, Uganda; months away from obtaining his private pilot's license. Photograph from Brad Baker Photography

I was just trying to trace who I was and figure out where I belong. But she never gave up on me." I had seen it myself.

"How blessed am I to have gotten two incredible mothers in my life!"

Life might not always be fair, but Fred has learned that adversity can be transformed into a glorious blessing.

"My life is just so different now!

"I never had godly examples of a real man to follow. After three years of being in the homes, we had a chance to see where I came from for the first time. It was hard to see the family on my father's side who abandoned us then and now they come running as if nothing happened. When my mom was sick, *none* of them showed up. Not on her death bed, not even for her burial."

He used to be so angry. So bitter. Just wanting to get even.

"My family had something to do with my dad's death. They took what they wanted but God never forgot us. I still see those guys today, my uncles, but now I forgive them and I even have peace calling them Uncle."

I am speechless.

"I used to stammer when I was young. I could barely say a word. Everyone would laugh at me at school, even the teacher. I would run away and cry. I was so angry at God for making me this way. I grew up with a lot of anger. I kept things inside and I was not a friendly person."

The day we shared our stories, he cried—the first time in a long time. I couldn't imagine Fred being anything other than the most kind-hearted, sincere, and gentle person I had ever met.

"I told myself that one day, one day, I will be able to speak. I will stand in front of people and speak without stammering," he said, without a hint of hesitation or stutter.

"I hear myself speak now and I know this is something bigger than me."

I had tears in my eyes, but he wasn't done reminiscing.

"We all stammer, or at least used to, my siblings and I. We all stammer and we all sing. We used to sing together because when we were singing, we were not stammering. My mom was a great singer and she taught us all the voices."

Today they still sing when they're together: partly to remember and partly to honour their mother. His sister has one of the most beautiful voices I have ever heard. Together, their music is heavenly.

Oh, and that little boy, Albert? The one who shared his toys and gave Fred some of his clothes? Well, Albert is a good friend of mine, too. If you haven't read his story yet, it's right after this one. To this day, he and Fred are inseparable.

Fred used to feel alone, friendless. But God crossed their paths in a time of fear and desperation. Albert's gesture was proof that an act of kindness, no matter how small, could go a long way.

Fred went from thinking his nightmare would never end to daring to dream that anything was possible. He used to be discouraged and angry, all bets against him, but now he's confident and hopeful about the future. His face radiates joy and his eyes shine with excitement.

After the initial disappointment of having to earn his airplane mechanic certificate due to a lack of funds, he pressed on. Grateful to be one step closer to his dream of becoming a pilot, he never gave up. Fred now has his private pilot's license in Uganda.

Fred has the maturity and experience to understand that, though the dream takes time, the ones who

Photograph from Brad Baker Photography

wade through the trenches with dirty hands and humble hearts are the ones who rise above. The ones who stand out in a world full of comatose people, devoid of passion.

Loved by all who know him, Fred is a well-respected young man of character and integrity, hard work and perseverance. He's a person of influence and impact. No one who meets Fred leaves the same.

He has learned the freeing power of forgiveness. He has reached out to his Heavenly Father: the maker of miracles, the giver of life, the restorer of the lost, the healer of the broken.

"God has been so good. God has been so, so good." Fred repeats this over and over and over again, in spite of himself, in spite of everything.

He has learned to be thankful, to believe, to use his voice. He has learned to treat others with grace and gentleness, with the same kindness he was once shown. He has understood the power of the love of his Heavenly Father: the extender of grace, the transformer of hearts.

Just as there are circumstances that can't be explained by chance, so there are people whose lives and character can't be explained by luck or coincidence. People of whom we ask, "How did you turn out so well?" People whose lives point to something else, something bigger.

What makes the difference?

It's tempting to believe it's a combination of luck and good timing—the right people in the right place at the right time. With more opportunities or more grace or more favour.

Father, forgive us.

The difference isn't random or by chance.

The difference is in the mind. In the life fully surrendered to the giver of life.
The difference is in the faith to believe that God is good—so, so good.
The difference is in the courage to walk with Him through it all, no matter what.

People like this don't forget where they come from—they embrace it. In this way, they embrace the miracle. People like this understand that who and where they are today is only by grace: grace and the transforming love of their Father God. Their transformation is unexplainable by human effort or reason, is nothing short of miraculous.

My brother Fred is one of these people.
He is a miracle child.

MORE THAN A SONG

≤ **Albert's Story** | Kampala, Uganda

"It was not like being a son. It was more like being hired."

Being born out of wedlock meant nothing but rejection for Albert. Tossed back and forth between parents, neither wanted to accept responsibility.

His mother was young and still in school, which meant she needed to drop out to look after him. She passed away before he could remember what she looked like.

"I'm told that she died while I was in her arms."

His father, an alcoholic, abused and neglected him. Albert spent a lot time at the bar because, well, that's where Dad was.

"Finally, one of my aunts decided to take me on." Albert winced a little.

Take him on. As though he were a responsibility or a project. A nuisance.

She took him on. But she already had kids of her own, so he was just that—a nuisance. And it was clear she didn't want him around.

"I was rejected by everyone that I called family."

His father passed away when he was five. His aunt looked for work so he could go to school. She found a job teaching English and literature at an orphanage in Luweero, Uganda. It wasn't a good place to live, but at least they had somewhere to stay.

"After a few years, she applied to work at one of the Watoto schools 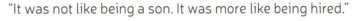and she was accepted."

But Albert didn't join Watoto right away. He attended Mengo Primary School for the first year and tried to take control of his situation by acting out.

"I was a bully. The other kids thought they could make fun of me so I had to show them another side of me. I fought a lot and often went home with dirty clothes."

One year later he joined his aunt at Watoto. That's when he met Fred.

"I was a shy guy, but Fred just kept coming back to me. I feared connecting with people, but Fred helped me to build my confidence."

Albert doesn't remember much about the day he met Fred.

"But what I remember is that Fred was a nice guy. Much nicer than all my other friends. I could share my dreams and passions with him."

Fred didn't make fun of Albert or call him names. He was safe.

Sometimes it's hard to believe. Hard to believe someone wants you around. Hard to believe you're valued. On purpose. For a purpose.

That someone has chosen to be *with* you rather than be *without* you.

But Fred showed him that. And that's probably why their bond is so strong to this day.

"He is the greatest gift ever." Albert grinned.

Both share an intense love of music, which has become an important part of life for Albert, a therapy of sorts.

Bottom: The day Fred, Albert, and I accidentally matched

UGANDA: MORE THAN A SONG

THESE BEAUTIFUL PEOPLE

"I used to wish that I could see my biological mom, but I knew that would never happen, so I would use music to calm myself down and bring me joy."

One day he was watching television and he was so inspired by the sounds coming from the guitar and the keyboard that he decided to learn.

"I had a friend who was trying to teach me but then he left for university and I had to start over. I decided to use the little money I had to buy a guitar book."

Now Albert teaches others how to play those same instruments. And his innate musical talent wasn't overlooked by the staff at Watoto.

"Almost as soon as I joined Watoto, I was selected to go on Choir #11. That was 2003. We went to Australia and then to the United States, where we had the opportunity to meet President George Bush and even our Ugandan president, H.E. Yoweri Kaguta Museveni. He was surprised to see us there!" he laughed.

When he returned from the tour, his aunt decided to continue her schooling, so she left Watoto and Albert behind. He still honours her for her care and kindness to him.

"I thank God every day for that lady. She believed in me and loved me the way I was. I owe everything to her. She is my hero. She is close to my heart and I love her so much."

Today Albert is living on his own and studying industrial art. He also spends much of his time in South Sudan serving at Watoto Church Juba. He's a talented artist and can draw just about anything.

In the future, he would like to do more interior design and photography, as well as pursue his passion for music. His dream is to have a studio someday.

Albert does all these things straight out of his heart. A place once dark and painful.

It's not that he will never again wish to see his birth mother. It's not that the pain of rejection will no longer sting. But when it does, Albert doesn't have to sit and stay in that place. He doesn't have to sketch himself into that picture of his life. He doesn't have to mumble along to the words of that song.

See, when dark times come, Albert stands up and turns on the light. He picks up his pencil and draws a now picture. He cradles the guitar and picks out a new tune.

To some of us, it's just another drawing, another catchy melody. But to him, it's more than that.

For Albert, it will always be so much more than a song.

UGANDA: MORE THAN A SONG

THESE BEAUTIFUL PEOPLE

AMAZING GRACE—FOR EVEN ME

≤ Smith Moses' Story | Kampala, Uganda

He was just one in a crowd of 75. One young man in a mix of Ugandan and international students at Watoto, taking a discipleship course for the next seven months.

I'd seen him around but never talked to him much. He was quiet and reserved. Always well dressed, he carried himself with a certain poise: a well-guarded charisma that simultaneously captivated and kept you at a distance.

A few months into the course, we lined up outside for lunch as we did every day, rain or shine. Today it was shine, and he stood in front of me.

Out of nowhere he turned around and said, "Hey, I need to tell you something."

Surprised, I couldn't fathom what it would be. We'd never had a serious conversation before, but I sensed it was urgent.

"Sure, what is it?" I asked.

"I'll tell you." He looked away.

"You're kidding, right? Just tell me!" I pressed.

"Don't worry, I'll tell you." His mouth pulled up at the ends. I was certain he had no intention of telling me.

≤ Photograph from Brad Baker Photography

UGANDA: AMAZING GRACE–FOR EVEN ME

THESE BEAUTIFUL PEOPLE

"You know you can't do that to me. You can't start something and not finish it. You *will* tell me," I poked in fun. Seriously, I can't stand unfinished conversations.

By now we'd reached the food. We filled our plates and found a place to sit among the circles of chairs in the semi-outdoor eating area. After chatting with other students, I turned to him.

"So, what did you want to tell me?"

He must have known I wouldn't give up. He nodded toward the church auditorium and said, "OK, but not here."

We sat facing each other on the pews near the back of the sanctuary. Around us people milled, praying, working, chatting.

On that bench, Smith Moses told his story for the first time. On that bench, his healing began.

"I was born right here in Kampala in 1994. My life was good. I had friends, family, and I went to school. Life was fun. Everything was good. When I got to secondary school, everything changed for me. I was exposed to the real world."

Smith stumbled across pornography and down the long, dark path of addiction.

"It was our school holidays and I went to the library to pick a movie like I usually do. I saw a label that said "Adult section," so I went to check it out. I didn't know what it was so I just picked a few movies from there, took them home and popped them into the DVD player. To my surprise, it was pornography."

He kept going back, watching more and more and more.

His face changed slightly. I could tell he was struggling.

"I've never told anyone this stuff before."

Already humbled, nothing could have prepared me for what he said next.

"I don't know what happened to my mind, but one day I found myself wanting to practice what I saw. So that night I went into my cousin's bedroom. She was two years older than me and I convinced her to have sex with me. That was my worst time."

My heart became heavy. I could only imagine the burden he and his cousin carried after such an act. But I stayed silent. Listened. Prayed.

"I kept doing that for some time but I didn't know that it was bad because I didn't even know enough to realize I was committing incest."

I could hear the regret in his voice, shame and despair dissipating as he spoke it aloud for the first time.

"I had so many questions and no answers. Things were out of control." He looked down, unable to look me in the eye.

A good-looking guy, it wasn't difficult for him to get girls.

"I could get them and I used them. I only wanted them for one thing. I didn't love them. I didn't even like them."

In Grade 10 he started drinking, trying to drown the guilt and shame.

"There was always something in my heart saying, 'What you're are doing is wrong.' Over and over and over, but I kept ignoring what I was hearing in my heart."

His family didn't know about his double life. On the outside, he was a good boy and student.

"I lived my life in secrecy."

I could see in his eyes that it was eating at him from the inside.

"Then one day I was, like, 'Yo, this thing is too much. It's wasting my life. How can I go about quitting all this stuff?' I tried to stop but I couldn't. I tried to stop chasing girls but I just wanted more and more and more.

"I was finished high school and I wanted to change my life. I didn't want to be like the friends that I had.

So when my mom told me about Watoto 360, I signed up."

But there were girls in the program, too.

"It was a burden for me. Usually when I'm around girls, it's not hard for me to get one, and I thought, 'Now what am I going to do about this? I'm at a church program and I'm going to struggle so much.'"

I laughed. Even he smiled at the irony. How we run from our problems but they're never far behind.

"It was during this time that my life started to change. We sang and worshipped and did all that normal stuff. Anyone can do that at any time. I would read the Bible and memorize it but then when I was hanging out with my friends, I would still be constantly thinking, 'You can get that girl, or that one. That one will accept you.' But the other half of me knew it wasn't right.'"

I smiled. So much about how I'd perceived him until now finally made sense.

I wouldn't hear the next part of his story for some time.

"So then this one day we were going to have lunch and something in my heart said I should speak to one of my friends about what I was going through. *There's that one over in the corner. Go and talk to her.* I didn't know much about her but I just felt like I should try even though she was a stranger to me.

"Her name was Twila and we ended up in the food line together.

"I turned around and said, 'I need to talk to you about something.' She was like, 'What?' I said, 'I'll tell you.' She's like, 'OK, I'll be around if you want to talk.'

"We got our food and I hoped she would forget but she came back to me and asked me about it again. I told her to forget about it, but she insisted. I was scared. I didn't want to tell her everything that was happening in my life. I wanted her to give up but she kept going and going. She wasn't giving up.

"So I told her everything." Right there on that church pew, as people milled around, no clue such a beautiful thing was taking place.

"I thought she would judge me but to my surprise she was friendly and kind and she talked to me and gave me good guidance. From the day that I opened my heart to speak to someone, that's when everything started changing."

I still get a lump in my throat when I think about it.

Isn't it beautiful? When the wound finally breaks open. When the grace of God pours into the gaping hole, over the broken pieces of the soul. When vulnerability triggers healing.

It's amazing. It's grace.

"It did not die easy. It was a struggle that was deep inside my heart."

Smith continued to struggle, but he kept going back to his friends after the discipleship course ended.

"Twila kept encouraging me that I can do this. She was someone I was accountable to and I knew I had to tell her everything that was happening. I found myself watching less porn. I found myself saying no to the girls.

"On the outside, it looked like I had everything I needed, but inside there was something I was still longing for.

"There's that thing of knowing Christ, then there is that thing of knowing Christ and that He's real! Yeah!"

His enthusiasm came from the heart—a place once filled with darkness. He laid it all at the feet of the One in whom there is no darkness, and it became as light to Him.

"Soon after the program ended, Twila had to move on to other parts of Africa and I had no idea who I was going to talk to. I was accountable to her and now she was gone. I knew that she was right, I needed to find a man I could talk to."

After praying about it, he contacted a classmate who'd gone through a similar struggle. "Now we meet and talk and pray together. We share God's word and encourage each other. My lifestyle has changed completely!

Smith Moses and me at our discipleship course graduation, 2014

"I no longer watch porn. I see girls in a completely different way. I changed the things I used to do and I have found new friends. I can now hear God's voice and He speaks to me clearly.

"Right now I am walking with Him. Those things are no longer a burden. Now I control them and they don't control me.

"I know Christ died for me and made me righteous and I'm no longer looking at my past. I have made things right with my cousin and I am looking toward the future."

———

I can hardly keep the tears from falling.

Over a year has passed since that day on the church pew, and I can't believe the healing and restoration and transformation I see in him.

It's amazing. It's grace.

Yes, he committed incest. Yes, he committed fornication.

He could be sitting in his shame. Wallowing in a cloud of self-hatred and remorse. Running from the arms extended toward him. Hiding behind his unworthiness.

But grace will have none of it.

Grace won't let you sit in your shame. Grace won't let you cower under the cloud of self-hatred. Grace extends His arms and seeks you out. Grace doesn't give up. Grace keeps going and going and going... until you finally get it.

Grace is for Smith Moses. And for me. And for the ones we don't think deserve it. And for the ones to whom we'd rather not extend it.

Smith Moses could have reasoned that this grace wasn't enough for him. But he made a different choice. He traded in his shameful rags for a cloak of righteousness. He dispersed the darkness with the light of truth. He threw off his unworthiness and ran toward those arms, crying, "Amazing grace—for even me."

AMAZING GRACE, HOW SWEET THE SOUND
THAT SAVED A WRETCH LIKE ME.
I ONCE WAS LOST, BUT NOW I'M FOUND,
WAS BLIND BUT NOW I SEE.

—JOHN NEWTON

JESUS SET ME FREE

≤ **Precious' Story** | Kampala, Uganda

"Let me start out with a positive statement. Jesus has always enabled me to pass through all my struggles and I do *not* complain in my life."

I suppose I could write that quote next to her picture and it would pretty much sum her up.

Precious is just as her name sounds: sweet in nature and appearance, with a contagious giggle and an irresistible smile.

But I think my favourite part about her—besides how much she loves to eat—is that everything about her comes from a place of inner strength. But not her strength—God's strength *in* her.

Born in 1991 in Kyunga District, Uganda, Precious grew up in Kampala with her mother, father, and siblings.

"I have always enjoyed school! I performed well in class and I absolutely loved what I did. I liked to read, go to church with my family, and wear my Converse shoes. They brought me great joy!" She giggled, picturing her beloved sneakers.

"We also loved to play games. We would make a small ball out of plastic bags and play dodgeball. Or we drew four circles on the ground and ran around them while dodging the ball—we called that Round Game. Things were mainly positive."

Then she lost her father.

≤ *Photograph from Brad Baker Photography*

"I was nine years old. He was a farmer, businessman, and politician. He gave me my own land and I started my farm. I loved to work the land and grow things, but I think my favourite was eating all the food! There was always so much food until he passed away. Then the story changed."

When the main breadwinner of the household is suddenly gone, finances cause the most stress for those left behind.

"My mom became tough on me because of the stress. We didn't have enough money for food anymore."

She loved school but often there wasn't enough money to pay for school fees. Things were so difficult that she attempted suicide at 12 years of age.

"Glory to God that He sent people to guide me through that time."

They would tell her about Jesus, but most of her family weren't believers. Her mom stopped going to church after her father's death, and many members of her family were involved in dark spiritual practices.

"I would help put on crusades for Christ and all that stuff, but I didn't believe. Somewhere inside I knew that God was there and that He wanted to meet me, but I wasn't a believer."

Meanwhile, things at home were getting worse. Her aunties wanted her to get married so they could get the dowry. Instead, she got a job. After being mistreated at the job, she ran away from home to stay at a friend's place.

"That's when I met my uncle, who sponsored me to go back to school. When his family decided to move, they sent me to live with a friend of theirs. That lady became my foster mom."

≤ *Photograph from Brad Baker Photography*

UGANDA: JESUS SET ME FREE

THESE BEAUTIFUL PEOPLE

When she was 16, Precious had a horrible nightmare. A friend advised her to give her life to Jesus.

"So I did. It wasn't easy because spiritually at home my family had believed in something different and the devil cannot just let you go like that."

The spiritual attacks were bad. She remembered living in the woods with snakes for weeks at a time, incoherent and insane.

"I was supposed to be the queen of all the devils in my family's clan."

That was the plan. That was Satan's purpose for her.

"But by the grace of God, I did not become that. He delivered me when I accepted Him into my life!"

An irresistible smile spread wide across her face.

Her journey to freedom hasn't been easy. The attacks were frequent and severe, but God placed people in her life to pray and fast and do deliverance sessions. Today she is completely free.

"Without Jesus, I can't live," she said as if it were common sense, unfathomable any other way.

Precious used to be in a family that rejected her. Now she lives with a foster family that has accepted her as its own.

"I do not regret joining that family. She is a single mom with only one biological child and I am so proud to be a part of them. We struggle financially sometimes, but we are always content."

She used to be running wild in the bush, out of her mind. In 2014 she received the highest marks in the country and was offered a full scholarship to university.

She used to be unable to attend school regularly. Now she has graduated with a bachelor's degree in procurement and supply chain management.

She used to have plans for destruction, but now she has plans for a future. After her bachelor's degree, she will obtain her master's and become a professor. Once she has saved enough money, she'll pursue her original dream of becoming a lawyer.

"I used to be without hope. I was out of school and still God brought me back. I cannot forget such a great testimony. So I want to become a professor to implant knowledge and hope in the minds of young people. Lord willing, I will become a professor of law. What Satan meant to harm, God turned around for good."

I asked her to describe herself in one sentence.

She smiled and said, "Jesus set me free!"

A PLACE TO CALL HOME

⩽ Katono, Edward's Story | Kampala, Uganda

Never despise small beginnings.

Nobody understands this better than Edward. His name, Katono, means "small thing" in Luganda, the national language of Uganda, where he was born.

Edward is one of those people you need to meet in person. I've tried countless times to describe him to friends and family. Every time, I end up grinning and saying, 'Ah! You just have to meet him!'"

But here I am, trying to do it again… Trying to tell his story.

He's one of my favourites. Kind, generous, and sincere, he's an encourager, everybody's friend. Easy to be around, easy to like. A talented football player, he's also the best translator I ever had.

And he's downright hysterical—or "fantamaglorious," as he would say—to the point where you see him coming and you're already smiling because, well, it's Eddie.

Eddie. He's my brother. And he came from small beginnings.

"September 30, 1994, I was born in Mulago Hospital."

But his mother left the hospital without him. She couldn't afford to take care of him so she left him there.

⩽ *Photograph from Brad Baker Photography*

Abandoned. Vulnerable. Small.

"They took me to the children's section of another hospital. From there I was taken in by Sanyu Babies' Home, where I stayed for three months until I joined Watoto, where I got a new mom and siblings. I've been there ever since."

Edward was one of the first babies to join Watoto, a ministry that has now rescued thousands of children in Uganda. Watoto is the only family he's ever known, the only place he's ever called home.

"I was a fat boy." He chuckled and slapped his six pack. "With a big belly. I would cry if they didn't give me enough food."

He told these stories in his own dramatic way, drawing me in.

Then he flashed a contagious grin, did a little dance step, and kept walking because that's his nature.

That's Edward.

"I was stubborn, too. I got caned a lot. Oh, we were so mischievous. One time in primary school, we snuck out for pork and because we didn't invite one boy along, he told on us. When we got home that day, my house mom—eh, she caned us seriously! She would cane us according to the days of the week: Monday to Friday, one to five."

He stood up to demonstrate.

"Like the one day we were supposed to go to school but we went to Farm Fresh to fish and she found out. She asked us what day it was. 'Friday!' we squealed. 'How many strokes?' she would ask? 'Five!' we wailed."

I doubled over with laughter as he acted out the scene.

"Sometimes we would invite people to play football with us. They were older and bigger than us and we would still beat them seriously! We had to have our sticks and stones ready every time they would come. *Ako* means 'stones.' When we would hear that being yelled, all of a sudden they would be flying all over the place!"

His arms waved frantically in front of his face, illustrating the stones.

"We had to have our stones ready so that we would be organized!"

And there would be more caning.

"But I can see the good effects of that. It has made me grow up to be responsible. I believe I am now a responsible person. And I love my Watoto mom so much! Although she is not my biological mom, she raised me and I love her from the bottom of my heart.

"I may have grown up without many people around me, but I now have friends from all over the world and I love that!"

Edward has been given incredible opportunities. He was part of Watoto Children's Choir #8, which travelled to Norway, England, the United States, and Canada in 2001–2002.

"I was eight years old and I thank God for that privilege. It was so fun and so good. It sparked in me my desire to travel. Maybe someday I will get my degree in travel and tourism."

Although he didn't enjoy school, he was able to complete his schooling, and for that he's grateful.

"I graduated from high school in 2013, and man, was that a good experience."

Things had not always been glamorous at school.

"I wore diapers until 2009. I had a problem peeing the bed. I would pray and pray and nothing would happen. I would shower but the smell never really left. My friends at school made fun of me and I was always uncomfortable in class."

No one wants to be "that kid." Edward felt like even more of an outsider.
"I was so ready to just be done! That's a long time to be studying."

He let out an exasperated sigh.

"Here in Africa, people are kicked out of school because they don't have school fees but my fees were always paid for. I just hated school because there were so many subjects and you have to put so much information into your head. You study for several years and you have to remember it *all* for the tests at the end. We once spent four hours on one paper. *Four hours!*"

His eyes nearly popped out of his head as he waved four fingers in my face.

"Ah, man, it's too much. I am not a person who likes reading and writing. It makes me," he paused, "uncomfortable."

I was dying of laughter.

"That's why I'm doing things with camera and film. Working with my hands."

Edward recently received his diploma in media studies, journalism, and mass communication.

I asked him, "What's next? What about your biological family? What's on your heart now?"

"I met Jesus in 2012 and recommitted my life in 2015. I've always grown up in a Christian environment but it was not my own. I simply never knew anything else. Precious is the one who challenged me on this and I went on a journey of reading my Bible from cover to cover."

You might think, "So what? What does that have to do with right now and the future?"

Because Eddie wouldn't want you to think that his walk has been easy.

"I've never told anyone this before, but I struggle with pornography and sexual sin. I'm trying to overcome it. I'm hearing testimonies of people overcoming it. I've fought with myself and it's not working out. I need to find someone to talk with. Someone who can walk alongside me. A person I can trust who has been through the same thing. It's happening to me; I can't deny it. It is disturbing me. People call me "brother." But how can I be their brother with the things that I've done? I do things that other people don't do. I watch movies other people don't watch. How can I be someone's brother?"

My heart ached for him... but I knew someone. Remember Smith Moses? I connected them and they've supported each other ever since. Like family.

And his biological family? Looking for them was daunting.

"The records at the hospital are just thrown into some room. No one knows where anything is," he said.

"I decided to first settle and finish studying. I am not the first or last person living without my biological parents. I won't say I don't need them, but I can do without them to some extent. I have God, who looks after me. I will find them in the right time, though sometimes I think about it and it hurts me. I feel the pain and the bitterness.

"I know I'm not the only one, but why did it have to happen to me?"

In spite of his strength and resilience, he ached for a place to call home.

"Right now the biggest thing on my mind is transition."

Edward graduated in 2017 and he is no longer under the wing of Watoto.

"I'm thinking about how to start my own life now. How am I going to find a place to live and a job that can provide everything I need? I won't let myself get to the point where I am on the street. Too many people have invested in me and I will not allow that to happen to me. But I'm worried. Where am I going to start from? How can I even get a job when I don't have biological family to give me a reference? There is no one to fall back on.

"But I won't lose hope. I won't lose hope!"

And he won't. Even though he came from small beginnings, he has big dreams.

"My dream would be to start my own video company, get my own cameras and studio. I will still play football, of course, for as long as I can, and I would love to build a good football stadium for my people in Uganda. I don't want to be selfish with my money."

His eyes lit up as he talked about making Watoto proud and making something of his life.

UGANDA: A PLACE TO CALL HOME

THESE BEAUTIFUL PEOPLE

Goodbye lunch, 2015

"I know that I will overcome in this world. And I will become the person God wants me to be, even when everything is still seemingly out of place."

He might not have a place to call home on earth, but he has a family that transcends human definition. He understands better than anyone the deep void of the soul. A void that can only be filled by a Heavenly Father. A void that we all carry, orphans or not.

"If I could tell the world one thing? *Get back to Jesus.* If everyone would get back to God, my friend, people wouldn't be thinking only about themselves. Instead of keeping all the money to themselves, they would be using it for the good of everyone. Get back to God. Give our whole selves to God. He knows us all inside and out. God is good, loving, and caring. If we get back to Him, we will also be all of those things. You will have love in you. It would change the way you look at your neighbour."

Getting back to God would give you a place to belong. A place to call home.

———

Edward, I know your name is Katono and it means "small thing." I know you don't like it, and that's why you chose the name Edward.

But you know what, Katono Edward? Do you know what Edward means? It means "wealth and fortune." It means "prosperous."

You might have come from small beginnings, but they are not to be despised.
You might have the name "small," but the best things always start that way.
You might have started life without hope or home, but you helped make Uganda a place I call home.

You are big enough. You are good enough. You are not alone in this.

You will always be my brother and I know you will create a place for yourself.
A place to call home.

JUST WHAT WE NEED

≤ Nicholas' Story | Kampala, Uganda

"He doesn't even realize his potential!"

I was sitting with Edward on the cement benches outside Watoto Church Central. Lunch break at our discipleship program was long enough that we could eat a mountain of food and still have time to chat.

Nicholas was today's topic.

Edward and Nicholas were good friends. They loved to play football, to laugh and carry on about the same things. They quickly became like brothers to me.

Today Edward was frustrated.

"Nicholas doesn't see his full potential!" Edward exclaimed. "His problem is not that he isn't capable. It's that he doesn't believe in himself!"

Edward was adamant. His arms gesticulated wildly, as usual. And he was right.

Nicholas was born and raised in Kampala by his mother after she left his polygamous, abusive father. A tailor by trade, she was still alive and working in the Watoto homes. His father was good at "spanking, slapping, and giving heavy punishments," as Nicholas put it.

Nicholas was the youngest of seven children. Because his mother couldn't afford school fees for all his siblings, he often missed out. That was how he came to Watoto. And that was where he met Edward.

Nicholas, me, and Edward on one of our many escapades

If you met Nicholas, you'd wonder if he had a voice at all, but I assure you, he does! You wouldn't be able to hear him next to you, but he loves to sing.

You see, Nicholas had big dreams—but he often doubted his ability to achieve them. Fear of disappointment? Maybe. Fear of failure? Perhaps.

And can't we all identify with that? Don't we all need that one friend who is frustrated with our self-doubt and insecurity? We need them to look us in the eye and say, "You don't see your full potential! The problem is not that you're incapable; it's that you don't believe in yourself!"

Over the last few years, I've watched Nicholas learn to believe in himself. With friends like Edward nudging him forward, and his relationship with his Father growing stronger, he has transformed that childlike stubbornness into determination. The sky is not even his limit.

Just because he was afraid to speak didn't mean he had nothing to say. Just because he grew up without his father didn't mean he couldn't grow up to be a man. Just because he missed some schooling as a child didn't mean he was unable to learn.

UGANDA: JUST WHAT WE NEED

Nicholas had always wanted to play the guitar and sing but he never believed he could. Now, he plays and sings on a regular basis. People comment on how quickly he's been able to learn.

Before I left the country, I sat in awe as he played and sang a song for me in front of other people. The last time I saw him, he was heading to worship practice at his church.

Now he's doing his bachelor's degree in business administration.

"Jesus loves me, and I am not lacking anything. That is my joy," he said with a grin.

Maybe that's the key. Realizing that when Jesus loves you, you lack nothing. It doesn't matter if you feel scared or inadequate or incapable.

All that's irrelevant because the maker of the universe looks down and sees what you can't. And He grabs you by the shoulders and says, "Come on, child. Don't you see your full potential in Me? You aren't incapable. You just don't believe in Me. You don't believe in My ability in you. You don't trust My love."

Nicholas needed to hear it, and isn't that just what we need as well?

SHUT UP

⩽ Emma's Story | Kampala, Uganda

He was sitting next to the window, his long legs crumpled up behind the seat. His dark, lanky arms supported his chin as he watched the class outside.

We were boarding the bus, heading out on a mission.

I had seen him in class. He was quiet, never much to say. If he was called on in class, he would struggle to reply, all shut up inside.

His stutter was so pronounced that it was almost impossible to understand him. But I was oh-so curious to know his story. So I plopped down beside him on the seat and struck up a conversation, fully expecting it to be one-sided.

I was wrong. From the moment the bus rolled out of the lot to the time we parked at our destination, he didn't stop talking once.

I admit, I struggled to understand him. Listening to him tripping and stammering over every syllable of every word was almost painful for me. Imagine what it has felt like for him his whole life.

From that day on, I learned so much about Emma. His mom passed away when he was young. He was raised by his father, who was in the military. He was beaten and burned by those who cared for him in his father's absence.

"Th-h-h-h-they w-w-ant-ed t-t-t-t-o… ssstop me f-f-f-rom… s-s-stut-t-t-ering."

He went to Juba, South Sudan, with his father and became a child soldier at six years old.

UGANDA: SHUT UP

THESE BEAUTIFUL PEOPLE

The day I discovered Emma no longer stuttered

"M-m-m-y dad w-w-was... a... g-g-g... good dad."

Trained as a child soldier for three years, he was paid by the army to bring back those who ran away. He loved being in the army. Most of the children were forced to be there, but Emma was there because of his father. He didn't want to leave.

He was told that in Watoto he would have a mother and a family.

"...B-b-b-but I s-s-s-said... n...no, m-m-m-m-y m-m-m...mother died l...long ag-g-g-go."

They insisted, so he joined the Watoto homes.

As he was telling his story, I could see he was full of life and mischief. He had a unique way of doing things and a creative mind.

Because he stuttered, that was usually all people noticed. But he was also a writer. He wrote poems, hundreds of them.

I encouraged him to write his story in poem form. I'll never forget the day he sat in front of our class of 75 people and recited it. I was so proud—and then I learned he had made it up on the spot! I only wish it had been written down so I could share it with you.

He started his vocational training with Watoto and discovered that he enjoyed working with his hands. But he was always under a kind of stress. The stress of trying to figure out where he belonged, how he was going to do what he wanted to do. The stress of being forced into a mould he didn't fit.

School wasn't a good match for him. It's difficult to make a living from writing, so what was he to do?

One year later, I returned to the Watoto village. To my surprise, there was Emma! I ran over and gave him a hug, jumping up to reach him. I asked him how he was doing. Right away I knew something had changed.

The stutter was gone! He spoke with passion and confidence about how he was asked to go to Mombasa to work with construction machinery. He loved every minute of it.

The stress was gone. He had found his place, his passion… his niche. He had a purpose and a plan and there was no stopping him now. His eyes were bright and full of possibility… and a little mischief. I was dumbfounded.

When I asked him about his stutter, he smiled and said, "Yeah, it only becomes worse when I am stressed or afraid."

Of course. What things he must have seen when training to be a child soldier. What things he must have felt when being beaten and burned for his speech impediment.

Of course he was silent. Of course he stuck to himself. Of course he didn't want to participate or speak out in front of people.

He was shut up within himself—shut up and shut off from the world.

But man, when you give someone a purpose… just watch them come to life.

The light returns to their eyes.
The spring returns to their step.
The smile tugs at their lips.

And when given the platform, they won't be able to shut up.

BETTER THAN YESTERDAY

⩽ Henry's Story | Kampala, Uganda

It feels like just yesterday.

Yesterday... when I sat on the front steps of Watoto Church Central, overlooking the busy street. Henry sat next to me with his face in his hands and my arm around his shoulder.

Yesterday... when I sat silently with him because there were no words. He was grieving the loss of his best friend.

"She was a writer, too." He broke the silence with a whisper. "She loved art and music and everything I love. And we would hang out and meet up all the time to share and encourage each other. We made each other better... and now she's gone.

"Why does everybody I love die?"

It feels like just yesterday.

Yesterday... when Henry was born into a healthy and loving home. But after his father was poisoned by his business partner, everything changed.

"I can still see my mother crying. I remember asking when dad would return. She burst out in fresh tears. She held me and said in Luganda, 'He is dead. He will never return.'

⩽ *Photograph from Arm Up Media*

UGANDA: BETTER THAN YESTERDAY

THESE BEAUTIFUL PEOPLE

"I knew he would return. Within me I knew he was just sleeping. I saw him sleeping. I knew he would be back with bread, lots of milk, and a toy for me to play with. I knew he would come and take me with him to his workplace and buy me a soda. That was life with him around, a life of abundance," Henry recalled.

But that was yesterday.

Yesterday... when they moved from the village to the city so his mother could find work. When he had to live with one of his uncles but was treated like a slave. When he was reunited with his mom and sister but had to move from place to place because there wasn't enough money for rent. When he was beaten because there was so much stress in the home. When he started fighting at school. When he decided he hated people.

It feels just like yesterday that he was alone, praying to get away from today. Praying for a better tomorrow. Now, even those tomorrows are yesterdays. Henry discovered that he liked reading and spent more and more time in the library. "The librarian took notice of me and encouraged me to keep reading. She didn't care if it was a big book or a small book; she would just hand me books to read and I would read them. One day she handed me *Lord of the Flies*. I was appalled by the way these boys treated their fellow people and I vowed that I would stop fighting. It changed me!"

He and his sister joined Watoto in 2000, where they were given the chance to travel together with the children's choir.

"I found myself waking up excited every day because I was going to get to meet new people! It was life-changing." The excitement still danced in his eyes.

That's also where he met Jesus.

"I remember getting on my knees and asking God to show me my purpose. I didn't want to live an empty life."

In Watoto Henry met an artist who took him under his wing.

"Him giving me a chance to paint and work with him helped me to start opening up. I had such trouble opening up to people, but he didn't push me; he just gave me opportunities. The painting I did would tell what was on my heart and later on I would speak about it."

≤ *Photograph from Arm Up Media*

UGANDA: BETTER THAN YESTERDAY

THESE BEAUTIFUL PEOPLE

He studied journalism and pursued his passion for music and media.

"I love music and making the world a better place. I've realized that my life's calling is to improve the world for children and women, as well as the environment. I recorded one of my songs, and even shared the stage with several renowned musicians in the country, when I was selected to present at a fundraising concert for babies with heart problems. I'm also involved with National Environmental Management Authority, and we were recently able to save part of a wetland in Uganda from being turned into commercial property."

He has also started a media house to photograph the people and nature he loves so deeply.

"It's in its infant stage. A lot of what I would love to do in the future lies in its existence. I would love to use photography to impact people's lifestyles—I want to tell stories. I would love to have an art and music school that helps disadvantaged children express themselves through art, as well as a place that tells Uganda's stories of her people and wildlife through film."

Passion oozed out of him.

"I don't want to have a career that is all about money. I want to better people's lives. Money can come and go but people last longer than money. Helping someone and encouraging them has more impact on lives than making money."

Yeah, he had a messy and painful yesterday... and he probably has more of those to come. But Henry has a unique hope and a unique calling.

"I deliberately choose to love and care because at one point in life I will need the love; I will need the care," Henry said.

He might have lost people he loved yesterday, but today he is working to make sure fewer people are lost tomorrow.

He might have been neglected and beaten yesterday, but today he is working to protect women and children tomorrow.

He might not have trusted people yesterday, but today he trusts in Someone who already exists in tomorrow.

He might have been anxious yesterday, but today he is confident and passionate.

And it's not because he is doing one big thing.
It's not because he has more time, resources, or energy than the rest of us.

No, it's because he's doing the small things well. It's because he's choosing to do something today. It's because his gratitude spills out onto everyone he meets.

And he is making the world a better place, better than yesterday.

UGANDA: BETTER THAN YESTERDAY

THESE BEAUTIFUL PEOPLE

FROM MURDERER TO MOTHER

≤ Mamma Nancy's Story | Gulu, Uganda

"Kill her!"

She felt the hairs rise on the back of her neck as he hissed in her ear. His breath reeked of alcohol, his voice of hate.

"KILL HER!"

His foot found the back of her leg, sending her crumbling to her knees.

"Kill her, or I'LL KILL YOU!"

Saliva sprayed from his mouth. She could feel him leaning closer, but didn't dare turn her head toward his blood-stained face.

There wasn't much time—she had to choose. Shaking, her hands gripped the gun. Sweat and tears blurred her eyes as she focused on the woman in her crosshairs.

He was waiting. They were all waiting: those who had been forced to kill, and those who had just witnessed their loved ones die.

Would she do it? Her options were kill or be killed. She placed a trembling finger on the trigger and pulled.

≤ *Photograph from Brad Baker Photography*

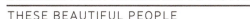

UGANDA: FROM MURDERER TO MOTHER

THESE BEAUTIFUL PEOPLE

Silence. Except for the explosion of the shot, the clatter of the gun falling to the ground. Except for the voice screaming in her head, *What have you done?*

After they hauled her away, she looked down at her hands. They had changed somehow. Like it or not, they were the hands of somebody she was not.

A murderer.

———

Nancy grew up an orphan.

Well, that's not completely true. She did have a father, but he had three wives, and she was passed from one home to the next. Her mother had died when Nancy was young, and her father's wives mistreated her. She was an outcast and she didn't know why.

It wasn't until Nancy took poison in an attempt to end her life that her father finally told her the truth about her mother's death. She was promptly sent to live with her grandmother. This would be her first "permanent" home.

But even that wouldn't last forever.

"When I was 16, I was captured by the Kony rebels," Nancy shared with me and a friend. Sitting in her armchair, she relived the horrors of her time in the bush.

"You see how these people killed people. How they slaughtered. Ah, they did bad things to people."

You can tell by the faraway look in her eyes that the memories are crystal clear. What she said next made my jaw drop and my heart ache.

"And I can't lie—I was among the people who killed. If I count, I killed five. Three women and two men. If you don't kill, you die. They are standing behind you the whole time, ready to knock you down. I killed to survive."

That had happened here, on the land where we were now seated. I couldn't imagine it. I couldn't believe the strong, loving hands in front of me, wrapped around a cup of tea, were also the hands of a murderer.

After some time, the rebels moved to a different location and split the women into three groups.

"I was among the first group. I was taken to become the fifth wife of the captain of the rebels. But when I arrived, I realized I knew him. And he recognized me!"

What seemed to be the worst-case scenario ended up saving her life. The captain turned out to be the husband of her cousin, and he was just as surprised to see her.

Thankfully, he couldn't take her as his wife because he was already married to her relative. Instead, he offered her protection. He made her swear she wouldn't tell anyone she knew him.

The girls who were captured were treated as objects, used and abused by any, if not all, of the men in the army. Had Nancy been sent to any other rebel officer, her story could have been drastically different.

But she was placed here.

"You can stay in my house," the captain said. "Everyone will think you are my wife, but you will not be married to me. You will just stay here."

And stay she did. For two years she remained with him, until the army headed to Sudan. The captain arranged for 20 soldiers to escort her to a place she would recognize, so she could find her way home.

"Go. Run. Get away," he told her.

So she ran.

When she reached home, she found it in shambles. She continued to Gulu Town, where she discovered that people were looking for her.

"People thought I had died, and others thought I was escaping, so I had to keep running."
She ran to Kampala, where she met her husband.

After giving birth to six children, she and her husband were tested for HIV. He tested positive. She tested negative.

"It is the grace of God that caused this thing to happen," Nancy said with a smile in her eyes. "I am

Visiting (almost) the whole family, 2015

Mamma Nancy with five of her eight children, Laminadera village, Gulu

negative. I am healthy and I don't have any problem!"

Miraculous. But this miracle was also wrapped in a struggle. After they were tested, her husband left.

She began the humble, back-breaking work of crushing stones for money. From morning to night, she would sit hammering rocks into smaller pieces or powder for construction.

"This kind of work is only for strong people. It is hard work," Nancy said.

Strong describes Nancy. Hard and fearless. Faithfully crushing stones to provide for her children.

Ten years she worked, putting her children through school, food in their bellies, and clothes on their backs. Sometimes she walked two hours just one way to work.

One day in 2013, she saw something in a market in Banda Kireka that changed her life.

Like other markets in East Africa, booths crafted of sticks and tin lined the narrow dirt pathways. Littered with trash, these pathways turned to mud during the rainy season. Women sat cross-legged, stacking tomatoes and mangoes in neat piles. Children chased each other, weaving in and out of the crowd. Vendors hollered out prices and bargains, waving their wares.

Like other markets in East Africa, refuse covered the ground.

That day in the market, Nancy saw young people cleaning, picking up garbage, sweeping the streets. Voluntarily.

They thought they were just cleaning, but Nancy was watching, wondering what kind of church or organization would do such a thankless job.

A few weeks later, she entered the doors of that same church and heard about children's homes for orphans and vulnerables. Thinking it would be in Kampala, she applied to be a mother in one of the homes. At least it would help her provide for her children, who needed school fees.

"I didn't even know there was a home in Gulu. I went for my interview. I passed, and they asked me if I know Gulu because they heard that I spoke Acholi, one of the languages of Northern Uganda. I said, 'Of course,' and they asked if I would be a mother at a home in Gulu."

After much prayer and consideration, she accepted. She left her six children behind in Kampala and took the eight-hour bus ride to Gulu Town.

When they drove her through the gates of the children's village, she was overwhelmed with emotion.

"Nancy, why are you crying?" they asked.

"I know this place," Nancy cried. "I lived in this place. This home is built on the exact bush where I was captured. The place where I killed."

Thinking she was upset, they tried to comfort her.

"No," she insisted. "These are not tears of sorrow, but tears of joy!"

Confused, I leaned in as she continued.

"I just had to think, 'God, how great you are!' This area was the worst for shedding blood, the worst for slaughter. And for sure God has chosen this place to be different. This place is not the same as it was before. The demons that used to disturb people are no longer here."

Me and my Mamma

So she moved to Gulu. On reaching the home, she was given six children to care for, most under the age of five. Before long, it became too much.

"I wanted to quit. I wanted to run away like Jonah! Imagine, I wanted to go back to crushing stones in Kampala where my children were, so I could look after them. I even tried to run away, but the day I was to leave I got malaria and had to spend four days and all my transport money in the hospital."

In the hospital, she clearly heard the voice of God say, "I have chosen you, Nancy, to be a mother to these children." She returned to Gulu.

In the same place where she was held captive, she now celebrates freedom. In the same place where she was crippled by fear, she now leads fearlessly. In the same place where she used her hands to kill, she now uses her hands to heal.

Her hands wipe away tears. Her hands hold and cherish. Her hands bind up wounds and celebrate life. She restores hope to children who are victims of the same circumstances she escaped less than two decades earlier, on that same land.

And the children she left in Kampala? I've met them and spent time in their home. You won't find more hard-working, polite, responsible children—a direct reflection of their mother's love and strength. Her two eldest sons were taking turns with their university studies, one working to support the other until graduation. Such selfless sacrifice could only have been learned from a mother like Nancy.

I looked at this women, possibly the strongest I've met, and I was simultaneously humbled and proud. The only words from her mouth were praise for all God has done for her.

She looked down at her hands, changed like her name. They now called her Mamma, as did I.

Mamma Nancy has been transformed.

From prisoner of war to ambassador of peace.
From helpless victim to fearless warrior.
From murderer to mother.

ABUNDANTLY MORE

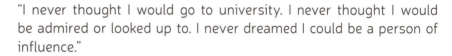

≪ **Martin's Story** | Gulu, Uganda

"I never thought I would go to university. I never thought I would be admired or looked up to. I never dreamed I could be a person of influence."

Martin was born in 1993 into a family with an absentee military father. His mother abandoned him when he was eight months old.

"My grandmother picked me up and I lived with her until my father came back when I was three."

This situation would prove not to be permanent. His father continued to go into the bush for long periods of time, leaving Martin with various relatives. He recalled living in more than seven homes from the ages of three to five.

"Some I would live in for one month, some just for one night. But I would always get kicked out for no reason and I would have to find a new place to live."

He rolled up his sleeve to reveal a scar.

"This is the only sign I have of my suffering as a child. I was cut once because I refused to wash clothes for one auntie and the children. Meanwhile, I was already required to do all the chores at five years old."

Finally, his father resigned from the army and found a job in Kampala. It seemed as though things would stabilize, with his father working and his grandmother caring for him. But after two years, his father remarried and things became worse.

"My stepmother mistreated me. She would constantly beat me and burn me with fire."

UGANDA: ABUNDANTLY MORE

THESE BEAUTIFUL PEOPLE

Martin's father lost his job and Martin was sent to live with his grandmother. She made him work for her, selling sugar cane and doing odd jobs.

"I wasn't going to school," Martin remembered, his eyes lost in the memory that came next. "Then in 2005 she chased me away. She called the cops on me and to this day I have no idea why. I remember standing there on the edge of the street, looking both ways, not knowing which way to take. I became a street kid."

I tried to imagine that.

In Kampala on any given day, you'll find hundreds, even thousands, of children and adults on the streets, usually working for someone else. The disfigured and handicapped are stationed at major intersections and highways, forced to beg for someone else's living. Young girls carry babies to evoke sympathy. Impossible to ignore, they approach you in your car or on the street. Others fend for themselves, their only goal—survival.

Like Martin.

"I was not going to school. I ate out of rubbish piles. I stole things and got into a lot of fights, causing trouble. I even learned martial arts with the sole purpose of revenging on my relatives."

"I had so much bitterness and pain in my heart. All I wanted was to be a killer. I wanted to be a terrorist."

The young man who stood before me now was nowhere close to being a terrorist. Although I couldn't picture it, I could sense the weight of bitterness and pain he had carried. Although the memories didn't cut as deeply as they used to, I could sense they remained crystal clear in his mind. He hates that city to this day.

"I go to Kampala and I see those kids on the street and I just see myself. It brings back all the terrible memories. I remember owning just one pair of pants, a T-shirt, and a sweater. And they took everything I had. I thought to myself, 'Will I ever have any other thing again?'

"I would tell myself during my time on the street that I don't have any future anymore. I never had any love in my heart. I never thought I could be a friend to someone."

After a year of being homeless, Martin decided to return to Gulu and look for a fresh start. He knew his auntie was still living there; perhaps she would take him in and help him go back to school.

"I wanted so badly to study. I had missed a lot of school because of not having school fees and living on the street, but I was intelligent. Every time I would come back to school, they would allow me to skip grades, so I managed to keep up."

Back in Gulu with his aunt, he wanted to continue with school, but there was not even money for food.

"Everyone would go for lunch in school and I had no lunch so I would just go and cry. I would have only water and three pieces of cassava in a week's time, but I so wanted to study."

Martin was near the end of his rope.

"I believed God hated me, and I hated Him."

Martin decided to rid himself of the anger, bitterness, hunger, and pain once and for all. Three times he tried to take his life: with pills, knives, and poison.

"I tried three times to kill myself, but *every time* my auntie would walk into the room just as I was about to do it. After the third time, I gave up! I figured I'm just not made for this," he said with a grin on his face. "To this day, she has no idea she interrupted my suicide attempts three times."

So, what changed? How did Martin go from wannabe terrorist to responsible, passionate, influential young man?

Here was the rest of his story.
He approached his uncle, who also lived in Gulu, and told him everything.

"He was broken and he said to me, 'Martin, from this day on you will be my son.' That was the first time I ever heard someone say they loved me."

Martin's uncle was actively involved in church, pastoring, mentoring, and praying for others. Uncle Patrick was the one who introduced Martin to Jesus.

"I wasn't so sure. I mean, if God loved me, I don't think he would have allowed me to go through all this. But I also knew that if I wanted to quit my wandering life, I needed to surrender my life. So I did. Partly because I wanted to, and partly because I wanted to stay with my uncle."

His transformation began.

"It took me five years to change. To smile, to be kind, to speak. I wanted to find out who this God was who loved me yet abandoned me and let me pass through all this pain. I needed to find out."

Martin's uncle, me, Martin's aunt, and Martin's sister, Gulu

It has been a journey marked by light piercing the darkness in his heart. A journey of learning to believe in himself, to see what God sees. A journey of seeing the impossible become manifest.

"One year after I accepted Christ, the pastor at my church came to me and said, 'I see something in you.' I responded in disbelief. 'You must be kidding! You don't know what I'm going through or what I've gone through.'

"He looked at me and said something so profound. 'It doesn't matter. God wants you.' And so I became a youth pastor in my church."

Martin and I attended the same discipleship program in 2014. After hearing his wisdom and gift of teaching, and witnessing his servant heart and compassion for others, I never would have expected his past struggle.

And what about the family and relatives he once wanted to wipe out?

"I forgive them," Martin said, at peace.

"I bought my dad a motorcycle and he could hardly believe I would do that. I told him, 'You're my father and you still remain a person of value in my life.' I gave my grandmother a place to live with me. The grandmother who had kicked me out and called the cops."

As we sat, we marvelled and wondered how this could be possible. For Martin, it was simple.

"The One who lives in me is the One who forgives. So let go of every past—we are following the future."

And he was chasing his future with more passion and energy than most.

"I never thought I would go to university. I never thought I would be admired or looked up to. I never dreamed I could be a person of influence. God has turned everything upside down," he said with a grin.

Martin's family now looks up to him as head of the family. They call him when important decisions need to be made or when a situation calls for wisdom. He is getting his bachelor's degree in education, English, and literature at Gulu University. He is the leader of several youth ministries and, whenever he has a break from school, he works with to local organizations that empower orphaned and marginalized youth.

"I have the vision of starting an orphanage. I want to be a father to the children who are going through what I went through. I think back to when I lost everything on the street and I wondered if I would ever have anything to call my own again. Now I look around and I have food to eat and clothes to wear and everything that I need. I want them to know that if God was able to pick me from where I was and place me here, then anything is possible for them!"

Martin now uses his testimony to transform the lives of hundreds, even thousands, of people.

"I do not regret where God picked me from. I no longer need to understand all the 'why's' of my suffering. I have a future as a vessel to transform others and I am excited!

"I'm a hundred percent different," he said, shaking his head with awe.

From abandoned and abused by his relatives to head of the home.
From no school fees to a university degree. From rejected to esteemed.
From bitterness to joy, anger to forgiveness.

See, Martin understands something so few do: he isn't entitled to a life free from suffering.

He recognizes what he has been given as just that—a priceless gift.

He recognizes there are two choices: curse the path that got him here or be thankful for it, knowing it has given him abundantly more than he ever dared to dream.

A SOMEBODY

≼ Justine's Story | Kajaansi, Uganda

"There's somebody I want you to meet."

Fred was grinning from ear to ear as he crossed the room in a single stride and reached for the latch on the door. When he swung it open, a timid but smiling face appeared and a young woman jumped into his arms. They laughed and bantered in Luganda, then he turned to me, eyes shining.

"This is Justine," he said, his arm around her shoulder.

Justine stuck out her hand to shake mine; I jumped up and pulled her into a bear hug. It's possible I frightened her at that point but, as she pulled away, she grinned and said how nice it was to meet me.

Little did I know, the pleasure was all mine.

We sat on the floor of Fred's two-room flat and laughed and talked and sang until long after dark. At first, Justine only observed, but as time went on, I could see her becoming comfortable.

Several months later, I was visiting Fred again. Justine came rushing in the door the moment she found out I was there. We spent the afternoon making—and eating—apple crisp and no-bake chocolate oatmeal cookies on a propane camping stove.

Gone was the timid and shy Justine I had met earlier. Here she was sharing her life with me, a complete stranger. I didn't realize what a privilege this was until I heard her story.

UGANDA: A SOMEBODY

THESE BEAUTIFUL PEOPLE

"I am Rwandese by nationality. My parents passed away when I was only three years old. I am the last-born in my family of six children and when my parents passed away I thought it was the end of the world. I didn't understand what was happening, I was just crying all the time because that's what all my brothers and sisters were doing."

Following the death of her parents, Justine was moved from home to home.

"The first home was with one of my elder sisters, but her husband never wanted me around so I had to go. None of my relatives wanted me because it was too much responsibility. Finally, when I was 10 years old, a friend of my mother's took me in."

Justine needed somebody. She was not wanted, not worthy, not a *somebody*—or so she felt.

"I spent two years with that friend of my mother's. What happened there is still too difficult for me to share. I've lived in five homes and am now in my sixth."

At 19 years of age, she has been through hell and back. But she refuses to see herself as a nobody.

"My life has not been easy. I have faced so many difficult situations but I still have so many dreams that I want to achieve. And I know that I will achieve them because of God."

She knows she is a somebody.

"I was only three years old when my mother died but I will never forget one thing about her: she taught me to pray. Before we ate, before we slept, all the time. I will never forget this."

And God has used those prayers to plant big dreams inside her.

"Since my childhood, I have told myself that when I grow up I want to make enough money to be able to take care of other children who are going through what I went through. I told myself that even if I don't have a lot of money, I will share the little I have with people who need it.

"My other dream is to be a journalist."

At this point, I asked her to write out her story for me. And she did, beaming at the opportunity to share through writing.

"I love to listen to people's stories and ideas, to study what's going on around me, and to share and interact with others."

"I'll tell you what…" she said, a grin on her face.

This is my favourite part, how two stories intersected to make a world of difference.

"I'll tell you what. I've learned that friends are important. More important than relatives, as has been my experience.

"In 2014 when I was alone and desperate and didn't know what to do anymore, when I had lost hope and was drowning in the grief of my heart, God brought somebody to me. A friend. He brought me Fred.

"Fred gave me a reason to live. He showed me the way forward and never left my side. Whenever I needed somebody, he was there to lean on. He has become my God-given brother.

"I know everything happens for a reason and I *know* that I needed to meet Fred. I cannot think of the hardships I have endured without tears in my eyes, but I am still alive because of God's mercy and that's why I love Him with all of my heart. And that is why I hang on to my dreams.

"I know I'm going to make it."

———

When Fred read this for the first time, he couldn't hold back the tears. Everybody needs a somebody, and sometimes we don't realize the impact we can have on a life. Sometimes it takes somebody to show us we *are* somebody.

You are a somebody, and you can be a somebody to somebody else. It's as simple as being there.

Justine needed a somebody. She was not wanted, not worthy, not a somebody—or so she felt. She needed a somebody who saw in her what nobody else could.

And now she no longer sees herself as a nobody. She has too much hope, too many dreams to pursue. Too much life to live, too many stories to write, too many people to impact.

All because somebody looked at her and didn't see just anybody.
He saw a somebody with a hope and a future.
A somebody named Justine.

UGANDA: A SOMEBODY
THESE BEAUTIFUL PEOPLE

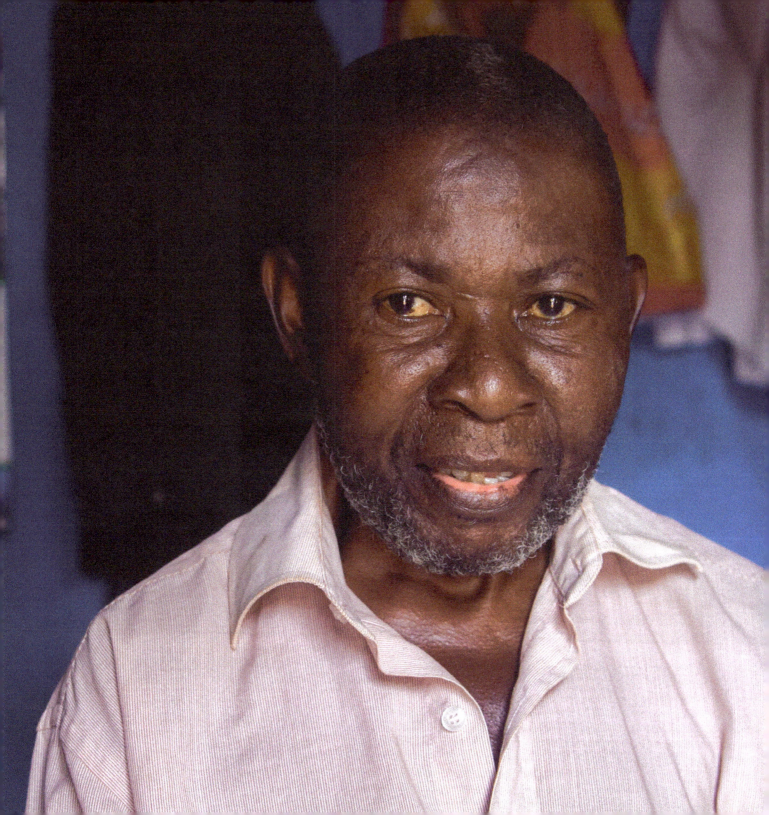

WHAT FAITH CAN DO

⩽ Uncle Peter's Story | Kampala, Uganda

You know, faith can be easy for us sometimes. Too easy.

Easy to say we trust when nothing is going wrong. Easy to say we have faith when there are no risks. Easy to say we endure when the road is smooth.

Many of us have that kind of faith—the fair-weather kind. The kind swayed by feeling and circumstance. The kind swallowed up in the storm, engulfed by fear or unbelief or just plain exhaustion.

But there's another kind of faith. The kind that has challenged me ever since I met Uncle Peter.

―――

The road was long and uphill. "Road" is too generous a word—it was more like a dirt path.

Tiny shops lined its edges: a butchery with meat hanging in the sun; a hair salon with a hairdresser fixing a weave on the front step; a *boda boda* stand whose drivers beckoned pedestrians from under their shade tree.

Women carried baskets of fruit on their heads and babies on their backs, making it difficult for the occasional car to navigate around potholes. No matter how slowly the cars drove, they always left us coughing in the dust.

We rounded the corner, where a man was skillfully rolling out dough, sending it sizzling into a hot cast-iron pan. Our bellies rumbled at the smell. Maybe later we could stop for one.

⩽ Photograph from Brad Baker Photography

UGANDA: WHAT FAITH CAN DO

THESE BEAUTIFUL PEOPLE

The path became more narrow until small mud houses appeared. We squeezed down narrow alleys, trying to avoid stepping in the muck. Our guide stopped and knocked on the wall of a hut, calling out Uncle Peter's name.

There was a rustling inside. After a few moments, the curtain being used as a makeshift door slid across and Uncle Peter stepped into view.

He looked at least 80, and his eyes were tired. You could see instantly that he wasn't well, overwhelmed by the three steps from the bed to the doorway.

Nearly bald and very frail, he still smiled. And welcomed us without hesitation. Seven strangers showed up unannounced, and he was thrilled.

We piled into his one-room home. A bed was on one side with some clothes piled around it. On the other side were two old wooden chairs, a small table, and a tiny black-and-white television. That was it.

Uncle Peter spoke about as much English as I did Luganda—so nothing. But oh, how I wished in that moment for the gift of understanding his language. I had to rely on translators.

To my surprise, Peter was only 62 years old. He loved football and had played it often when he was young. But he couldn't do those things now. He couldn't even work with his hands or do his laundry or take a walk.

Not for the past 12 years.

You see, 12 years ago Uncle Peter was in two *boda boda* accidents. In the first accident, he was on the bike but he survived with little damage to his body. In the second, he was struck by a bike as he was walking across the street, and the damage was severe.

His neck was cracked and broken in several places. The fact he lived is miraculous—but that's not even the most astounding part of his story.

When Uncle Peter arrived at the hospital, they could see he had no money. They laughed at him and told him to go home because he was old and would die anyway.

So he went home.

What choice did he have? His daughter did her best to look after him, but she only had a little money from the tuck shop she ran near their home.

Painfully, he pulled out the package of pain medication he was taking: the equivalent of pain killers for a headache. My jaw nearly dropped to the floor. That's like Advil.

For a broken neck. For 12 years. *Advil?*

For more than a decade, he'd been unable to move his neck or sleep properly or do anything physical without experiencing pain. The break had never healed properly. The bones had fused together and would require surgery for him to regain any kind of movement or relief.

As we left that day, my mind reeled. I was angry.

How could he be denied care simply because of his social status and age? What kind of hell had he lived in for all these years? They couldn't do anything? Really? Not even a simple neck brace?

As a Living Hope client, our outreach team was supposed to visit him regularly to pray for and encourage him. Living Hope was part of a Watoto ministry to support those living in poverty or with HIV/AIDS.

Living hope. It was laughable. He was in a living hell, and had been for years. How could we go back week after week, claiming to help and encourage him, without addressing one of his greatest needs?

I felt God tap me right on the heart and say, "Twila, you need to do something."

Oh, how I struggled with that. Because I'm white. And there's often an expectation that a white person is a saviour. A white person has all the money and power to completely fix your life.

This was always so frustrating because, no, actually, I don't have those things. That's Jesus you're thinking of. *He* has the answers. He *is* the answer.

I knew if I agreed to do this that I would be footing the bill. It's not that I minded spending the money: the money wasn't mine anyway—it was God's. I just hated the way it looked. Hated the way it encouraged the "white superior" mentality all too common here.

Uncle Peter as a young man in his twenties

But I couldn't shake the feeling that something had to be done. And why should I care how it appeared to other people? So what if they thought I was a rich white person? So what if they thought I could fix all their problems because I come from a "superior" place?

Should Uncle Peter not receive the care he needed simply because I was concerned how it might appear? Ridiculous! He wasn't a project—he was a person.

So I decided to adopt him.

My team and I did some research. We discovered that his post-accident medical test records were likely lost, and waiting for them to be found—well, we didn't have that kind of time. I wasn't going to be in the country for much longer.

Watoto 360, the discipleship class that had assigned us Uncle Peter, would be ending in a few months. We needed to use our time wisely. My team advised me it would be faster to have the tests redone to assess the results and determine the options.

The next time we crowded into Uncle Peter's humble abode, we brought good news. We had booked the CT scan and we would arrange a car to take him to the appointment. On hearing the news, Uncle Peter began talking one blue streak in Luganda, exclaiming and gesturing and hardly containing himself.

And so we discovered even more.

When he was turned away from the hospital, his family and friends insisted on taking him to a witch doctor for healing. They taunted him, saying things like, "Where is this Jesus? You keep saying He will help you, but it has been years and He has done nothing! Just come to the witch doctor and have this taken care of once and for all."

Every day they would come, and every day Uncle Peter would say, "No, Jesus is going to do something."

I sat there dumfounded. I'd like to think I would have had the same response. It's easy to think, "Yeah, I'd do that, too! I'd *never* go to a witch doctor!"

But wouldn't you? If you had a broken neck and only Advil for the pain? If you couldn't lay your head down all the way? If your arms and legs were mostly numb?

For 12 years.

Don't you think the thought of relief would be tempting, regardless of the form it came in?

Because wasn't that our default faith? The fair-weather kind. The kind swayed by feeling and circumstance. The kind swallowed up in the storm, engulfed by fear or unbelief or exhaustion.

I think that would have been my reaction.

But not Uncle Peter. And now today he was rejoicing because, for the first time in 12 years, there was a tangible glimmer of hope.

"They told me Jesus would never come to help me, but look! *Look!* Twelve years later, He is doing something now!"

No tests had been done yet, no promises of restoration made.

He simply believed.

And when he reached over and grasped my hand with his worn and weathered ones, when his once-tired eyes shone straight into mine, when he slowly sounded out, "Thank you, Mummy. Thank you,

Almost one year after his surgery, Uncle Peter in his home in Ntinda, Kampala

Jesus," in perfectly broken English, I had to have that faith, too.

I had to believe something could be done. *Would* be done. That God would do something.

I could only squeeze his hands because the lump in my throat was too large. And the determination in my heart too strong.

I realized in that moment that I didn't care what it looked like anymore. I only cared that his faith would be honoured and that God would show up.

From that day on, it was a whirlwind of appointments and results and meetings with doctors and options and divine connections. We were connected with people who knew all the right doctors, with people who could translate, visit Uncle Peter, and oversee his medication.

God was working and my faith was growing. I shelled out money for drugs and tests and doctors' visits.

I never knew how much anything was going to cost. There were days I worried: *I still have a year and a half left in Africa. If I use all my money now, then what?*

And Jesus whispered, "It's not yours anyway." It had gone from a project to something personal. Because seriously, what would I gain from travelling to other parts of Africa but knowing I'd refused to serve the ones right in front of me?

So I determined that I would rather run out of money and go home early than leave this uncle without help. *My* uncle.

My teammates gathered small food items for him, just to bless him. On our days off, they would translate for me or take him to appointments.

Finally, it was decided he should have surgery. But no one knew when he could get an appointment. No one knew how much the surgery would cost.

So we prayed. And waited.

Then I got a call from a friend who'd been helping relentlessly with the whole process.

He said, "We need to take Uncle Peter to the hospital immediately. He is on the waiting list for the surgery but he has to be in the hospital to be in line. It could still be weeks or months, but he has to be in. We don't know how much it will cost but you need to decide right now if we are going to go through with it."

I was silent but my mind raced: *How am I going to pay for this? Where's the money going to come from?*

The surgery was as risky as it was expensive. The money simply wasn't there.

Then I remembered the faith of Uncle Peter. And I felt it rise up in me: *if he can believe God for a miracle for 12 years without wavering, surely I can believe God for some money and divine timing, can't I?*

I heard myself say, "Go ahead and book it. The money will be there. I don't know how, but it will be there."

A few days later, we moved Uncle Peter to the hospital.

The medical care system is different in Uganda. For most of us, if we're admitted to the hospital, we're fed and taken care of physically. Family members and friends visit and bring treats, but they're just that—treats.

UGANDA: WHAT FAITH CAN DO

Uncle Peter in his neck brace after surgery

In Uganda, not so much. The hospital bed is the only thing you're given. Food, personal hygiene, and care—everything—you must provide. That means cooking utensils and containers, food, a kettle, a mat for his daughter to sleep or sit on beside the bed—she would be with him constantly—basins for washing and laundry, soap... You name it, we purchased it.

We had no idea how long this hospital stay would be. All we could do was pray. And visit.

I remember one time going to see him in the hospital. I took him one of my Watoto 360 shirts. He was so excited. He sat up in bed and insisted we put it on him. There he sat, clenching my hands, beaming from ear to ear.

We still had no idea when the surgery would be or how much it would cost or how it would be paid for. We just took it one day at a time. One week at a time.

Many people from Canada—yes, even some of you—donated funds to assist in his care. I wish you could've seen the look in his eyes when I told him he had friends all across Canada praying diligently for him.

After years of feeling unseen and unheard, suddenly he was enveloped in care right here and across oceans.

That's what faith could do. And Uncle Peter had loads of it.

I'll never forget the day I got the call.

I was in a taxi headed to Jinja to see friends from Canada when my phone rang.

"Uncle Peter has a surgery date. And I don't know why, but the doctor is doing the surgery for free." My friend sounded as flabbergasted as I felt.

My hand gripped the phone even tighter and my breath caught in my throat.

"I'm sorry, what? Are you sure?" I stuttered. Silent shock was being replaced by inexplicable joy.

"That's not normal, is it? That doesn't normally happen, does it? Surgery is not normally free in Uganda, right?" My questions spilled out one after the other.

"No." His response solidified it. Nothing short of miraculous.

But should I have been surprised? That's what God can do. That's what faith can do—when it's a faith that lasts.

The surgery was successful. We had a neck brace for his post-surgery to assist in the healing process. He was also enrolled in physiotherapy for the next six months.

By now I was in and out of the country. My time in Uganda was finished but I still had several countries in Africa to visit. Every time I passed through Uganda, I would check on him and his physiotherapy.

Sometimes I went with a translator. Sometimes I didn't.

One time I showed up with juice to find him hunched over a basin doing his laundry by hand! Once his neck had healed, the pressure on the nerves was released and the numbness in his arms and legs was almost completely gone.

I could hardly hold back tears.

God gave us another special gift that day—the gift of understanding each other. As if his English had improved overnight, we were able to have a conversation, something which had never happened without a translator before or since.

He told me how he good he felt, how he would go for walks around the compound, how he was able to

UGANDA: WHAT FAITH CAN DO
THESE BEAUTIFUL PEOPLE

sleep. But even if he hadn't been able to say a word, it only took one look at him to know something had greatly improved.

I was so encouraged by the visit, but there was still concern for sustainability. I knew I couldn't keep this up forever.

It was our final doctor's appointment. I was leaving the country for good and we needed to make sure his recovery was on track. He had completed his physiotherapy and our prayer was that the doctor would say he didn't need anything else.

The doctor's words washed over me with a flood of relief.

"He is good to go."

The little bit of pain he had in his knees and back was simply related to old age. Everything related to his neck injury was healed and the pain medication could slowly be reduced.

"They told me Jesus would never come to help me, but look! *Look!* Twelve years later, He is doing something now!"

I went back to visit him in 2016 and he is not doing as well as he was. Advancing age and a lack of resources and care are putting him in pain again.

But he was still so grateful. And he was still praising the God who showed up—even after 12 years.

Hope deferred makes the heart sick, but a longing fulfilled is a tree of life

—PROVERBS 13:12, NEW INTERNATIONAL VERSION

A hope 12 years deferred could have turned Uncle Peter into an angry, bitter, old man with no use for a God who could allow such a thing.

But instead, Uncle Peter dug his roots deep, set his face toward his Father, and refused to lose faith.

Now, a longing fulfilled 12 years later has brought not only life and hope and joy, but also faith.
A faith that doesn't avoid storms but embraces them.

UGANDA: WHAT FAITH CAN DO
THESE BEAUTIFUL PEOPLE

A faith that isn't swayed by feelings but remains steady, regardless of circumstance.
A faith that refuses to give up or turn back. A faith that drives out fear.

A faith so powerful that God had to wait 12 years to bring me from Canada, to join a discipleship course, to be placed in the specific group assigned to Uncle Peter, so his longing could be fulfilled and my faith could be challenged.

But that's what faith can do.

I sometimes wonder if Uncle Peter understands the depth of the impact he has had on my life. All the lessons I've learned from him, he taught me without saying a word!

Simply by living out faith.
A faith that lasts.

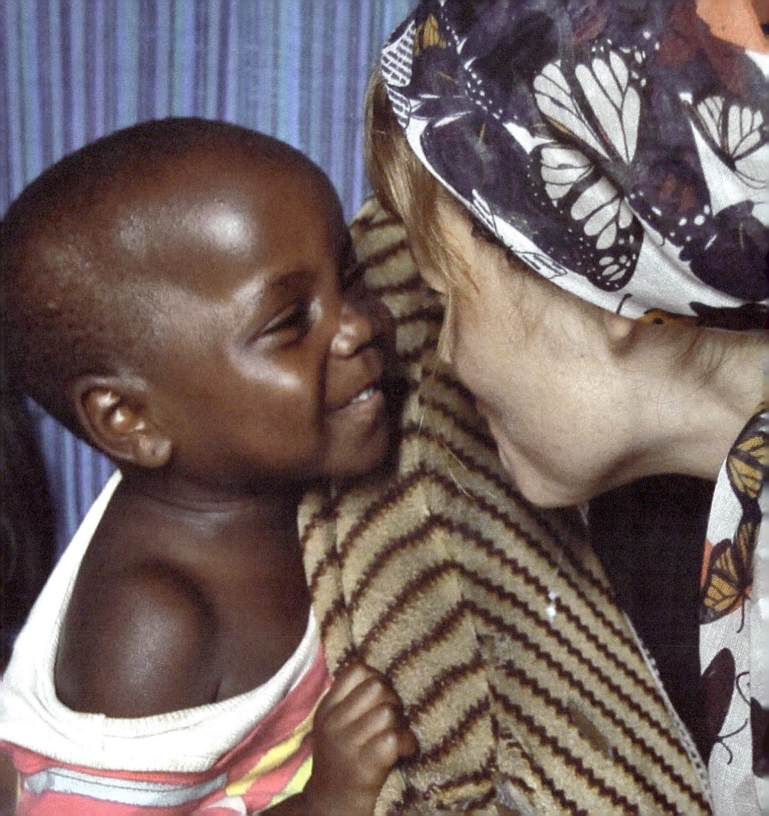

A LITTLE CHILD SHALL LEAD THEM

≪ Vivian's Story | Bwaise, Kampala, Uganda

"Hey, Julius. I think it's going to be a child."

The afternoon sun beat hot on my shoulders as we made our way down the busy street.

An hour earlier, my outreach group had been standing in a circle in our classroom, praying for direction.

We were headed to the slums to adopt a family that we could love and support for the next six months. We needed God to lead us to the right family.

As we stood praying hand in hand, Isaiah 11:6 came to my mind: "A little child shall lead them."

My immediate response? How out of context this section of the verse was in this situation!

But God gave me a picture of a small child taking me by the hand and leading us to her mother. I sensed this was how we would find our family.

"Julius, I feel like it's going to be a child that leads us to our family," I said.

"Really?" Julius flashed me a smile and grabbed my hand as we carefully crossed the street, dodging *boda bodas* and weaving in and out of taxis.

"Yes. I got the verse and picture while we were praying earlier," I said.

"Well, we shall see." He was skeptical but smiling.

≪ *The day we met Vivian*

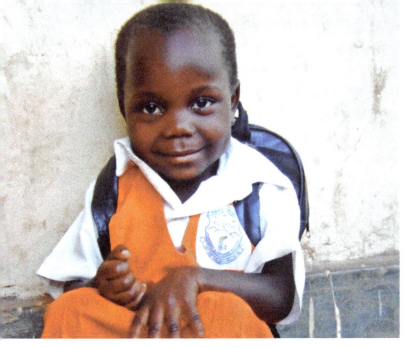

Vivian in her school uniform, 2016

Smiles before the goodbye tears on one of our many visits

We stepped off the main road and onto the red dirt path leading toward our side of the slum. You could smell it before you could see it: not the slum so much as the river of refuse next to it. I'm convinced it contained more trash and feces than water.

We took the first path to the right and walked toward the heart of the community. Buildings almost unrecognizable as houses dotted the sides of the road, watermarked from previous floods. Windows and doors were built up in hopes their one-room abodes wouldn't be washed out by the rainy season.

But still, children played and laughed. In the midst of the dust and trash, life went on.

We had just entered the street when I saw a little girl, no older than three, running down the street with her arms wide open. As she approached me she fell to her knees, a customary act of respect and honour in this community.

She grasped my hand and led me and my team back to her mother, who was cooking food in giant cast-iron pots over a fire. She would sell her food in the evening from the side of the road.

We had found our family. I was speechless. We walked through the rest of the community just to make sure, but three-year-old Vivian had my heart.

Despite the language barrier, we had found

our family. Sara, Vivan's mother, invited us into her home, a one-room stone structure that was home for five people: herself, her three children, and her sister. A curtain separated the bed from the rest of the room, which contained two chairs, a couch, a television, and a fan.

No bathroom. No kitchen. No toys for Vivian.

But the smile on that girl's face could light up a whole village. And she had captured my heart.

"Julius, I told you! I knew it would be a little child!" I beamed.

"You fell in love with that little girl, didn't you?" He grinned in my direction.

Sure, I did. But more importantly, Jesus did first. And these are the moments I just *love* being on His team.

———

I wrote that blog a few days after I met Vivian. More than three years have passed, and I've had the privilege of visiting her several times.

There's still a language barrier. We can't talk to each other, but we can laugh and smile and colour together. Vivian is now in school and performing well for her age. She's bright and bold, mischievous and cheerful.

She might be surrounded by piles of trash every day, but *she's* not trash.

She might have fewer opportunities than others, but she's *making the most* of the opportunities she has.

She might not have fancy clothes or pockets full of change, but she has a beautiful heart and a future full of possibilities.

Yes, I fell in love with Vivian that day. Because just as she led me to her mother, so she will lead others. Lead her community, her country, and her world.

Just as this little child led us, so she will lead them.

FORGET I'M WHITE

⩽ **Sisters' Story** | Kampala, Uganda

New places can be difficult to navigate and adjust to. But how about a new country, a new *continent,* where you're an esteemed minority? Where you walk down the street and you look like an ATM, a plane ticket, or a green card. Where you're only desired because of the colour of your skin.

It's hard to know the difference between who wants to be *your* friend and who wants a *white* friend. All you want is to blend in and forget you're white.

Day after day it continues. And day after day you become more and more frustrated. It's easy to think that they all see you the same way. That you can't fully trust anyone.

And this mentality is as horrifically wrong as the one that believes in white privilege.

For as many people who look at me and see only white, there are many who look at me and see only Twila.

These girls are some of the many.

HARYET

I'll never forget the day we were walking down the street, talking and laughing and carrying on as we normally did.

UGANDA: FORGET I'M WHITE

THESE BEAUTIFUL PEOPLE

As we stood waiting for a taxi, Haryet exclaimed, "Why is everyone staring at us?"

I looked over at her in disbelief. I mean, isn't it obvious? She looked at me and broke into a smile.

"Oh yeah, I forgot you are white!"

I could have cried.

Thank you! Thank you, thank you, a million times thank you. For forgetting about the colour of my skin and simply seeing me as a person.

Thank you for forgetting I'm white.

UGANDA: FORGET I'M WHITE

THESE BEAUTIFUL PEOPLE

LINDA, JO-ANN, AND JORDANA

During my last week in Uganda, these girls planned—without me knowing—something now fondly known as "the seven days of goodbye."

They came to me one day and said, "You need to keep your evenings open during your last week. You'll find out why."

Every day for the following week, they planned outings to favourite restaurants or live music functions, and arranged activities I hadn't been able to do yet, like eat a whole chicken on the side of the road or frozen cheesecake with plastic forks. Every day was a reminder that these relationships were more than skin deep.

Too many times to count, without even trying, these girls made me forget I'm white. Birthday parties, road trips, long talks, tears, hugs, fights. Real-life stuff because we're real-life kind of people.

———

Sometimes it's easier to let the shallowness of our differences keep us from deep, meaningful relationships. We see the colour of someone's skin or nationality, instead of their heart and humanity. When I tell people about these girls, I refer to each one as my sister. And people look at me surprised, like, "You have a sister in Uganda?"

I just grin and say, "I have four of them."

They're part of the reason why going to Uganda is like going home.

Because they love me for me, not for my ethnicity.
Because they forget I'm white.

FIVE SISTERS, *NJERA*, AND A SCARF

≪ **Sisters' Story** | Kampala, Uganda

It was a beautiful, warm Thursday evening. We had all met at Mosana, the juice place—it's kind of our favourite. You can get a large glass of freshly squeezed layered juice for a couple of bucks.

Mosana also sells *njera,* another one of our loves. *Njera* is an Ethiopian sponge-like bread topped with meat or whatever you want. Then you use your hands to tear the bread and scoop up the meat.

It's pretty addictive, and it's been known to cause people to go a little crazy. At least that's our theory. Every time we have *njera*—so every Thursday night—we get loud and end up in fits of obnoxious laughter.

Tonight was no exception.

I was the first one there. Then Haryet and Jo-ann arrived from work. A little while later, Jordana breezed in. I had been away for more than a year, so the hugs and smiles were bigger than usual.

Long after we'd ordered, Linda bounded in, late as usual. We grinned and hugged all over again, nothing out of the ordinary. Except that today Linda was wearing a scarf.

Not just any scarf—a scarf designed by and made for her. See, Linda has an eye for fashion design. She has a gift for taking ordinary

≪ *Haryet. Photograph from RGfondo*

clothes and revamping them, using authentic African material, to create wardrobe perfection.

"I have to make one! Tomorrow!" exclaimed Haryet, as she snatched it from Linda's neck and wrapped it around her own.

We agreed we all needed one, and then we moved on to the jacket she was wearing, something stunning she had also created. That's how it all started.

"We should sell these!" Haryet piped up.

"Yeah, Jordana can sew them, and do all the makeup and style design for photoshoots," added Linda.

"And Jo-ann will handle the finances and modelling." Haryet pointed emphatically at Jo.

"We can all model," I said, "and I will do international sales!"

We all laughed. Then we all looked at each other.

"Seriously, guys. We could do this!" Linda exclaimed.

Then it got loud and obnoxious. The notebook came out and the planning began. The ideas were flowing faster than we could record. Scarves, accessories, phone covers… The list went on and on. And, naturally, every idea deserved a loud cheer. By the time we left, we had a company name, a plan, and an order for 20 scarves.

Within a week, we had bought material and hired our first seamstress. We had an order for 10 more scarves and a potential seller in Rwanda

≪ *Jordana. Photograph from RGfondo*

UGANDA: FIVE SISTERS, *NJERA*, AND A SCARF
THESE BEAUTIFUL PEOPLE

and Burundi. We also had a photographer willing to do a photoshoot using refugee youth and ourselves as the models.

And so Naked Roots was born.
Naked Roots: Be authentic. Be you.

The best part is we're employing refugee women in Uganda. These women are extremely vulnerable; some are already in compromising situations. We want to help them to become less susceptible to trafficking and other traps they might fall into.

Why wait until they are trafficked? Why wait until we have to free them and rehabilitate them? Why not stop it before it starts?

As we drove home that night, our heads were spinning and our hearts were full.

"Is this really happening?" we asked. Yes, it's happening!

As Haryet cried out to Jesus and placed this plan in His hands, we all knew we were about to be part of something bigger than ourselves.

So you never know when something will begin. You never know where or when God will give you an idea that changes everything. Maybe it will come when you're driving to work, walking the dog, bathing the kids. Whatever it is, it will start when you are truly being you.

For us, it just happened to be with five sisters, *njera*, and a scarf.

≪ *Left: Linda. Photograph from RGfondo*
≪ *Right: Top; Jo-ann. Photograph from RGfondo. Bottom; Photograph from RGfondo*

UGANDA: FIVE SISTERS, *NJERA*, AND A SCARF

THESE BEAUTIFUL PEOPLE

THE CLIMB

≤ **Ibra's Story** | Kampala, Uganda

There's nothing like the climb.

When you're driving toward the mountain and you see it standing in the distance, small in perspective but towering above everything else, you say to yourself, "That's big, but doable."

At the foot of the mountain, you stand, eyes lifted, neck strained. The peak is immersed in clouds and parts of the path peak out from behind trees. You're nervous but excited.

"That's big, and parts of the path are hidden, but I think I can do it. Yeah, I can do it… I think," you tell yourself, as you lace up your boots and tighten your pack.

Now you're part of the way up. Your breathing is laboured and your quads are in pain. The scenery is beautiful, sure, but your focus has shifted to how difficult this is.

"This is harder than I thought. Longer. Steeper. I can't see the end and I can't turn around now, can I?" Thoughts like this fill your mind but you push them aside. You take one more step. Then another. And another.

Just when you think you can't go on, you see it. Your heart skips a beat and you stop in your tracks. "That's the top, I can feel it." Out of nowhere, your legs and lungs find new strength. Your steps quicken. Is that a smile tugging at your pursed lips?

UGANDA: THE CLIMB

THESE BEAUTIFUL PEOPLE

Ibra waving his flag at Mount Everest base camp

It's the summit. You made it! You breathe deeply and stand still, looking east to west, north to south. Gone are the doubts and the thoughts about quitting. Forgotten is the pain and the pressure of the climb.

All that matters is the here and now. You made it. And the view is worth it.

There's no better feeling in the world than to stand at the top of a mountain, knowing you could have given up, but didn't. Knowing you could have missed this, but didn't.

UGANDA: THE CLIMB

Ibra understands this like few others.

Myself, I've climbed less than a handful of mountains. The most memorable was a volcano in Rwanda. One of the guides finally grabbed me by the arms and dragged me for the last hour.

Ibra, on the other hand, has climbed the top five mountains in Africa, with a combined total of 114,829 feet in elevation. And he loves it!

"The mountaineering bug bit me hard two years ago and I dream of standing on the great seven summits!" he proclaimed.

Born and raised in Uganda, Ibra has always been a free spirit, meant for travel and new experiences and challenges.

After travelling to 12 countries and starting several small businesses, he always has a new idea brewing.

"What's Ibra up to now?" was the constant question among friends and family. And the natural answer: "He's all over the place." Because he is. He's the epitome of making the most of every opportunity—and creating as many opportunities as you can.

In December 2014, my friends and I went to Zanzibar for Christmas. A few days in, we got a message from Ibra, asking where we were. We told him and he made a comment about flying over. After several minutes of stunned silence, trying to figure out if he was serious, we started laughing. Because that is exactly something he would do—just get a notion and show up. Not even two days later, he was there!

You see, to Ibra every moment is a blessing, everything is a gift, and everyone is an opportunity for relationship.

"I grew up with my parents and I am blessed to still have them to this day. I was always adventurous as a child, running around the neighbourhood instead of taking a nap as I was told. But my favourite memories are the ones with my dad. He would watch *The Lion King* with me, and bring me books to read with little notes from him. My favourite said, '*Ssebudde Ibrahim,* my dearest son in whom I delight.' I hold on to these things dearly," he remembered.

UGANDA: THE CLIMB

THESE BEAUTIFUL PEOPLE

Ibra surprises us in Zanzibar for Christmas

"My father was an alcoholic when I was young, so to be able to have this kind of relationship with him now is nothing but a gift. My mother led me to Christ when I was young, and she is still the biggest influence in my Christian life today."

His faith became his own at 16 years old. Since then he has been walking toward his purpose in entrepreneurship.

"I am growing a water processing, bottling, and distribution company," he said, "but my dream is to found a social enterprise that will impact a billion lives."

Ibra doesn't know yet what that will be, but his dreams are big like that. He also isn't content to keep them as dreams—he acts on them. I'm sure that for every successful endeavour, a hundred have failed.

When he tells me he has fallen in love with the mountains, I'm not surprised. In fact, I think he has fallen in love with the climb.

"Life is all about relationship. Relationship with our creator, with people, and with His creation," Ibra said.

Relationships, like climbing mountains, take work. They take perseverance and effort and grit.
But there's no better feeling than having healthy relationships. Than knowing you could've run from the hard thing, but didn't. Than knowing you could have missed it, but didn't.

It will probably be messy and more than a little painful, but it will also be worth it.

The climb is always worth it.

A POWERFUL ENCOUNTER

≪ Innocent's Story | Serere, Uganda

It was hot. It was dusty. I had to strain my ears to make out what he was saying over the roar of the bike, the wind, and the occasional passing car or shouting bystander. And I wanted so badly to hear because he was telling me his story.

I was in Serere, Uganda, about to speak at a conference for pastors and youth. (I was doing the *youth* part.) I was staying at a place about a 45-minute *boda boda* ride from town, and Innocent and I were making the trip on the popular but rarely safe motorcycle.

"I was born in 1983 in Eastern Uganda, the fifth of seven children from my father's thirteenth and final wife," Innocent shouted over the hum of the engine.

I was sure I hadn't heard right.

But it was true. In fact, he had recently met a sister for the first time, another ramification of being raised in such a large family.

"Daddy died when I was six and Mommy struggled a lot to provide for the family. Our basic needs were rarely met and education was a challenge."

Growing up in a polygamous family made life after his father's death even worse.

"My mom did not stay with the rest of the other women, and everything that belonged to my dad was owned by the bigger family. Even within that large group, only one wife had all the papers so no one else would

UGANDA: A POWERFUL ENCOUNTER

benefit. There was no unity in the family—a lot of division—so we never gained anything from my father's properties at all. At one point, one of the other wives told my mother to sell one of us to get food. That was how terrible life was."

Many of the details of his life were too painful for him to express in detail. He recalled often considering suicide due to the rejection he felt from the people who were supposed to be family.

Bitterness defined his life and he turned to violence.

"Before I met Jesus, my life was a mess, a real mess." He turned his head slightly around to make sure I had caught that part, as a large truck full of people hanging out the bed clunked past on our right.

I shielded my face from the onslaught of dust but to no avail. I leaned in closer to keep from being blown off. "I was a serious drug addict. I lived a reckless life without meaning and without purpose. I was taken to the police twice in 2004 and 2006 because of my habits."

It didn't matter that he had grown up in a setting where his mother was a believer and had done her best to raise him and his siblings in His ways. He still made his own choices.

"In school, I got friends who were living immoral lives and I got mixed up in it all. We pretended to be good but really we were thugs."

I laughed a little but instantly regretted it as a wad of dirt filled my mouth. I just couldn't picture this guy as a thug; the thought was almost comical. But it was true.

"I met Jesus in 2007," he continued, shouting over the wind. How could his mouth not be completely dried out? I leaned in closer, not wanting to miss a single word.

This was going to be the good part—I could just tell. The part where everything changed.

"It was August 14, 2007. Midnight. I was at home in bed and I woke up from what felt like an earthquake, but really there wasn't an earthquake. The whole house was shaking. I looked up at the ceiling and it looked like fire but it wasn't burning the house. I attempted to run out but found myself weak and I ended up kneeling down, which I had not intended. I crawled out but ended up flat on the ground with my hands glued down, crying and wailing, and I couldn't get up.

"A voice called me by name and asked, 'Innocent, will you follow Me?' Three times, the voice asked. The first and second time, I didn't respond. The third time, with power and authority that I can't even describe to you, I couldn't resist and I said, 'Yes, Lord, from today on I will follow You wherever You lead. Yes, Lord, I will serve You.' Then the voice said, 'Covenant signed,' and everything returned to normal. I was able to get up and go back to my bed."

But how can anything go back to normal after such a powerful encounter? And though the physical state of the room might have returned to reality, Innocent's life would never be the same.

"After that, I started going to church, participating in church activities. Doors opened for me. In 2008 I attended a six-month discipleship training school in Arua, Uganda. After returning, I served in my home church as a secretary for missions and evangelism. In 2010 I joined Youth with a Mission in Yei, South Sudan. From 2012 to 2013, I was appointed to pastor a local church back near my home, and in 2014 I got a new appointment to head the education department overseeing 10 churches in the area, which I am still doing to this day."

UGANDA: A POWERFUL ENCOUNTER

THESE BEAUTIFUL PEOPLE

See, it never goes back to normal. Not after an encounter.

"My life has totally been transformed and changed by the grace of God."

No kidding!

I kept thinking of the story of Saul. On the road to Damascus, he had a powerful encounter with the Almighty God. His environment returned to normal, but Saul was changed. He was given a new name—from Saul to Paul—and a new destiny—from persecutor of Christians to fearless proclaimer of the gospel.

Innocent had been on the road to disaster. He, too, had a powerful encounter with God. He, too, was given a new destiny.

"I am at Alpha Omega Seminary in Jinja, Uganda, pursuing my bachelor of arts in theology part time and serving the church part time. My pastoral calling is meant to serve the continent of Africa, so that is what I am going to do for the remaining days of my life. I want to establish a strong teaching ministry here to serve my people. Wherever He leads, I will follow. Whatever He asks me to do, I will do."

Innocent was also recently appointed a government role as secretary head of health and education for his district. He has dreams to apply for his master's immediately after completing his four-year program. The school is paying half of his tuition; the rest he relies on God to provide. This faith and trust he attributes to his late mother, who taught him and his siblings to depend on God. He knows they are who they are today because of who God is and what He has done in their lives.

"My heart has finally found what it was missing. This is where I was meant to be and so I purpose to take this direction for the rest of my life."

Words like this cannot be spoken with such passion unless they come out of a direct encounter with the Father.

How fitting that God had used a long, dusty bike ride to reveal a story of His power and grace, and His longing to meet each one of us on our road. And you can never go back to normal after seeing the face and the grace of Jesus, however He comes.

Whether it be a bright light on the road to Damascus, a quaking hut in the villages of Africa, a quiet whisper in your soul on a long day, a verse or a song that pierces your heart, or two dust-caked faces sharing life stories on a backroad in Serere.

These are the moments that change everything.
These are the moments we'll never forget.
These are the powerful encounters.

KENYA

They say the name Kenya comes from a combination of three tribal languages, each with a similar-sounding word that means "God's resting place."

Kenya does have a restful, calming feel—except for maybe Nairobi, the capital.

My first impression of Kenya was arriving in the tiny town of Eldoret at 4 a.m., not knowing where I was going or if anyone would be there to meet me. My phone had died. The streets were quiet, dark, and empty. And I was freezing.

I didn't know then that I was at a much higher elevation than the rest of the country. Although it was hot during the day, temperatures dropped significantly overnight and people would dress like it was winter.

Ever wonder why Kenyans win all our races? I used to, until I went there. Eldoret is home to an Olympic training ground where athletes come from far and wide to train at altitude. No wonder they win when they come to Canada and the United States—they have more air in their lungs than they know what to do with! I, on the other hand, was huffing and puffing for the first three days just walking.

Kenya is a young country, with 40 percent of her nearly 47 million population under 15 years of age. This is attributed mostly to earlier marriage and child bearing, as well as a shift from family planning to HIV/AIDS prevention. The average life expectancy is 64 years, and in 2015 it was estimated that more than 1.5 million people were living with HIV/AIDS. That same year, 36.8 percent and 69.9 percent of the population lacked proper drinking water and sanitation facilities, respectively. This leaves Kenyans at a greater risk of infection and disease. In 2012 more than 43 percent of the population was found to be living below the poverty line.

≤ *Airstrip in Kisii, Kenya*

KENYA

THESE BEAUTIFUL PEOPLE

Fishermen in the morning, Mombasa, Kenya

Kenyans, however, are known as businessmen. Highly educated, literate, and innovative, they work hard and get things done. You'll notice this by Nairobi's faster pace. The joke is that taxis in Nairobi don't stop: you have to jump on and off while they're moving. Rolling stops were one of the first things I noticed while riding Kenya's loud, vibrantly decorated buses.

Recognized as East Africa's hub of transportation, Kenya's economy is threatened by corruption and weak governance. The unemployment rate is 40 percent, even with a growing middle class of entrepreneurs. Relying mainly on agriculture, 75 percent of the nation's output is from livestock production or small rain-irrigated farms. Many of Kenya's neighbouring countries are recipients of these exports, especially fruits and vegetables.

The medical field took a significant hit in the last half of 2016, with doctors going on strike due to underfunding, under-remuneration, and poor working conditions. The public health care system almost stopped functioning completely after 5,000 doctors walked out. Kenya's health minister, together with President Uhuru Kenyatta, saw the doctors' demands as too costly to meet. This caused heavy strain on nurses, who weren't able to provide the care their patients needed. As a result, the whole country suffered.

KENYA

THESE BEAUTIFUL PEOPLE

Despite these challenges, Kenyans are a joyful and expressive people. Slightly more assertive than other East Africans, they're natural musicians and storytellers. They're also insistent on teaching everyone they meet how to speak Kiswahili, one of Kenya's official languages, which they've combined with English to create what is known as "Shang." To them, it's "so easy to learn." To most, it's a butchering of both languages.

Tanzanians say, "Swahili was born in Tanzania, it was corrupted in Kenya, and it died in Uganda." And it's absolutely true.

Kenyans' fluency in English, however, is beneficial to the nearly 400,000 Somalian refugees who now find shelter within Kenya's borders. This doesn't include refugees from South Sudan, Congo, or Ethiopia. With this influx of cultures comes diversity in religion; unfortunately, some groups have turned violent.

When most people hear "Kenya," they think "West Gate Mall." The attack there was just the beginning. Since then there have been more isolated attacks by extremist groups, but it's not the country as a whole. Most of the country continues to live in peace despite ethnic differences.

Much of Kenyans' music and culture reflects an adaptation of Western culture, mirrored in the hustle and bustle of Nairobi's thriving metropolis. I stumbled across Subway, Coldstone Creamery, and other foods that made my eyes widen and my heart leap for joy. But your experience would not be complete without the one thing a Kenyan can never live without: ugali, a maize-based starch present at nearly every meal. Kenyans say, "Ugandans eat rice, but for us, we eat rice while we are waiting for the ugali to cook. You have not eaten if you have not had ugali." It's delicious with skumawiki (fried kale) and omena (tiny fish), or intestines or any kind of meat. Ugali will always be my request when I arrive, along with African (milk) tea and mandazi (a huge, often triangular, donut-style pastry).

But while Kenya might be home to familiar food, an ice-skating rink, and East Africa's largest airport, her villages are home to some of the original nomadic and warrior tribes: the Masai (warriors) and the Kikuyu (farmers). These tribes—especially the Masai and Masai land, or Masai Mara—draw thousands of tourists every year, hoping to get a glimpse of the colourful costumes and ancient practices of the people who first made the land their home. Though the Kikuyu tribe was bigger, the Masai dominated by frequently raiding their neighbours.

Slavery is also a big part of Kenya's history. By the time slavery was abolished in the mid-nineteenth century, thousands had already been taken and sold in countries throughout the world.

KENYA

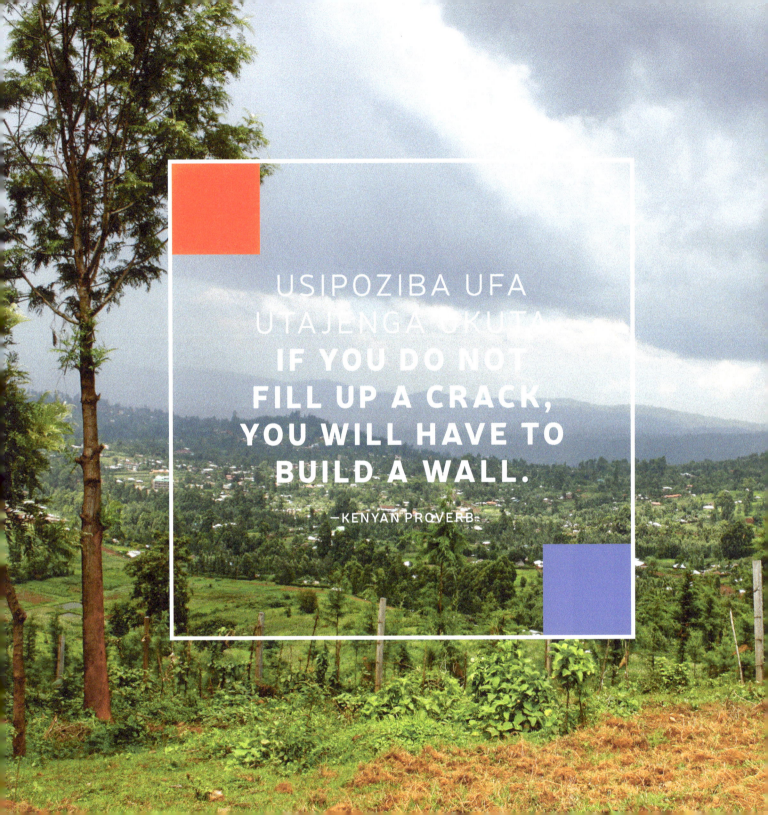

USIPOZIBA UFA
UTAJENGA UKUTA
**IF YOU DO NOT
FILL UP A CRACK,
YOU WILL HAVE TO
BUILD A WALL.**

—KENYAN PROVERB

But these things are in the past, and though we can look back and learn from them, we can't stay there. Kenya is growing and changing, with much to be proud of and much to give.

Kenya is known for her wildlife. You can find the "Big Five"—lion, leopard, rhinoceros, elephant, and Cape buffalo—as well as breathtaking views and landscapes, including the famous Rift Valley near the west and the beautiful beaches of Mombasa in the east.

The first African woman to win a Nobel Peace Prize was Kenyan environmentalist professor Wangari Maathai in 2004 ("Wangari Maathai: Biography" 2011).

Bones of one of the earliest human ancestors were found in Kenya. Scientists believe northern Kenya and Tanzania could be the original birthplace of humanity (Zimmerman 2013).

The world's twenty fastest marathon runners in 2011 were all Kenyan (Adharanand 2012).

Oku, a 34-year-old Kenyan in a wheelchair, has developed an online job-pairing resource that connects the disabled with employers throughout the country (Hodal 2016). This is completely changing the game for Kenya's disabled, making job searches, once next to impossible, a reality.

Kenya is full of promise and possibility. Not because there is no struggle or hardship in her past or future. But because there is creativity and courage in her people.

Go ahead, meet them. I dare you not to be inspired by these beautiful people.

≤ *Kisii, Kenya*

WHEN I MET THE OBALAS

≼ **The Obalas' Story** | Eldoret, Kenya

I arrived in Eldoret at four in the morning.

Not knowing where I was going. Not knowing if anyone would be there to pick me up.

Because my bus information had changed, I couldn't get through on my cell phone.

But it worked out. Somehow, miraculously, someone received my message, and someone was freezing their face off at 4 a.m., when my bus arrived.

The next day, I slept till noon in a stranger's room. When I woke up, I finally met her.

Mercy was put in charge of me: making sure I had everything I needed, showing me around, and moving me into her house with her family. A family that instantly became my family. They even named their chickens after me… but that's another story for another book!

I spent only two weeks with the Obalas, but I needed only two minutes to feel at home. Greeted immediately by hugs and excitement and more food than I should ever consume, they jumped right into my heart.

I could go on for pages, telling you how this family impacted my life, but I'm going to let them impact you themselves. Through the eyes of Mercy.

≼ *Six of the seven Obala siblings enjoying their first campfire—with s'mores; left to right: Mercy, Dennis, Greg, Faith, Irene, and Christine*

Sisters. They insisted that "cooking over fire was for poor people." I insisted that campfires are for everyone.

The first time I met Mamma and Papa, 2014

"My name is Mercy Adongo Obala. My mother named me Mercy because of God's mercy upon her. Adongo is the name always given to the second twin. Yes, I am a twin! Christine is my twin sister. Gregory, Fredrick, and Dennis are our older brothers, and our youngest sister is Faith. She came seven years later and my mom likes to call her the 'pension child.'"

Mercy describes growing up in a big family as so much fun. After sitting around a campfire and teaching them how to make s'mores for the first time, I wholeheartedly agree!

"My best memories are, without a doubt, Christmas memories! Decorating, storytelling, singing and dancing, gift giving, and so much more. But the main thing for me is that we are all home at the same time. This is rare for our family now that my brothers are out of the house, and we miss being together."

The closeness of this family is evident in every conversation, every action, every quiet exchange, every heated discussion.

This closeness pulls you in and makes you never want to leave—and they genuinely never want you to leave.

"Christine always made friends easily, while I was the quiet one. I was introverted and I

KENYA: WHEN I MET THE OBALAS

THESE BEAUTIFUL PEOPLE

depended on her to have friends. I had some issues with self-esteem and seeing myself as not good enough because I struggled to make friends. I shone in academics but that's it. When my family moved, my sister and I were put into separate streams of our class and that was difficult. My self-esteem hit an all-time low, but in the end it caused me to gain my independence, and slowly I was able to build relationships on my own. It allowed me to dream, and I plan to someday own a hotel and a children's home because I love children!

"My father's name is Andrew Obala. He says the family name Obala is a name given to heroes in our tribal naming system. He was born in 1957 in a village far, far away! OK, not that far, but in another town. Now he lectures at Moi University in Eldoret. He is a microbiologist and works on various projects in conjunction with universities in Kenya, and studies epidemics such as tuberculosis and malaria abroad. In short, my father is a scholar, the darkest man I know—a running joke in our family—and he is a great provider!

"My mother is Mildred Obala. Born in 1962, she is a nurse and a counsellor for victims of gender-based violence and domestic violence at the Moi Teaching and Referral Hospital. She is compassionate and loves to help. She also loves to cook and feed people and she has a heart of gold. My parents love Jesus. They go to work together every day and come home together every day. My mother is talkative and makes friends easily, whereas my dad is quiet and hardly ever knows what is going on!" She laughed.

"They love us and we love them!"

I can vouch for this. Hearts of gold is an understatement.

Andrew was always asking me questions, hungry for information like a true scholar. Mildred—or Mamma Obala, as I was instructed to call her—was always cooking me food. They were so generous that I gained at least five pounds. They showed me love and acceptance, generosity and sacrifice, no strings attached. Just a pure, unadulterated, joyful giving of their time and resources and energy and laughter. I will forever be impacted by such a picture of grace extended to me, a stranger.

"My eldest brother Greg is an excellent chef! He doesn't cook often but when he does it is crazy delicious! He studied medicine and is now a doctor in Aga Khan University Hospital in Nairobi, Kenya. At the same time, he is pursuing his master's in radiology. He loves music and can play the guitar and piano. He also bought Christine and me a guitar so we could learn. Music is something we share. We always loved hanging out with him and usually ended up watching cartoons. He is the most amazing older brother and has set an example with his love for Jesus and for us. He loves being a doctor but he doesn't get a lot of time off so we don't get to see him often."

I met Greg when he was home for a few days. I could instantly see the impact this man has had on his younger siblings, his sisters, especially in their excitement to have him around.

"Fred is an engineer. He thinks and eats very fast! He loves anything to do with technology and he is definitely an extrovert. He easily speaks his mind and is strong willed. He lives and works in Zambia, so we only see him three times a year. We miss him terribly!

"Dennis is the youngest of my brothers. He is quiet but probably the closest to me. He has few friends but they are all close. He loves sports and food and he studied actuarial science, graduating in 2015. At the moment, he is living with Greg in Nairobi and doing an internship as a credit analyst."

It's true—Dennis can eat. It's also true that he's quiet, but there's a depth to his relationships that's refreshing.

"Christine, my twin, is in her final year of law school. She is easily the closest person to me. I got a sister and a friend! She is a talented musician and dreams of releasing her own music someday!"

As she should. I loved listening to her play the guitar and sing. She's energetic, smart, beautiful, kind... Yup, a lot like Mercy. So similar in character but different in personality. So hospitable and downright fun to be around. They made my stay an absolute dream and I consider them sisters to this day.

"We do almost everything together and one of those things is volunteering at Youth for Christ Eldoret. It was one of those things you just do without any expectations and it ends up changing your whole life! We joined in February 2012 and I cannot even find the words to describe how awesome the experience has been!"

I'm particularly happy they joined Youth for Christ, because that's the only reason I know them. When their leader asked if anyone wanted to host this stranger coming from Canada, they immediately volunteered and welcomed me as family.

"My youngest sister, Faith, is the sunshine of our family. She is loud and she is still finding her way. Some days she wants to be a doctor; other days a model or a designer. So we will wait and see!"

She *is* a ray of sunshine. I would always expect a knock-you-over hug any time I walked through the door. Or at any point during the day. Or I would expect to find her curled up next to me stroking my hair, asking me questions and laughing boisterously. She's a little ball of energy and whatever she chooses to be, she will be it with all her heart.

"Irene is also part of our family. She came in 2008 to help my mom in the house and she just never left. She became part of us and is now my elder sister."

I guess they make a habit of taking people in as their own, huh?

Yeah, I loved Irene. I spent so much time watching her cook, laughing till we nearly cried, and trying to learn Kiswahili. We even participated in a walk for diabetes and could hardly contain ourselves when they served a cake while discussing healthy eating. It took me the whole time I was there to find out she wasn't their biological daughter or sister.

This is what's so incredible about this family—they model what a real family looks like. Real family is not where you come from. Not the same colour of skin. Sometimes not even the people who raised you.

Real family is the people who are around you now. Pouring their genuine love and care and acceptance all over you. Taking you in without batting an eye. And not even going out of their way because it's simply the way they live every day.

What if we all portrayed this kind of family? What if we all poured out our love and care and acceptance without holding back? Without strings or restraint?

What if every time someone entered my home, it was like walking into the family of God?

Because that's how I felt... when I met the Obalas.

NO MATTER WHAT

≤ Anne's Story | Kisii, Kenya

"I'm pregnant," she whispered, burying her head in her arms to stop the tears. Her voice shook and her eyes were full of questions. Full of fear.

"I'm HIV positive," he said, not looking her in the eye. He couldn't. Too ashamed. Too afraid of what she might do. Or worse, what she might think.

"I lost my parents to HIV."

"My auntie beats me for no reason at all."

"We don't have any food in the house."

"My grandma doesn't have school fees for me. I'm not sure I will be able to attend next term."

Day after day. School after school. Student after student.

Their faces were different, their stories varied. But their pain was eerily similar.

And every day, when Anne looked into their frightened eyes, held their trembling hands, and spoke to their wandering hearts, she saw something she recognized. She saw herself.

She saw how her family of eight had lived so happily. So carefree. Her parents had government jobs, so things were taken care of—until her mom passed away when Anne was eight years old. Her father went into a deep depression and never recovered. She lost him one year after her mother.

She felt the pain of burying her younger brother just two years after that, leaving only five siblings in her family. She can still remember going from one relative to the next, unsettled, rejected. An orphan.

She recognized the rebellion that had boiled up in her teenage years. At university, thinking she would finally be free, she retreated further and kept people at a distance.

And she could still feel the heat rise to her face and her stomach climb up to her throat when she uttered those same words out loud.

"I'm pregnant."

In her first year of university, she gave birth to her son.

She remembered. How could she forget?

Because it was the whole reason she is who she is and does what she does today. The reason she saw herself in those kids. The reason she was able to identify, and counsel, and console. The reason she will be there for them—no matter what.

"God wanted me to grow up," she said. "I realize today that the gifts He has given me and my life purpose, what I am doing now, could not be done by someone who had the mentality of a child."

God took her from that frightened, rebellious, young girl to a single mother with purpose and determination to reach those struggling in the same way.

"Single motherhood was my school. After I had my son, I knew I could not keep cutting people out of my life. For the first time, I learned that I had to resolve conflicts. I had to sit through a situation and stick it out until it improved."

No matter what.

During that time, she met Jesus and began volunteering with Youth for Christ Kisii. They would speak in schools and Anne developed a love for working with youth.

"I realized those kids were at the same point that I had been. They were struggling. They were hurting."

She saw herself.

"And I realized that when I was going through those things, all I wanted and needed was someone to walk through the situation with me. To help me understand myself better and build the capacity—the resilience—to deal with my issues."

Anne went to college and obtained her bachelor's degree in education. Upon graduation, she got a job teaching at a girls' boarding school.

"My passion for young people grew immensely in this setting. After class the girls would hang around and tell me their stories and I would try to translate it into why they were who they were."

She would listen, guide, counsel.

"I realized that it gave me a lot of joy to see these young people develop and grow beyond their problems." Anne smiled with her eyes. Her enthusiasm was contagious.

After teaching for several years, Anne and her friends formed Timiza Trust Initiative, a community-based organization that goes out to schools to provide student counselling and share the gospel.

"During one of these sessions, I came in contact with a student living with HIV/AIDS."

Not long after, their organization was chosen by US AID to implement a program in the primary schools in Kisii County.

"We worked with many schools and we realized there was a lot of suffering among children living with HIV/AIDS. Most were total or partial orphans. Some had both parents, but most were living in abject poverty."

Timiza Trust is now working with schools to raise awareness and reduce the stigma for children living with HIV/AIDS. They also equip teachers and staff to be able to care for and accommodate these children in a culture where living with HIV/AIDS is disdained.

"It has always been my cry and commitment that, as we mentor and lead and guide these young people, we would be able to do something significant in their lives."

Day after day. School after school. Student after student.

Their faces are different, their stories varied. But their pain is eerily similar.

And every day, when Anne looked into their frightened eyes, held their trembling hands, and spoke to their wandering hearts, she saw something she recognized.

She saw their value. She saw their potential. She saw someone worth fighting for.

She saw herself.

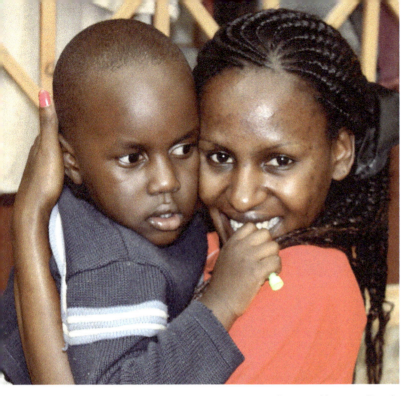

Anne and her son, Bravin

Saying good-bye to Anne after the first of many visits, 2015

"Young people are a bunch of possibilities. I grew up an orphaned child. It took someone sacrificing for me to go through school so I could grow up to be the person I am today. Now I don't just look at orphaned children—I *see* them. I really *see* them, and I understand. Every step of my journey has prepared me for what I am doing now and I absolutely love my life. My life is awesome!"

She grinned.

"What I do on a day-to-day basis is hectic and draining, but every time I get a phone call at the end of the day saying that someone is getting better, or I walk through a schoolyard of children laughing and shouting and playing, no matter their status, it makes me come alive!"

And Anne loves her son. I lived in their home several times during my travels and witnessed firsthand their bond. He is her world.

"I love my son. He is six-and-a-half years old now and it has been quite a journey. Coming to terms with the rejection of knowing that his father has never seen him and will never be a part of his life is hard, and it hurts. But that's my weak point. That's what keeps me coming back to God. It keeps me in faith—no matter what.

"While I was working in the area of HIV/AIDS," she said, "God gave me a gift. He gave me the idea for a book called *The Peer: Knowledge and Life Skills for Young People on HIV Care and Treatment."* Published in 2018, this book is a milestone for Anne.

"God has been so very faithful to me and I could not have come this far if it were not for Him," she said.

Anne is strong. Independent. Compassionate. Tenacious.

She loves to laugh and smile and bring out the best in everything and everyone. Anne is pretty much superwoman, in my eyes.

"God has given me so much in terms of experience. I don't just let my experiences pass by. He expects a lot from me because it has cost Him." Her voice softened, and her eyes pierced mine.

"God is a loving God. He's our Father. It was painful for Him to let me walk through some of those experiences. It has cost God a lot to pass me through this pain so He can make something beautiful out of me."

Anne will not waste her experiences. No matter what.

When Anne was nearly drowning in her fear and frustration, she came across Psalm 139.

"I remember reading this and it gave me purpose for my life. Knowing that God has a deep knowledge and understanding of me. Everything that has happened in my life, God knew it before I was even born. None of it escapes Him, not even one little thing. He knows every minute, every detail. That has given me complete confidence in life and in His love.

"No matter what… He knows. When He seems to be quiet… He knows. When it seems too deep, too painful… He knows.

"That meant everything to me. Despite all the things that have happened, they have not destroyed me."

Even when He seems quiet… He knows.
Even when it seems you will be stuck forever… He knows.
Even when it feels as if your world is crumbling… He knows.

And knowing that He knows… you will get through. You will overcome. You won't be destroyed, and you can count on that.

No matter what.

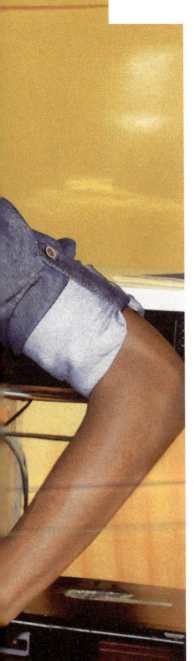

FOR THE LOVE OF MUSIC

≪ **Boaz's Story** | Kisii, Kenya

"This is all I've ever wanted to do."

His fingers flew across the keyboard. Clicking, adjusting, typing. I sat there mesmerized. I'd never seen anyone so confident. So talented. And he had taught himself.

It was my first time in Kisii, a small, vibrant town tucked between the hills in southwestern Kenya, not far from the Tanzanian boarder. I was sick— and dreading meeting new people all over again. But when I arrived after a long bus ride, I was taken straight to the Youth for Christ office where I received one of the warmest welcomes I can remember in my travels.

A good number of people in the room were musicians and I was soon whisked away to their studio down the road. This is where I met Boaz.

Boaz was born and raised in Kenya with four sisters and two brothers.

"My life revolves around this town. I have never lived anywhere else."

Loving and traditional, his family took care of him like an egg.

"No going to the neighbours, no going to the kitchen—that was for girls—no missing church, no disrespecting your elders or anyone older."

His fingers continued to move on the keyboard, adjusting dials.

"Do you sing?" he asked me.

I was a little taken aback. I *like* to sing, but that doesn't mean I *can* sing.

"Just sing something. Anything. You have to record a song while you are here. Just sing something and I'll do the rest."

KENYA: FOR THE LOVE OF MUSIC

THESE BEAUTIFUL PEOPLE

Recording my song in the studio

Um, OK. So I did. Awkwardly, to start.

"OK, that's good."

His fingers flew around and a song took shape. Within an hour, he had created the background music for a song that wasn't even written yet. I was amazed. Where does this kind of talent come from?

"My father couldn't afford much for me as a kid. I didn't own a bicycle or any kind of toy. But I remember the first time I played the piano."

It was an old organ in the church store, which they used in music class.

"I used to sneak in there to play during my school breaks. I was eight years old."

Boaz was nine years old the first time he walked into a music studio. He was in awe.

"I knew right away that I wanted to do this when I grew up!"

He taught himself how to play the piano, then how to use computerized music software. He is teaching himself guitar.

You can't do that if you don't love it. You *won't* do that if you don't love it.

"I had always grown up in a Christian home but, for a few years in my teens, I backslid. I made some poor choices and things changed. One of my ex-girlfriends tried to commit suicide when I broke up with her. I didn't know how to have healthy relationships and I felt so bad that I just got back together with her. Everything was a mess. It wasn't until high school when a speaker came and I just knew I had to change my life. I needed help. I've always been easily influenced by my friends and, unfortunately, they weren't a good influence. It was difficult finding new friends and healthy relationships after accepting Christ."

What remained was his passion for Jesus and for music.

As I sat in the studio watching him create and produce a song, I was awestruck.

Boaz has traveled to Tanzania, Uganda, and Rwanda, among other places. But he always prefers to come home, home to Kisii. It's where is heart is, where his music is.

"I am a music producer and I have worked and volunteered in this field for the last three years. I trained in our church studios and the only reason I excelled so quickly is because of the passion I had!"

He now owns a recording studio for single artists and small bands. A trained peer educator, he volunteers at Youth for Christ in the guidance and counselling department. His band performs at live events and has even won local music awards.

"I would like to achieve many things in my lifetime. I want to take my music as far as I can go. I want to mentor and nurture artists. I want to be good to people, make friends for life, and have a God-fearing family."

I have no doubt he will.

Because it doesn't matter if you had a good upbringing. If you had one toy or one hundred. If you took all the lessons and joined all the clubs. If you backslid then or if you're backsliding now.

"My talent and passion won me a scholarship to get my diploma in mass communication and journalism from 2010 to 2012," Boaz smiled.

His talent and passion made the difference. Not upbringing or accomplishments.

He doesn't do it for the money or position or bragging rights. Yes, those can all be good incentives. But at the end of the day, they won't bring happiness, not the lasting kind. They won't keep you going when the going gets tough.

No, he does it for a much more fulfilling reason.

Boaz does it for the love of music.

TO GROW OLD LIKE HER

≤ Boaz's Grandmother's Story | Kisii, Kenya

I don't know her name, don't even know much about her. But every time I remember that face, I can't help but grin. And want to grow old like her.

In 2015 a friend and I were visiting Boaz's home. After meeting his parents and siblings, we were ushered off to see Granny.

She emerged slowly from her mud brick house and sat on a stool in front of us. We greeted her and she grinned from ear to ear.

We didn't speak the same language. But I knew that if we could communicate, I would have liked her. I already liked her.

"She is 90 years old. She lives here on the compound with us, but she still goes out to dig in the fields," her grandson Boaz told us.

My jaw nearly dropped to the ground. *I beg your pardon? She still digs?* She continued to grasp our hands and smile.

When I spoke to Boaz more than a year later, he said, "She is doing well, although we no longer allow her to go out and dig. She just looks after the chickens now."

Over 90 years old and they have to tear you from the fields and leave you with *just the chickens.* I want to be old like that. Spry and active. Thankful for what I can still do. Smiling and content, no matter my age.

The day I met her, as we were walking away, she raised her arm in a wave and uttered with delight the few English words she knew.

"See you!"

I can't get out of my head the grin on that wrinkled face and the sparkle in those bright eyes. And I know, without a doubt, that I want to grow old like her.

KENYA: TO GROW OLD LIKE HER

THESE BEAUTIFUL PEOPLE

BENT BUT NOT BROKEN

⩽ Sally's Story | Nairobi, Kenya

It was a warm, humid day, like most days in Mombasa, Kenya. The port was teeming with people.

Shoulder to shoulder, they bumped and shoved to get their spot on the ferry. A mother clasped a child's hand, another child strapped tightly to her back. Men and women dressed in suits were going to work. Others were going on holiday, suitcases stacked neatly on top of their heads. Laughter and light chatter filled the thick air, already pungent with sweat and salt. Somewhere in the middle of that chaos was Sally.

She pushed her way through the crowd, steps determined, jaw set. But she wasn't going to work; she wasn't going on holiday. No bags or belongings with her, the letter she'd carried earlier had been slipped into the post.

Sally moved forward with the crowd and boarded the ship.

Leaning against the rail, she let out a long, slow breath and gazed into the sea, letting the salty air whip her hair in her face. She didn't brush it away. It wasn't long until the horn blew, and the boat moved away from the shore.

She turned her head to watch the shoreline disappear. The waving people with their shouts and cries became more and more faint.

But it didn't matter—no one was on that shore for her. No one knew she was on this boat. And there was no going back now.

⩽ *Photograph from Flawnt It/Kevin Gitonga*

KENYA: BENT BUT NOT BROKEN

THESE BEAUTIFUL PEOPLE

Looking back across the water, her heart began to race. *Am I going to do this? Is this the only way?* Tears stung her eyes and her knees threatened to give way.

The water was deeper now. She glanced over her shoulder at the other passengers. Some were eating; others were sick and lying on the floor. Children laughed and pointed as parents warned them to stay clear of the edges. Elderly women sat while younger women stood in clusters.

Chaos. But it was nothing compared to the turmoil going on inside Sally's heart and mind.

It's time.

Before she could give it a second thought, she hoisted herself over the rail and jumped.

———

Sally is the youngest in a family of 10, with whom she lived until she was seven. Then she moved in with her older sister. She grew up dreaming of being a secretary.

"I wanted to always smile at anyone who walked into the office, to type letters and do all the things involved in working in an office setting. I would always watch carefully as people typed and often got in trouble for hanging out in the office talking to the receptionist!" Sally's eyes sparkled.

After high school, she completed a secretarial course and got her dream job as a secretary, working first for her sister, then for two other employers.

During that time, she married and moved to Mombasa.

"My first child, Jack, only lived for two months. I miscarried my second pregnancy at seven months."

After losing both children, she became sick and was hospitalized for a week. Soon after, she was called back for a follow-up. She was never told that an HIV test had been performed.

"Just when I thought I could not deal with anything more, I was diagnosed with HIV and there was still no medication for the condition. Plus, the person who told me the news was unprofessional and not the least bit compassionate. They simply walked into the room and said, *'Uko na ukimwi.'* You have AIDS. That's it."

The news hit Sally like a ton of bricks. She was bending under the weight, about to break.

"I went into a deep depression, not eating or sleeping for days. After two months, I said to my husband that I was going to die. His response was, 'You know what? You are over 18 years and you can make your own decisions. If that is what you have decided, go ahead.'"

This was the approval she was looking for to end her life.

"I quickly wrote a letter to my sister, posted it, and boarded the ferry."

The water swept over her body. She didn't fight it.

By now most of the passengers had noticed what was happening. They were pointing and shouting at her in the water.

After five or six minutes, people started to wonder. She wasn't trying to stay afloat—but she wasn't drowning.

"I was trying so hard to drown, but I could not! I do not even know how to swim," she said.

They were calling her a ghost because she was floating on the water, despite her efforts to go under.

"I remember God speaking to me clearly while I lay in the water. He kept saying, 'I have good plans for you. I brought you and I will take you, but not now. Go and save my people. Go and show love.'"

This went on for at least 10 minutes before a diver forced her back to the boat. She was taken to hospital with one of the women who had witnessed the whole thing. Unable to believe what she had seen, this lady followed Sally to the hospital to make sure she was a real human being.

"Because attempted suicide is considered attempted murder in Kenya, the police were summoned. But when they arrived, I told them my story and they let me go."

Sally returned home to her husband, but things weren't good. He was unfaithful and they were often separated.

"I thought I would die of heartbreak, but I did not."

In March 2007, she went to the doctor for a routine check-up. Just like that, she was diagnosed with stage 2 cervical cancer. A hysterectomy was her only option. Three years and 13 surgeries later, she was informed it had spread to her colon.

KENYA: BENT BUT NOT BROKEN

THESE BEAUTIFUL PEOPLE

Photograph from Flawnt It/Kevin Gitonga

"My doctor told me another surgery was inevitable. They needed to remove part of my colon but they did not explain to me what the consequences would be."

Sally woke up from the surgery with a stoma, an artificial opening that allows waste to pass from the intestines. In her case, it would be permanent. She was an ostomate.

"The surgery was traumatizing. I could not imagine how I was going to live a normal life."

Sally was introduced to a nurse who specialized in stomas. He taught her how to change and clean the colostomy bag, which fits over the stoma and sticks to the surrounding skin. This nurse held monthly support meetings for others with this condition, and he invited Sally.

"I will never forget the first meeting I attended. There were beautiful women wearing form-fitting dresses and jeans, going about their daily lives as if it were not there."

As if they didn't have a bag for waste beneath their blouses.

"It completely changed the way I saw my condition. It was the first time after my operation that I felt hopeful."

Only two weeks after being discharged, Sally went to Kenyatta Hospital to visit the ostomates there. What she found was shocking.

"The patients did not have access to colostomy bags. They were using tissue, gauze, paper bags, diapers, and even the sheets and mattresses they were lying on to cover the stoma!"

Imagine the inhumanity. Imagine the stench.

"A colostomy bag makes life bearable," Sally said.

Adjustable and easy to attach, colostomy bags contain charcoal to eliminate odour. Each bag costs roughly 600–1,000 Kenyan shillings (CAD$8–12), and the average person needs two to three bags per day. Many can't afford even one bag, so they are denied this "luxury"—the luxury of a dignified life.

Sally couldn't stand by and do nothing; that's not who she is. She had some of her own bags with her, so she shared them with the patients.

"That visit birthed something in me. I wanted to help."

Sally and her friends formed Stoma World Kenya in 2010 and registered it in 2012. What started with six members has grown to more than 200 in at least seven hospitals across Kenya.

During this time, her husband got sick.

"I moved back home and took care of him the best I could. It was hard. I cried a lot and was on anti-depressants but I decided to show him love."

He passed away in 2012 and Sally attended the funeral, using it as a platform to spread awareness about HIV/AIDS.

"If God has seen me through all of the above, I know I will be OK," Sally said confidently.

That day in the hot Mombasa sun and the cold Indian ocean, Sally heard the voice of her Father. He didn't call her out of the chaos—He pulled her through it. And He gave her a purpose: to save His people and to show love.

"I'm still here, and I have made it my life's purpose to show love."

Besides her intensive involvement with Stoma World Kenya, Sally worked for Médecins Sans Frontières in the Kibera slum as a health promotor, a role she acquired simply by sharing her story,

"I started sharing my story in the patients' waiting bay at the hospital and someone asked me if I would do this daily for pay! I worked with an incredible team that understood my condition, and the organization paid all my medical bills."

KENYA: BENT BUT NOT BROKEN

THESE BEAUTIFUL PEOPLE

Her contract with Médecins Sans Frontières ended in March 2017, so she was still out of a job, but she continued support her community.

When I asked Sally for the best ways to help, she said stoma care appliances and financial support are needed.

"We have a donor from Canada who sends two shipments of colostomy bags every year; we only pay the shipping costs. This works out to 300,000 Kenyan shillings per shipment (about CAD$4,000). Most of our members cannot afford the 1,500 membership fee, but we manage by God's grace. Stoma care appliances are severely lacking in my country and I wish to change that."

Every day Sally is faced with more emotional stress than most of us encounter in a lifetime. She spends almost all her spare time handing out bags and counselling patients and their families.

"I have taken it upon myself to be a kind of motivational speaker. Not many people are willing to share their stories, so I feel it is imperative that I share mine. I'm also a born-again Christian and I share the love of Christ any opportunity I get!"

Besides their stomas, many of Stoma World Kenya's members have cancer. Others are rejected by family and friends.

"One member's husband would open windows whenever she walked into a room, claiming that she was making the house stink. She didn't want to leave the monthly meetings to go home and face him. When she passed away, her husband would not let us attend her funeral."

Sally has lost many friends along the way, but she has gained many more.

"Some were afraid I would be a burden to them. Others just didn't know how to treat me and slowly faded out of my life. But I have a wonderful family that never once discriminated against me and I am so grateful for that support!"

Forty-six years old. Outlived both her children. Diagnosed with HIV/AIDS. Failed suicide attempt. Cheated on. Depressed. Cancer survivor. Widow. Ostomate.

Many words could be used to describe Sally. Some are from the past, and some will be permanent. But one of the words you can't use to describe Sally is "broken."

"I am beautiful and I still have men that want me but I set the record straight from the word go that I have HIV, I cannot have children, and I have a colostomy bag."

If ever there was a person who *could* claim the label "broken," it would be Sally. If ever there was a person who could be self-focused, it would be Sally. If ever there was a person who should be excused from serving, it would be Sally.

She has been knocked down, twisted, and bent until she thought she might break.

"But I did not."

And here she is, still loving people.

She no longer fears the wind—she's flexible now.
She no longer fears the storm—she has weathered the worst.
She no longer fears the future—she is carried in a steady hand.
She no longer fears futility—she's a world changer.

"I have accepted myself as I am. God can heal you or give you the grace to live with a condition, and that is what He has done for me."

She might bend, but she will never break.

TANZANIA

Have you ever met someone who was really nice? Like, super kind, and you couldn't help but wonder why? Or if they were always like that? Well, that pretty much sums up Tanzania.

I don't know if it's the relaxed pace of life, or the fact that it's the largest country in Africa with the lowest population density, or if it's just the way Tanzanians have always been. Even their language is soft and kind. It trips so gracefully off the tongue that it would be difficult for it sound anything but nice.

"Swahili was born here," Tanzanians say with swelling chests. "It was corrupted in Kenya and died in Uganda."

We laugh because it's true. If you want to learn true Swahili, learn it from Tanzanians. And if you want to be treated nicely and perhaps learn to be nice yourself, go to Tanzania. You're sure to be greeted with a gentle hug, a kind word, and a chance to become family.

This is significant because life has not always been kind to Tanzanians.

Originally two states until 1964, the name Tanzania is a combination of Tanganyika and Zanzibar. To this day, the island off the coast is still called Zanzibar. Operating almost like an independent Arabic-speaking country, Zanzibar is actually part of Tanzania. Together, the island and mainland boast a population of almost 52.5 million (2015) but death rates are shockingly high. Inadequate maternal and pediatric health care push the numbers higher, with malaria and HIV the leading killers of children and adults, respectively.

To make matters worse, in 2015 it was estimated there were only 0.03 physicians for every 1,000 people, more than 1.3 million were living with HIV/AIDS, and 22.8 percent were living below the poverty line.

≤ *Zanzibar*

TANZANIA

THESE BEAUTIFUL PEOPLE

HARAKA
HARAKA
HAINA
BARAKA
HURRY HURRY HAS NO BLESSING.
—SWAHILI PROVERB

Left: Mwanza, Tanzania. Right: Night market, Zanzibar.

Despite Tanzania's status as one of the world's poorest economies (determined by per capita income), her growth rates have greatly benefited from tourism and natural resources.

Women are especially vulnerable due to traditional customs and gender roles. If a woman becomes financially successful, it's not uncommon for a male relative or her husband to assume ownership and control of the project and the money generated. Children are also at high risk (21 percent, excluding Zanzibar) of being trafficked internally by friends and family, usually out of desperation and the inability to provide.

But even amid all these struggles, Tanzanians are more likely to be kind than harsh. To treat you like family rather than a stranger. To be nice, even if unwarranted. And even though there might be things about their country they would change, they aren't deceived into thinking they have nothing to offer.

TANZANIA

THESE BEAUTIFUL PEOPLE

Tanzania is home to Mount Kilimanjaro, the highest peak on the continent. Bordering three main lakes and the Indian Ocean, the fish is always fresh and delicious. In Zanzibar, you can hit the white sand beaches in the morning then find fishermen frying up their catch of the day. After dark, go to the night market for any kind of seafood imaginable, cooked and sold by candlelight. Take a spice tour or stroll through Stone Town to learn about the rich history of the island and taste the unique spices cultivated there.

Tanzania's landscape and animals are featured on coins, used as brand names for products, and protected as national treasures. And why wouldn't you, when you have the world's highest concentration of animals per square kilometre?

Not just rare species of animals are found in Tanzania—the African Blackwood tree is the most expensive hardwood tree in the world.

Sometimes the moon shines so brightly, you don't need a flashlight to see where you're going at night. Jane Goodall studied chimpanzees in Gombe National Park of Tanzania in 1960. Farrokh Bulsara, otherwise known as Freddie Mercury, lead vocalist of Queen, was born in Tanzania.

Next time you see a lion climbing a tree on television, you'll know it was filmed in Tanzania—Lake Manvara National Park, to be exact, home to the world's only tree-climbing lions.

But whether it's the world's highest pizza delivery to the top of Mount Kilimanjaro (Meades 2016), or Livinus Manyanga's innovative enterprise, Kakute (Ubwani 2017), which has transformed thousands of lives by upgrading skills and increasing productivity, it still won't be the best part about this beautiful country.

The best part will always be her kindness.

Though easily mistaken for weakness, her kindness has the unique potential to softly, gently, change the world.

Just keep reading, you'll see. She's going to do it. In fact, she has *already* been doing it.

One beautiful person at a time.

THE LOUDEST ECHO

≪ **Pascal's Story** | Mwanza, Tanzania

I've always been fascinated with echoes.

They can stop you in your tracks. Make you think twice. Make you wonder about their source.

Some echoes take longer to come back to you; some return immediately. Some resound several times; others, only once.

But the coolest thing about an echo is that it starts somewhere— there's an initial sound. You can't stand silently in a cave and expect an echo. No, you must speak or create a noise.

If you took my friend Pascal to a cave or an empty concert hall, his voice would create the loudest echo, without a doubt.

I met Pascal in 2011, when I was living in Botswana. He had a boisterous laugh and so much energy that he left our heads spinning with his wild and wonderful ideas. But here's the thing: he didn't just have ideas— *he did something with them*. This guy made things happen.

A curious learner, he saw every challenge as an opportunity and every opportunity as a gift.

Pascal was born in the western part of Tanzania, close to the Burundian border. When he was 13, he and his family moved to the island of Zanzibar, where witchcraft was practiced rampantly. His parents didn't agree on which church to go to, so the kids went with their mom to the Roman Catholic church.

"You don't have a choice; it's just what you do on a Sunday," he said. "It was technically a Christian home but it had no impact." Or so he thought. It was the beginning of an echo.

TANZANIA: THE LOUDEST ECHO

THESE BEAUTIFUL PEOPLE

He was one of seven children, with only five siblings alive today. His mother lost her firstborn and later a daughter at only two weeks of age. Told of their sister's death at school, the children were taken home. They rushed to the body of their sister, curious. *What would a dead body be like?* Pascal touched his deceased sister, just to see.

"According to tradition, it was believed that the child who died was bewitched. That she was not fully dead, but rather her spirit was taken. Everyone believed that we buried the body but it was not really the child. They also believed that the person who touched the dead body would receive her spirit. Even though we didn't know anything about this stuff, or necessarily believe in it, we had a target on our back. I was to be the next one taken."

His family was afraid, especially when he became ill.

"I could see the child," he recalled. There was an intensity in his eyes, as if it were yesterday.

"No one else could see her, but I could. And even though she was a baby when she died, I knew that the young child I saw was my sister. She would say, 'Come, brother. I'm not really dead; I'm in another house. Come.' I was 14 years old and people thought I was out of my mind."

The community insisted that traditional healers cast the demons out of him.

"I experienced things that nobody ever should. Against my will, witch doctors would take me to the graveyard at night, find a fresh grave, and try to transfer the demon from me into the dead body. I even had to live with them because my family was too afraid to have me in their house."

Pascal recalled one instance where they took him to a river to wash the demon out.

"They spoke words over the river and the water became powerful. When they put me in, it was burning hot."

They were fighting witchcraft with witchcraft. But it wasn't working.

"We killed so many chickens. They would put white or red or black chickens, dead or alive, in big traditional pots with some of my hair or nails. But it never worked." He laughed as he told me this, but I knew it hadn't been funny in the least.

His family was surrounded by fear, up against a hard wall. The perfect place for an echo.

"One day, someone walked up to my parents and said, 'Remember you are Christians. You will die in this witchcraft,'" he remembered.

And there it was. The echo. The reminder to Whom they belonged.

TANZANIA: THE LOUDEST ECHO

THESE BEAUTIFUL PEOPLE

"My parents were proud and it was hard for them to accept this. But going to the church is free so they agreed," he said, starting to grin. "However, the Anglican church they went to does not have a practice of casting out demons, so they took me to the Pentecostal church, and they prayed. They prayed over me and our house. In every room and in every way they could think of!"

It wasn't instant.

"But slowly, over time it worked. I no longer had those night terrors!" he exclaimed. "And so we believed. We sold our place and moved away from there."

The church continued to walk with them, teaching and discipling them. His family started reading the Bible and going to fellowship.

"Zanzibar is a bit of a closed country with a lot of tourists and not a lot of English, but I loved living there."

He didn't realize it then, but God was turning his heart toward his own people.

"There were mistakes and walking away for sure, but all that teaching and discipleship, they were like echoes."

His gaze shifted. He was remembering.

His stepfather wasn't around much. Pascal found himself in gangs and even spent a portion of his teenage years on the street.

But the echo always returned and, in true Pascal fashion, his natural charisma and endless energy found him involved in a variety of positions, making decisions based on his desire to serve his beloved country.

He received his diploma in customer service and marketing in the United Kingdom at Commercial Management College. He took many jobs to pay for school and practice English: at an international school; in hotels; as a private music vendor, late-night television presenter, and tour guide.

But the echo returned. He wanted to better himself to serve his country more effectively.

In 2006 he had the opportunity to go to college in South Africa. He took theological studies and participated in summer school for drama and the arts. Friends and family thought he was crazy.

"They couldn't understand why I would give up everything to go there. I had a good job and my own apartment full of nice stuff, and here I was leaving it all behind to go to Bible college."

Needless to say, it didn't take long for those same people to "share" all his belongings.

TANZANIA: THE LOUDEST ECHO

THESE BEAUTIFUL PEOPLE

"South Africa is like Europe. You won't need this stuff," they would tell him.

"When people go to South Africa, they don't usually come back. Why would you come back? For what?" His eyes were as wide as his grin. He thrust his hands up and shrugged.

"That is their mentality. So they took everything, right down to my bedding. When I came home to visit, I even had to ask people for a place to stay."

But those people didn't know about the passion deep in his heart for his own people, a passion that returned wherever he was in the world.

He spent several years in South Africa, where he met his wife, Esther. Originally from Zambia, she was attending the same college. They were married in Pretoria on July 20, 2008, and lived there until 2010.

"I always knew I would go back," he insisted. "Studying theology was a way of bettering myself. Not to become a theologian, but to better my country."

They had built a nice life for themselves in South Africa. He was working for a South African organization that was ready to sponsor his citizenship. Their house was fully furnished and their first two children were born there. But his heart had begun to shift toward youth.

"I identify myself with the kids living on the streets. I have been in a gang. I didn't have a father figure telling me how to behave. When you grow up like that, you are missing certain puzzle pieces. God sent people into my life to fill in those missing pieces when it should have been my dad. Now I wanted to be that person for others.

"I asked God why He gave me all these unique opportunities when no one else in my family did. I started asking Him how I could say thank you."

God responded differently than he thought.

"He told me, 'No, there is nothing I want from you except that you use what I have given you to bless others. Use it to reach young people.'"

In true, bold, passionate Pascal fashion, he hit the streets. He would ride the trains early in the morning in the sketchy parts of Johannesburg and talk to the guys who were "train surfing" to steal from people.

"I would stand there and look at them and see myself," he said. "My passion for young people continued to grow. We felt we were being asked to give it all up a second time and move back home. And again everyone thought we were crazy!"

He raised two fingers in the air. The second season of starting over.

They had no money, no idea how things were going to work out. Their pockets were empty and the road would be hard. They were surrounded by unknowns, up against a wall. The perfect place for an echo.

"The church and ministry I was with in South Africa started manipulating me to take their ministry to Tanzania. This was the only way they would support me financially.

"I said, 'No. We want to go home to serve the young people. We don't know where to start, but if God has called us and I have had all these experiences to use for others, then I am the right person to do this. I know this is my calling and I need to go home.'"

He was confident in the Voice that told him to go. The Voice that continued to echo through time with a deep love for his country.

So they went. God provided enough money to get home. When they arrived, they slept in a church in Zanzibar. They began sharing their mission and mobilizing initiatives for youth, a feat next to impossible in such a closed country.

Little did they know, the church he'd been with the whole time in South Africa was connected to Youth for Christ. And Youth for Christ was praying for someone to pioneer the ministry in Tanzania. The church had recommended Pascal.

By now they had been living on the island for nine months. Pascal had managed to buy nice things for his wife and children, who were new to his country.

"I wanted to impress them. I wanted them to feel at home. Now Youth for Christ was asking us to move to Mwanza, which is the far west side of Tanzania (the opposite of Zanzibar) and start over. We were being asked to give everything up again for the third time." He raised three fingers above his head and laughed out loud.

"But Esther is a true woman of God. She willingly followed me to Kenya, Rwanda, Uganda—everywhere Youth for Christ asked us to visit. When we arrived in Mwanza, we had only a large mattress for all of us, but we knew we were to start Youth for Christ here and God would provide."

He was absolutely convinced of the goodness and provision of his Father. A friend from Australia visited and saw their poor living conditions. Three years later, he sent money for them to build a house.

"By that time, we already had a decent place to live and everything we needed—and we were afraid to buy

Pascal's wife, Esther

Clifton, Clarisa, and me. Claudia, the littlest one, wouldn't stand still long enough for a photo.

nice things in case we had to give them away again," he chuckled. "So we used the money to buy land. Soon after, the same friend told us he would be paying for our children to attend a better school. By now we had three children. Even after all that, they told us they have a team back home who raises money for building projects and wondered if we had anything we wanted to build."

So they laid the foundation for a house in the country on the land they bought for Youth for Christ.

I stayed with them in Mwanza for one month in 2014, teaching at their training centre for vulnerable women.

Pascal was still himself, all laughter and energy. He left my head spinning with everything he had accomplished in Mwanza in such a short time.

When he visited Canada in 2017, he was no different. I sat with him at Redeemer College, listening to his dreams and goals. I was inspired.

In the last four years since he and his family set foot in Mwanza, Youth for Christ has run a school for vulnerable women, which has now been transformed into a one-year program for boys and girls, with a focus on physical trades like tailoring and welding. Upon completion, participants are awarded a certificate from the Vocational Training Board of Tanzania.

"We want to use the house in the country for a retreat centre. People pay less, they have a nice place to stay, and Youth for Christ earns a small income. We are starting a small company to connect with international tourism and are hoping it takes off."

His eyes widened and he moved to the edge of his seat as he described this new dream taking shape. Again with the innovative ideas, and again with never letting them remain ideas. But this journey hasn't been a walk in the park. Besides all the starting over and the loss of physical belongings, there's more.

When their oldest son Clifton was four years old, he was diagnosed with Hodgkin's Lymphoma cancer. Without treatment and proper diagnosis in Tanzania, doctors administer treatment without knowing if it's effective. It's a cold, hard truth they face every day.

Even more recently, they had to say goodbye to their unborn child.

I'm certain there are days where their hearts feel empty. Days that are hard, impossible even. Days where they're up against a wall. But that's the perfect place for an echo. The kind that will stop you in your tracks, make you think twice. Make you wonder about its source.

"The Lord doesn't slumber or sleep," Pascal said. His eyes were focused, his voice sure.

"He works in ways we cannot see. God is powerful. It doesn't matter the situation you are going through. It doesn't matter where you are; He always has a plan. If you are in the right direction, you will always see Him come through. God has taken me through many situations, and He has always been faithful. There has never been a day that I feel offended. If something happens, it's not for no reason. It's not because God doesn't care or isn't concerned for me. His ways are simply higher."

The harder the place, the louder the echo. The emptier the space, the longer it resounds.

Let those words resonate in your spirit. Let them bounce off the hard corners of your heart and reverberate in the empty parts of your soul.

Because I'm convinced if you send Pascal out into the world—this hard, impossible world—if you send him out with the encouragement, comfort, and endurance that can only come from the Source—I have no doubt that will be the loudest echo.

TANZANIA: THE LOUDEST ECHO

THESE BEAUTIFUL PEOPLE

THE LANGUAGE OF THE HEART

≤ Sara's Story* | Youth for Christ Training Centre, Mwanza, Tanzania

Tanzania is not an English-speaking country, and I am not a Swahili-speaking Canadian, leading to some interesting scenarios when the two are combined.

I had been asked to teach for two weeks on identity at Youth for Christ to a group of vulnerable and marginalized women in Mwanza, Tanzania, and I was excited. There is nothing like introducing someone who has been broken and abused, afflicted and forgotten, to the truth that they are loved and valued, worthy and affirmed.

Just one obstacle: language.

Everything needed to be done through a translator. Every session, every conversation, every word. And it was unbelievably frustrating.

When a girl wants to pour out her heart to you and all you want to do is listen, but you can't.

When everything in you wants to find out the story behind those tired eyes, or tell her she's beautiful and loved, but you can't.

Because there's a barrier. A language barrier.

Each day of the two-week program tackled a different aspect of finding and accepting self, discovering eternal worth and value, and engaging in something fun and frivolous.

≤ *Sara* sharing her story at graduation*

TANZANIA: THE LANGUAGE OF THE HEART

THESE BEAUTIFUL PEOPLE

From forgiveness to nail painting. Family trees to dance parties.

Each day added another puzzle piece to the picture. The big picture. On the last day, we found a quiet place and wrote our stories.

For some the words came easily; for most they came painfully and slowly. But for all it ushered in an aspect of healing.

When they handed their papers to me at the end of the day, I wanted nothing more than to soak up every word. To enter into their stories. But I couldn't. Because of the language barrier.

On the final day, we prepared a graduation ceremony. The classroom was abuzz with excited chatter as the girls put on their traditional wear and painted their faces. Confidently, they strutted across the stage, showing off their beautiful cultural dress in a fashion show. They performed a dance they had choreographed, and sang their hearts out in a beautiful Swahili welcome song.

Then Sara got up to speak.

She was standing tall before the crowd, eyes steady, voice strong and unwavering.
She was telling her story for the first time, and I had no idea what she was saying.

But something in my heart began to stir. It pressed out and swelled and took my breath. Tears welled up in my eyes and I couldn't hide my pride.

Even though I couldn't understand her words, something in my heart understood hers.

Our tongues couldn't speak the same language, but hearts have a language of their own. A universal language. A language of care and compassion.

That day a supernatural form of communication allowed me to laugh, cry, celebrate, and dance with a group of breathtaking young women whose language I didn't speak.

It was the language of the heart.

≪ *Top: All the girls showing off their traditional wear before hitting the runway*

Sara's name was changed to protect her anonymity

TANZANIA: THE LANGUAGE OF THE HEART

THESE BEAUTIFUL PEOPLE

SOUTH SUDAN

They say challenges are opportunities in disguise. If that's the case, then South Sudan is ripe with opportunity.

I wasn't supposed to go to South Sudan—at least, it wasn't part of the original plan. When I announced that my visa came through, the flood of concerned emails and messages almost made me think twice.

Most places, particularly African countries, aren't portrayed accurately in the media. The focus is on war and poverty and negative conditions that, though true, are not complete pictures of the country as a whole.

South Sudan is misrepresented in a different way; that is, we don't realize just how heartbreaking the situation is. We know things are bad, but we don't grasp the everyday horror the Sudanese have been living for years.

Since 1955 Sudan has been in a constant state of unrest, through glimmers of peace and times of brutal war. Even after gaining independence from Sudan (officially, the Republic of the Sudan) in 2011 and signing peace agreements in 2015, South Sudan continues to be a place of perpetual bloodshed.

Although her greatest resource is oil, war has caused shortages everywhere. If you do find oil, the cost is high. In fact, the cost of everything has nearly tripled in the past few years, making subsistence nearly impossible for the hundreds of thousands of refugees fleeing Sudan. And rather than stopping the brutality, the government often contributes to it. Why? Because stopping the war would cost too much.

South Sudan might have won her freedom from Sudan, but the war isn't over. The roads to Juba, the capital of South Sudan, are rife with ambushes. Driving is only an option for those willing to risk their lives. Some make it. Some don't.

It's difficult to get statistics on South Sudan's situation. This is what we do know.

SOUTH SUDAN

THESE BEAUTIFUL PEOPLE

EMPTY
STOMACHS
HAVE NO
EARS.

—SOUTH SUDANESE PROVERB

Learning how to make donuts at Project Two–Five Culinary School

Between 1955 and 2005, Sudan and South Sudan together lost about 2.5 million people in a combination of conflicts, mostly due to civil war, drought, and famine.

In 2012 the government shut down oil production. By 2013 the constant state of unrest between Sudan and South Sudan displaced millions more Sudanese and caused severe food and oil shortages.

South Sudan is one of the poorest countries in the world.

A total of 80 percent of the population lives in rural areas. Maternal mortality rates are among the highest in the world, caused by the young age of the mothers and the lack of access to trained medical professionals. More than half the population lives below the poverty line.

Since 2013 more than 900,000 Sudanese have fled to neighbouring countries: 200,000 people fled in July 2016 alone. This isn't counting 1.4 million displaced people, or the more than 240,000 refugees who have fled to South Sudan to avoid the fighting in Sudan.

Severely underdeveloped, she has some of the weakest infrastructure in the world, with only 200 kilometres of paved road in the entire country.

In stark contrast, she has a wealth of natural resources, led by oil. When producing, nearly half a million

THE HANDS

THESE BEAUTIFUL PEOPLE

barrels flow out of South Sudan per day. She also has one of the richest agricultural areas in all of Africa: fertile soils and abundant water. This region supports 10–20 million head of cattle, as well as large numbers of elephants, buffalo, and other wildlife.

Hundreds of thousands of Sudanese are flooding the borders of Uganda in search of peace and safety. They have given up on their own country after years of seeing nothing but desolation and death.

As I walked the streets of Yei in 2015, now a war-torn and deserted village, I saw people sitting around, waiting. Resigned. You could smell it in the air. The spirit of defeat.

Even through the dust, this country is beautiful. Fertile. Friendly. And there is hope—if you look under the surface. People are making a difference, turning difficult situations into opportunities.

They put their hand over their head and say, "It's hard!" But they do it anyway.

For years the Sudanese have been getting up every day and fighting for their lives. They're still here, testaments to a hope within.

One step at a time. One painful page at a time.
Each line. Each word. Each memory.

These beautiful people come from a place of war. Of unrest. Of distrust. Their stories are filled with loss and abuse and insurmountable obstacles.

But I see something in them.

I see opportunity.
I see hope.

The challenges are too many to count. So, too, the opportunities. We must learn to see adversity in this way. And we must be willing to pay the price. We must be willing to stay.

Even though it seems South Sudan has given up, take a closer look. You'll see glimpses of hope, even in this place of constant struggle.

It's not over for South Sudan. It's just the start.

On December 24, 2017, a ceasefire was signed between Sudan and South Sudan ("South Sudan's Warring Parties Agree Ceasefire in Bid to End Four-Year War" 2017), with hope for a peaceful implementation.

So don't be afraid to lean in. Go on. Embrace one of her weary but beautiful people.

SOUTH SUDAN
THESE BEAUTIFUL PEOPLE

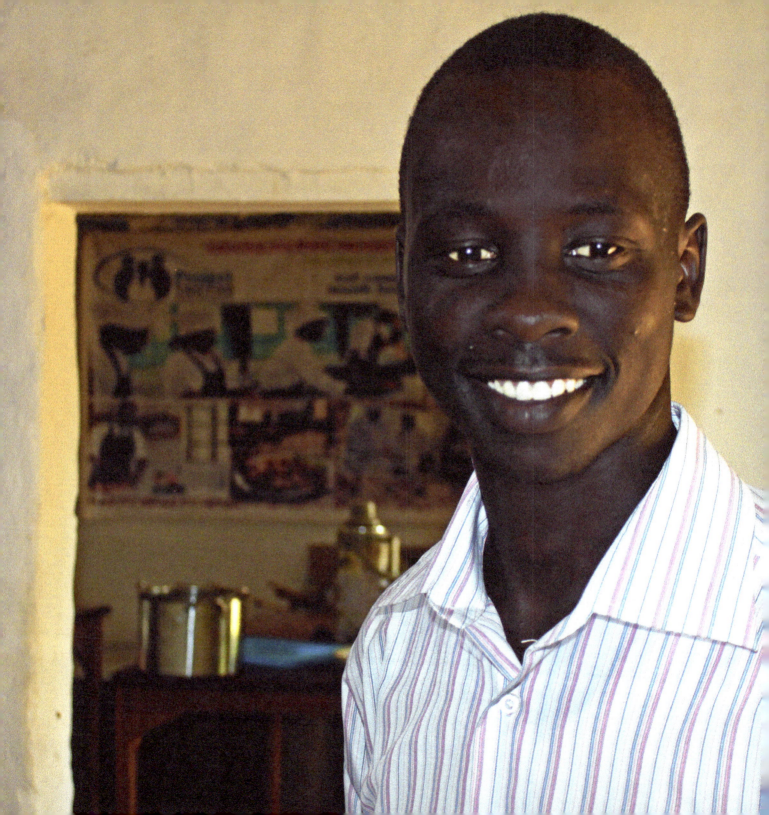

ONE STEP AT A TIME

≤ Naphtali's Story | Yei, South Sudan

It was hot and dusty. The sun beat down on her tired shoulders. Dirty and sore, her feet ached for rest.

A little like South Sudan, she thought. The war had been raging for years, but it felt more like forever.

The country was hurting. The people were weary, their knees buckling under the weight of the world they carried. She tried to remember a time when the country was at peace, but those memories were fuzzy and hard to recall.

Seeing the same weariness on her daughter's face as they walked together, she adjusted her pack and shouldered her daughter's. They walked in silence, worry on their faces but determination in their steps.

It had already been two days of walking. Two days of dreaming what the moment might be like. Two days of praying what they'd heard was right—that he was really there.

She hadn't seen him in six years. Because of the war, there had been no communication. She hadn't known where he was or if he was even alive. Until now.

Someone had told her he was in Yida camp. And although it was a three-day walk from home, this worn and weary mamma had to go. She just had to know. So she kept going, one step at a time.

She remembered when he was born in their small village on Nuba mountain, December 23, 1992. Because there were no schools in the village, he was away from home for long periods of time, looking after the cattle and goats.

SOUTH SUDAN: ONE STEP AT A TIME

THESE BEAUTIFUL PEOPLE

175

But this last time was different. This last time it was uncertain he would ever return.

It was 2003 before the government opened a school in the area. She and her husband enrolled their son immediately. He was already 11 years old.

He was always so clever. Remembering how he loved to learn, a proud smile tugged at the corner of her lips.

It was hard to have her son away from the farm. Her husband was a pastor, so the farm was their main source of survival. But he had climbed quickly to the top of his class and his education needed to come first.

Then came the day she went to a women's ministry course. Her smile saddened because this was the beginning… the beginning of what took him away. She'd met a lady there who helped enroll her son in school in Yei, a short plane ride away.

The look on his face when his father and I gave him that surprise. We had to show him the ticket with his name on it for him to believe us.

She couldn't suppress her chuckle at this memory. Her daughter looked at her, curious. Laughter was a welcome break from the tediousness of the journey.

"I can't wait to see him again, Mamma," her daughter whispered, as she reached out and squeezed her mother's hand. But Mamma couldn't even speak for fear the tears would come. She gently squeezed back and offered a hopeful smile.

Everything inside her said, *Me, too, sweetheart. Me, too. Please, Jesus. Me, too.*

She pictured him waving goodbye, excitement wrapped in nerves as he headed toward the aircraft. He had only enough money for his first term of school and a school uniform. That was it.

She stood at the airport with all the pride in the world, but with even more questions. *How will he manage? Will he survive? How will he get money to live?*

September 2, 2009. It might as well have been yesterday, the memory was so clear. And she still didn't know the answers to those questions. He hadn't been able to return from school because of the war and lack of funds. She knew she wasn't the only one who had waved goodbye to loved ones with no idea if they would see or hear from them again. The war had done this, and it was sobering how "normal" it had become.

Now, six years later, she was just a few hours away from that sweet boy's embrace, from the answers to all her questions and prayers. They finally arrived at Yida camp, dusty and sun-stroked. Shaking in their worn-out sandals, hearts pounding in their chests, they slowly approached the gate.

"We are looking for Naphtali. He is here with a mission team from Yei. Have you seen him?" Mother and daughter searched, one foot in front of the other, one step at a time. Just when they thought they could go no farther, Mamma raised her voice to ask one more time.

Before the words could even leave her lips, he turned around. Not the bright-eyed boy she'd waved goodbye to on that plane, but him nevertheless. Naphtali.

Her knees buckled while her legs locked. She wanted to run but couldn't take another step. She didn't have to.

"Mamma!" he cried, running toward her.

His arms enfolded her and she wished he would never let go. Tears streamed from their eyes and mixed on their cheeks. There was so much to say, so much to reclaim.

They could do nothing but weep and hold each other. When she finally pulled back and looked into his eyes, she knew he was OK. Her young boy had grown into a strong and confident man. A man of God. A man who knew what it was like to be in need and to humble himself to accept help.

"After I arrived at Yei, I met a friend that I knew from back home. He supported me and fed me until I finished my primary and I passed with distinction one," he told her proudly.

A man who wasn't afraid of hard work.

"My friend then invited me to Juba with him so we could work and make money between terms. I didn't have the money for the transport, so I borrowed it and I was able to get a job."

A man who wasn't too proud to start at the bottom.

"The only work we could find was in construction. I didn't know how to do construction but I could help mix the sand and carry the bricks up the stairs."

A man who didn't give up when things got tough.

"It was hard work but I had no option other than to endure. Some days I even worked with tears running down my face."

SOUTH SUDAN: ONE STEP AT A TIME

THESE BEAUTIFUL PEOPLE

Naphtali and his mom

A man who understood that *any* job is better than expecting hand-outs.

"When that job was finished, I found other jobs, like washing people's clothes. I was a waiter, an itinerant trader... and that's just a few."

A man who understood what it was to be homeless.

"The work in Juba did not pay well enough to have a home, so at night we would just lie down on the ground in someone's compound and rest."

A man who was gracious because he has been shown grace.

"I was always just a religious Christian. I went to church. I prayed. I would even preach and teach the children, but I wasn't a believer. My friends got me into drinking and smoking, and I fought a lot. On December 31, 2010, I finally gave Him my life and began my new journey."

A man who understands you don't get where you want to go in a single leap.

"I finished my schooling in 2014 with good results and that's when I met the guy who started and ran Project Two-Five. Now I help run his vocational school for men and women and I am the pastor of a local church here in Yei." He had a heart for his country and his people. As he spoke, her heart warmed and her chest swelled. She hugged him goodbye,

SOUTH SUDAN: ONE STEP AT A TIME

THESE BEAUTIFUL PEOPLE

took her daughter by the hand, and started the long journey home. She knew he couldn't take the time off to return home with her; his calling was in Yei. Her heart ached, but it was also full with seeing him after such a long time. Seeing him in safety and good health with her own eyes.

"I am a child of God who believes in hard work and faithfulness to God."

A child of God—that's right. I don't have to worry about him anymore. He is taken care of. And even more than that, he is taking care of others.

Her mind was at peace.

It has been eight years since Naphtali has seen the rest of his family. As soon as he gets the money, he'll visit. But for now, he's on a mission to serve his people right where he is. The war has recently become more volatile. He's no longer able to be in Yei because of the political situation, so he's in Juba until things settle down.

He has passion, heart, and perseverance.

He's on a mission: A mission to bring hope to his war-torn home. A mission to save the people responsible for tearing his country apart.

It's not going to happen today, maybe not even tomorrow. But if he has learned anything along the way, it's that life doesn't happen in a single leap. South Sudan won't be restored in a day.

The long dusty road won't be paved overnight. The aching feet will need time to recover.

But it's not a race—it's a journey.

You don't get there in an instant.
You get there one step at a time.

SOUTH SUDAN: ONE STEP AT A TIME

RWANDA

When I drove my Rwandan friends over one of the highest hills near my home in Southern Ontario, they looked at me in disbelief, laughed hysterically, and said, "This is just a speed bump. You need to come to Rwanda!"

They were right. A few years later, as the bus from Kampala bounced and swerved its way to Kigali, the capital of Rwanda, I realized it was called the land of a thousand hills for a reason. A very good reason.

One of my favourite things about Rwanda is that no matter where you are, no matter where you look, there's a view. Although the hills make running an absolute nightmare, they also create incomparable beauty. Although my legs throbbed and my lungs cursed me, I was stronger for those hills. Rwanda as a country is no different.

Her history has been as up and down as her landscape. What was once a brutal war zone is now one of the most economically advanced countries in the region.

For centuries, the Hutus and Tutsis lived in peace and harmony, hardly noticing their tribal differences. The Hutus were higher class herdsmen; the Tutsis were lower class farmers. It wasn't until 1933 that things began to change. Every citizen in Rwanda was issued an identification card disclosing their ethnicity. In 1957 Hutu leaders published a heinous, racist article known as the Hutu Ten Commandments (Southgate 2011), inciting followers to a political conflict based on ethnicity. In 1959, three years before Rwanda gained independence from Belgium, the Hutus overthrew the Tutsi king, killing thousands of Tutsis and displacing hundreds of thousands more to neighbouring countries. The next generation of Tutsi exiles rose up and formed a rebel group, the Tutsi Rwandan Patriotic Front (RPF), which attacked from Uganda and started civil war in 1990.

≤ *Traditional Rwandan dance*

RWANDA

THESE BEAUTIFUL PEOPLE

Musanze, Rwanda

Out of this environment of sociopolitical, economic, and ethnic tensions, the horrific genocide began in earnest in April 1994. On April 29, an announcement was declared over state radio that May 5 would be Clean-up Day, when Kigali would be thoroughly cleansed of Tutsis. In a matter of days, more than 14,000 Tutsis were systematically massacred, making it the worst coordinated campaign since the Holocaust. More than 800,000 Rwandans were slaughtered between April and July of that year, mostly by machete.

The RPF troops entered Kigali in July. By the end of August, almost the entire country was under Tutsi control. From the beginning, the RPF has been committed to racial equality. The first cabinet, however, was mostly led by Hutus: 16 members were Hutus and six were Tutsis.

Although Rwanda has been at relative peace for just over 20 years, ridding the country of racism is difficult to achieve. The first step was abolishing identity cards. Rwanda also became part of the Commonwealth in late 2009. Now, when you drive into Rwanda, you would never guess the horror that had happened only one generation before.

Despite the socio-economic turnaround achieved in such a short time, the effects of the genocide are still widespread in many areas, beginning with the population.

Rwanda is the most densely populated country in Africa, with almost 13 million people living in a country smaller than Rhode Island in the United States. A total of 84 percent are Hutu, 15 percent are Tutsi, and the remaining 1 percent are Twa. Less than 40 percent of the population lives below the poverty line, and the infrastructure is the best it has ever been in the country.

In 2016 the unemployment rate was 13.2 percent, another significant improvement due to enhanced infrastructure, education, and foreign and domestic investment. The average hourly wage, however, is a mere 450 Rwandan francs (CAD$0.72).

The average life expectancy for a Rwandan is 60 years, and 70.5 percent of the population above 15 years of age is literate.

Rwandans are fluent in Kinyarwanda and French. Many Rwandans speak English and a few understand Swahili. Kinyarwanda is said to be one of the most difficult languages in the world to learn. I concur. Communication proved difficult for me in this rural country where English isn't widely spoken.

A total of 90 percent of her population is involved in some form of agriculture, with tea, coffee, minerals, and tourism as Rwanda's main industries. None of this is surprising if you have gone gorilla trekking, climbed one of her many volcanoes, or driven through the breathtaking hills and valleys to birdwatch more than 700 species of birds. Or if you've been lucky enough to sip Rwandan coffee or tea over a plate of sweet potatoes and cassava.

Rwanda might have a messy past. But she's proud. She owns where she has been so she can know where she's going. And she's determined that her people go together.

For example, the last Saturday of each month is called *Umuganda*. On this day every Rwandan, including the President, participates in national community service. This has resulted in the building of schools,

ZIMUNGIRA UKUBÍLI
ALÍKO
ZIGAHÙLIZA IMBERE

BEETLES CHEW FROM EITHER SIDE, BUT ALWAYS END UP INSIDE TOGETHER. THERE IS NO POINT ACTING ALONE, WHEN THE AIM IS IDENTICAL FOR ALL.

—*Rwandan proverb*

hydro-electric plants, and medical centres. Cities, towns, and villages are cleaned, making Kigali one of the cleanest cities in Africa.

But that's not the only unique feature this country holds.

Rwanda does not allow plastic bags into the country. Banned in 2007, you'll be required to remove all plastic bags from your luggage at the border.

At a stunning 64 percent, Rwanda has the highest representation of women in parliament in the world.

Rwanda gives a crisp, clean, organized impression. But don't let the peace and stability fool you into thinking there was no cost. She has paid dearly in her fight for freedom. She has bled and cried and still mourns the loss of loved ones. She has not completely healed, and she is not completely at peace.

But it's not impossible for her. Because she's not just the land of a thousand hills—she's the land of a thousand souls.

So go ahead and find courage in the experiences of these brave, beautiful people.

≤ Top: Bisoke volcano; Kigali, Rwanda
≤ Middle: Trek after climbing the volcano the day before, 2014; some of Rwanda's genocide victims, Kigali memorial
≤ Bottom: Bisoke crater lake

OUT OF DEEP WATERS

≤ Adelaide's* Story | Kigali, Rwanda

**When you go through deep waters,
I will be with you.**

—ISAIAH 43:2

I knew she was different the moment I entered her office.

It was Monday morning. I had just arrived in Rwanda after a hectic couple of days and a long bus ride. Time to meet everyone. Again.

Every time I travelled to a new country, I feared not finding someone I could be completely "me" with. Someone who wanted more than a casual conversation. Someone who would be a real friend. In the last country, I had found more than one new connection—but would it be the same here?

She was the personal assistant to the national director of Youth for Christ Rwanda. Because school was soon closing for the term, there wasn't much to do. So I would spend my days in her office, three feet from her at the same desk.

This could be the best month or the worst month. And I was nervous.

Turns out, without cause.

Adelaide is an incredible woman. My Rwandan sister. Someone who has fought hard to become who she is. Someone who understands the ache and freedom of surrender. Someone who is familiar with deep waters. Someone who possesses the strength to swim out.

RWANDA: OUT OF DEEP WATERS

THESE BEAUTIFUL PEOPLE

Here's her story.

Adelaide was born and raised in Rwanda, a city girl with five sisters, one brother, and an incredible set of parents. Her happy memories of growing up are too numerous to recount and her academic success was praised and celebrated by her family.

"They spoiled me," she said with a grin. "When they learned I had the third highest mark in my school for the national exam, they spoiled me!"

Adelaide has always been a hard worker. She never stops, never quits, never gives up.

Life doesn't happen to Adelaide. Adelaide happens to life.

Except for a few times. And during those times, her resilience and determination were what saw her through. See, when you're thrown into deep water, your only options are sink or swim.

"I was seven when the genocide happened. We fled from the city and when we returned the house was empty. No furniture. Not even a single spoon, pot, or pan. Nothing."

Her parents worked tirelessly to put all their children through school, but the quality of education declined catastrophically during this time.

"Ever since that day, I have always fought for success, and I can say that I made them all proud!"

She was accepted into university, but while she was there… more deep water.

"The pressure was too much. My boyfriend and I had a baby."

This didn't stop Adelaide. Despite her parent's disappointment, she continued her studies.

"To my surprise, they paid for my master's and agreed to help raise my child as their own."

There is distance in her eyes, as if remembering that time. A time of fighting. A time of struggle. A time of deep waters that threatened to consume her.

"Despite the judgments I received from so many, I was saved at the time of my son's birth. Before that I had an attitude. I didn't give a damn about anyone or anything. I wanted to live my life however I wanted, but my dad was so strict."

A smile tugged at the corner of her mouth as she continued.

"I didn't have enough time to spoil my life. Between my dad sharpening me on one side and my mom praying for me day and night on the other, I didn't have a chance."

The smile has grown into a full-fledged grin. And she was so beautiful when she smiled. That was where I saw something different about her. Something stronger. Deeper.

RWANDA: OUT OF DEEP WATERS

THESE BEAUTIFUL PEOPLE

Adelaide grew up in church. Her parents took her and her siblings to every service, in the hope they would choose the same path.

"But there always comes a time when we need to choose for ourselves," Adelaide said. "We started refusing to go because church was 'old school.'"

Her smile was even bigger now.

"Honestly, I was afraid to surrender my life to Him because all the people who were saying they were saved were miserable! They were illiterate and I felt like I was better than them."

I laughed. Because she's honest, and I like that. And because she's kind of right. Often we "saved" people are the most miserable ones around.
"But Jesus pursued me." Even in the deep waters.

"I accepted Jesus as my Saviour in 2004, and it was great! I just had a problem with baptism."

Being baptized as a child, others kept telling Adelaide she should be baptized again as a public confession of her personal choice to follow Christ.

"They told me I had to be baptized in deep water." She looked at me with laughing eyes. "Look up the term for yourself, Twila."

I did, and found this: "When you go through deep waters, I will be with you (Isaiah 43:2)."

"I thought this baptism thing was ridiculous and I withdrew from church again."

She had the opportunity to study in Bangalore, India, for three years. God continued to pursue her and she couldn't stay away from His church for long. The senior pastor of the local church became her godfather and mentor. If she decided she wanted to be baptized, he would do it. All she had to do was say the word.

On March 5, 2010, Adelaide was baptized.

"In deep water!" she confirmed with a laugh. "From then on, I was released from the hatred in my heart, a resentful spirit, and worry about what others thought about me. I no longer live with a spirit of fear because I am chosen. I didn't choose Him; He chose me, regardless of my past."

She didn't jump into deep water looking for Jesus. Jesus jumped into deep water looking for her.

"Jesus has taught me that I should praise him in every situation, no matter how small. He reminded me that He has chosen me to be a mother to my son. He told me that His love differs from human love because He is Love!"

Adelaide now works as a communication agent in a government institution, which has been her lifelong dream. Her son is now eight years old, and in May 2017 she got married. You heard me—married! She recently gave birth to a beautiful baby boy.
"My dream is to be more socially involved and also to be a good mom to my kids and a good wife to my husband. Jesus brought me love. He gave me someone who loves me and my son unconditionally. I never thought I would find this and I definitely never thought I would be able to accept marrying anyone, but it is happening! And I'm so thankful for Jesus, His acceptance and His wisdom, His gifts."

Adelaide is an incredible woman. My Rwandan sister.

Someone who has fought hard to become who she is. Who understands the ache and freedom of surrender.

Someone who is familiar with deep waters. Who possesses the strength to swim out.

She's a stunning example of true beauty. Of depth and raw and real.

If she could tell the world one thing, she'd say, "Don't be busy doing useless things. Strive to bring God glory instead."

And she does. And she has.
And it often comes out of the places you would least expect.
Out of deep waters.

Adelaide's name was changed to protect her anonymity.

RWANDA: OUT OF DEEP WATERS

THESE BEAUTIFUL PEOPLE

LIVING ON A PRAYER

≤ Baaka's* Story | Kigali, Rwanda

"I just want you to pray for me."

It was possibly the last time I would see my Rwandan brother, Baaka. It was the rainy season in Rwanda, and we were sitting under a tent to stay dry.

Baaka is a hard-working young man from the district of Muhanga in the north. Having lived through the horrific genocide of 1994–1995, he has learned how to struggle. How to survive. How to see life as a gift.

If you know anything about the Rwandan genocide, you'll know that for his entire family to have survived is miraculous.

"I was four years old when the genocide started and we lost my father. He went missing. That's when we fled to the Congo."

His brave mamma packed her bags and her three young children and set out for a new land. A safe haven, if they were lucky. She was a strong, smart woman, his mamma. She had a good job in a hospital until Baaka was born, then she stayed home to raise her children.

"Whenever the army would stop us along the way, wanting to kill us, my mother would plead with them, telling them that she doesn't know where her husband is; she doesn't have his ID and doesn't know his race."

His eyes had a far-off look. He was remembering. Reliving.

"She would lie and tell them my father was in the defeated army so they would think we were on their side. They let us go."

Even in the Congo, safety wasn't guaranteed.

RWANDA: LIVING ON A PRAYER

THESE BEAUTIFUL PEOPLE

"I remember being at the camp in the Congo. The Rwandans came there looking to kill us. I stood at the door and saw the men come with their weapons. They spoke to my mom and she pleaded with them to let us live. Luckily, we had money so we could pay them and they would leave. But they always sent more people back to find us, so we had to keep moving."

My mind tried to comprehend a four-year-old witnessing such scenarios. Then I remembered that others have seen even worse. It was gut-wrenching. Excruciating. Undeniably wrong.

"I still see that picture in my mind."

He laughed, but it was heavy with memory.

"While we were in Congo, we got word that my father had joined the rescuing army and we knew nothing else." And so they believed their father was in the middle of it all, fighting for their lives and possibly losing his own.

When the genocide ended, they made the courageous trip back into Rwanda.
To pick up the pieces.
To start over.

"It wasn't until we came back into Rwanda that we found my father. He had not joined the rescuing army; he had been in hiding the whole time and could not communicate to us."

The rain started up again and fell softly on the tent.

"I just want you to pray for me."

That's how our conversation had started.

At only 25 years old, he was responsible for paying the school fees for his younger brother and sister. Every six months, he had to come up with 800,000 Rwandan francs (more than CAD$1,200.00) to keep his siblings in school. What faith. What trust.

"My father was a good daddy. He had a job as a contractor and easily provided for us. Then in 2013 he was poisoned by some people who were jealous of him."

I was in disbelief as he explained that no one was ever held responsible for the poisoning. Though his father survived, he has been sick ever since and unable to work. Baaka is the sole provider for the whole family.

"It's more than my salary so I'm always thinking of ways to work and get the money."

Baaka is in charge of maintenance at Youth for Christ Rwanda.

There was no resentment in his voice. No whining or grumbling. No complaining about having to support himself and his family. He simply stated the fact and I was blown away by his commitment. His willingness to do what it took. So sacrificially.

Because it was family, he wouldn't think of doing anything else. And because of these circumstances, this young man had been forced to grow up before his time.

What he said next floored me.

"I cannot accept someone coming to give me money."

I tried to hide my surprise. I would have thought a monetary donation would be welcome.

"If you want to help me, give me a job."

What?

"If you want to help me, give me a job."

As he continued, I was blown away by his work ethic and mindset. I was astounded. And so, *so* proud.

"As Christians, we say that we believe God can provide everything we need because He knows what we need. So if you come to me and hand me money, then I take the money and I use it and it's over. But if we pray together, God can provide a thousand times over what we need and more!"

RWANDA: LIVING ON A PRAYER

He was so sincere. And so right!

I had to remind myself he was only 25 and carrying the weight of his whole family on his shoulders. Still, he refused to settle for a handout.

He operated on absolute faith and trust—something I'm still trying to grasp.

I nodded emphatically, to the point where I was sure he wondered what the excitement was all about. To him, this kind of faith was normal.

"It's not good to continually ask people for money. It's not a good culture."

It wasn't a good culture. It wasn't a good way of doing life. It wasn't a permanent solution.

And Baaka got it.

He was singlehandedly living by faith, and sometimes in want, because he believed in a better way. A better culture. A culture of hard work and personal responsibility. A culture of prayer and faith.

How did he get this way? How did he come out of these difficult situations with an uncommon mindset and determination?

I've concluded that it didn't happen overnight. No, it was a long process beginning with one decision at a time. Simple life choices.

Baaka has always had a heart to serve.

At his own expense, he served in Burundi, Uganda, and Kenya on building and volunteer projects because he knows the value of giving over receiving.

He studied construction and electrical, among other trades, because he knows the value of experience over dollar signs.

Now he has a dream to build a house.

"I have the plans, the list of materials, and the exact cost of everything that I need. I even know which land I want. All I need is the means, and I will start to build."

We walked the dusty path to his house, where he carefully pulled out the master plan. A thrill of excitement lit up his face and voice as he walked me through the plans for each room of the house.

"And this is so your parents and siblings can have a place to live together, right?" I asked him.

His eyes shone. "Of course!"

———

Baaka's father passed away in 2015, leaving a gaping hole in their hearts and home. He continues to work at Youth for Christ and he has built a smaller home for now, until he's able to afford a big enough place for his family.

Even with all the challenges, he dares to dream, because he knows that anything is possible with hard work and a lot of faith.

He is living on a prayer.

*Baaka's name was changed to protect his anonymity.

JUST LIKE JESUS

≤ Jean Baptiste's Story | Kigali, Rwanda

I don't remember the first time I met Jean Baptiste, or JB, as he called himself. I do remember instantly feeling like I'd known him forever. Maybe that's why it's hard to recall. But I'll never forget the time he came to Canada. I had no idea he was even in the country when I got his email.

"Hi Twila, I am in Canada at some place called Waterloo. Where are you?"

I nearly fell off my chair. I work in Waterloo.

I sent him my phone number. Before long we had made dinner arrangements with my parents for that evening.

After work, I met him and another couple and we drove to my parents' home. They laughed at the small bumps I called hills. When I showed them the highest point in Southern Ontario, they nearly split their sides laughing. They know a hill when they see one, and this was not one.

We enjoyed a wonderful meal together. He shared story after story of his life, then firmly informed my parents that he was here to take his daughter home. My parents were bewildered until they realized it was me.

I was the daughter. That's just how he is: immediately pulling you in, wrapping you up in a bear hug, and welcoming you to the family.

To this day, Jean Baptiste will forever be etched in my mind as the man who just might be more like Jesus than anyone else I know.

He has that presence about him: humble and kind, relational and real, vulnerable and patient. He's an incredible storyteller of even more incredible experiences; there isn't enough space in this book for them all.

RWANDA: JUST LIKE JESUS

THESE BEAUTIFUL PEOPLE

JB and Luc (right) surprising me in Canada

His eyes are kind and his smile is warm. The epitome of a servant leader, he lives above reproach and with unmatched integrity. He makes you want to be better, to be more like Him.

He's like a big teddy bear but made of the good stuff, the solid stuff. He's soft on the outside but a rock on the inside. Steady in heart, convinced of purpose, and constant in mind.

He's probably the only person I know whose name I'd substitute for the word "love" in 1 Corinthians 13, although he didn't come from a place or a family that had it all together. If anything, he could have had every excuse to feel sorry for himself.

But that's not His way, so that's not *his* way. JB never takes the easy way out.

He pioneered Youth for Christ Rwanda from the ground up. Now, more than 20 years later, it's one of the most well-known and well-respected organizations in the country. He can be carrying the weight of the world on his shoulders, but he'll always have time for the person in front of him.

When I went to Rwanda in 2014, I watched as he stood by his wife in the final stages of cancer. She had been fighting this beast for years and it was taking a tremendous toll on her body. He had taken her to doctors overseas, tried every treatment, yet there she was. Dying in her hospital bed.

The day after I arrived, he came to the office for a staff meeting. He entered the room with a smile on his face, joking with everyone along the way, passing out bananas and snacks. He gave a brief update on his wife then encouraged us and asked how we were doing.

A few days later, I met him in the parking lot. I asked how *he* was doing.

"I just don't know what else to do anymore. I am out of ideas." Tears welled up in his eyes. "I have exhausted every resource I can think of. I don't think there is anything else I can do."

My heart broke. He was walking through hell and still encouraging others along the way. He was losing the love of his life but he still invested in everyone around him.

"I just feel so bad that I am not around more while you are here." He looked straight into my eyes.

I could hardly hold back my tears. Why was he apologizing? No one would blame him for focusing only on himself.

We went to the hospital to visit her. What hit me hardest was not what I expected. Not her lying in the bed. Not the thought of her passing. What hit me was how much he loved her.

Willingly, he went to the hospital day or night. Without complaint, he adjusted the sheets and the pillow behind her head. Gently, he kissed her tired, dry lips. Bravely, he joked to see a glimpse of a smile cross her weary face. He sat beside her and held her hand, singing and praying.

In 2015 he gazed into her eyes as she took her last breath.

JB has an otherworldly strength. He has influenced thousands of people with his wisdom, kindness, and genuine concern. But for me, his unconditional love for his wife impacted me the most.

The kind of love you can't earn.
The kind of love that takes hold and holds on.
The kind of love you long for.

The kind of love that's just like Jesus.

BURUNDI

"Welcome to the heart of Africa!"

That greeting is one of the three things you'll receive when you arrive in Burundi. The other two are a huge grin and a peck on each cheek.

Burundi is the smallest and second most densely populated country in Africa. Home to just over 11 million people, what she lacks in size, she makes up for in heart. Her heart—and geographical location—explains Burundi's beloved slogan as "the heart of Africa." She is also home to a tree said to be located in the exact centre of the continent.

One of the first things I noticed about Burundi was her resemblance to Rwanda. Like Rwanda, the people speak French and Kirundi, similar to Kinyarwanda. The landscape is a stretch of rolling hills, except for Bujumbura, a valley surrounded by mountains and the beaches of Lake Tanganyka. Burundi and Rwanda share the same three tribes— Hutu, Tutsi, and Twa. Even the food is similar, except for fresh fish, like the native *mukeke,* and "Russian tea," a local combination of tea and coffee. Coffee is one of Burundians' pride and joys. Friendly and welcoming, Burundians are slightly less reserved than Rwandans.

These similarities make sense because Burundi and Rwanda were once neighbouring kingdoms known as Ruanda-Urundi. Urundi experienced an influx of Tutsi refugees when ethnic violence broke out in Rwanda in 1959; in 1962 Urundi separated from Ruanda and became the independent Kingdom of Burundi. In October 1993, Burundi was thrown into an ethnic war that decimated more than 300,000 lives after the president was assassinated. Only one year later, the Rwandan genocide took place. It wasn't until 2005 that Burundi was able to make headway with an integrated defence force, a new constitution, and a majority-elected government.

Unfortunately, the discontent and unrest has continued until today.

≤ Bujumbura, by the beach

BURUNDI

THESE BEAUTIFUL PEOPLE

IGITI KIGORORWA KIKIRI GITO
**WHEN YOU PLANT A TREE,
YOU HAVE TO SUPPORT IT
FROM THE BEGINNING
SO IT WILL GROW UP
IN A GOOD DIRECTION.**
—BURUNDIAN PROVERB

In 2015 the president was re-elected for his third term in a disputed election, triggering violence, about 400 deaths, and another outpouring of refugees from Burundi into surrounding countries.

So yes, in many ways Burundi is similar to Rwanda.

But the difference? Rwanda was resilient post-genocide, whereas Burundi has struggled between incidents. She remains among the poorest and most forgotten countries in Africa, with 68 percent living below the poverty line.

Lack of clean water, food shortages, and poverty are the main sources of child malnutrition, and poor reproductive medical services have caused maternal mortality and fertility rates to soar among the world's highest. Two-thirds of the population is under 25 and the average woman has six children, putting additional strain on an already struggling nation.

Minimum wage in Burundi is reputed to be 160 Burundian francs (CAD$0.12) per day in urban areas and 105 Burundian francs (CAD$0.08) per day in rural areas.

Burundi might be struggling and straining. She might feel forgotten and left behind. But she is full of possibility because she is full of people—vibrant, beautiful people with hearts bigger than their struggles. Bigger than their betrayal. Bigger than their past.

Burundians are known for their drumming—and what a sight to behold! They know how to celebrate and how to welcome. When you don't know what else to give, you can always give your heart. And they do.

So come on and meet them. You'll be captivated, I just know it.

Into the heart of Africa.
Into the hearts of these beautiful people.

≪ Top: Gitega, Burundi
≪ Middle: Hiking the hills surrounding Bujumbura
◁ Bottom: Overlooking Bujumbura; traditional Burundian drummers

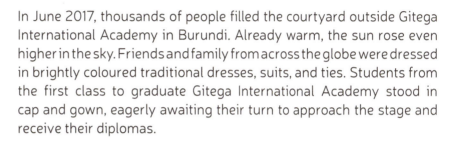

SOMETHING FROM NOTHING

≤ **Freddy's Story** | Bujumbura, Burundi

In June 2017, thousands of people filled the courtyard outside Gitega International Academy in Burundi. Already warm, the sun rose even higher in the sky. Friends and family from across the globe were dressed in brightly coloured traditional dresses, suits, and ties. Students from the first class to graduate Gitega International Academy stood in cap and gown, eagerly awaiting their turn to approach the stage and receive their diplomas.

But this was more than a graduation. More than a day of smiles and tears, hugs and high fives, it was a day of miracles. The founder of Gitega International Academy, Freddy Tuyizere, took to the stage and began to speak.

"Life was simple back in those days," Freddy said, looking out over the audience.

Freddy was the firstborn of 11 children from a small village in Burundi. Money was tight in such a large family, often without enough food to go around. They had nothing and thought nothing of it.

"In my innocence, our status seemed normal. I never envisioned life to be different than what I already experienced. My entire world was exactly where I was; thinking beyond that was inconceivable. I was simply a village boy. I did not dream of who I wanted to become."

≤ *Freddy and Marie Josée at graduation, 2017*

BURUNDI: SOMETHING FROM NOTHING

THESE BEAUTIFUL PEOPLE

Only five children from his village attended school. Before schools were made public by the government, they were required to attend the school affiliated with their church denomination, even if it meant walking three hours to school one way. Freddy did this for years, often on one meal a day.

"I thanked God because I knew that many in my village had no food at all," he said.

Freddy accepted Christ in secondary school. Baptized into his parent's church, he began to find the courage to dream.

This boy who came from nothing had the audacity to dream that he would attend the prestigious missionary school started by his church. He knew it was a pipe dream, but he prayed anyway.

When it came time for the government to choose which school he would attend, it was Lycée Kiremba-Sud. His dream school.

"I instantly, strongly believed that God had a plan for my life." Freddy leaned forward and grinned. "My friends and family rallied around me, somehow raising enough funds for my tuition and supplies."

From nothing.

"I was so excited! On my first day, I placed all my things into a bag that had been purchased for me, set it on my head, and balanced it all the way to school. It was a three-and-a-half–hour journey on foot."

His smile showed he didn't mind. Because it was a boarding school, he wouldn't have to leave for at least three months.

It didn't take long for reality to sink in. He was a village boy; most of the students were from wealthy families. And not everyone in the school held Christian values. Bullying and intimidation ran rampant.

To most at school, he might as well have been nothing. But when he went home, his pastor saw something in him. He mentored him and gave him a platform to speak to other young people in the church.

"It was the summer after Grade 8 that I felt a strong presence of God over my life. In my heart of hearts, I knew He was up to something and was calling me into ministry. I didn't know what that meant, but I knew I would spend my whole life leading His people and drawing many to Him." He shook his head as if still in disbelief over being chosen.

After graduating, the government sent him to study to be a teacher. It's here that he would meet his best friend and future wife, Marie Josée.

BURUNDI: SOMETHING FROM NOTHING

THESE BEAUTIFUL PEOPLE

In 1991 Bujumbura was attacked by a rebel group. He remembered being at school as the fighting drew closer and closer. Students were screaming and running for safety.

Soon after, he heard a prophecy over Burundi: "A generation will rise up and go out from plain to plain, sharing the gospel." Freddy was so inspired that his passion was reignited for ministry, as was the call God had placed on his life at age 16.

When his schooling was finished, he was sent to work in the south of Burundi, where he encountered many difficult people.

"God was showing me the kinds of people I would have to lead. He was preparing my heart to deal with them like He would," Freddy reflected. "He doesn't cast them away but rather embraces them, as shameful as they are. He rises up, covers their shame, and cares for them. That would be my mission—to be Christ-like. And to lead like Jesus would, to become a servant of all."

Things in the government were changing. People lived in an atmosphere of fear and unrest. During this time, God gave him a prophecy:

The country shall be covered by a dark cloud, which will bring tears and sorrow to every individual. But after the dark cloud, the sun will shine again over us and Burundi will be a source of light to the nations. Many people will come to Burundi from other places to see what God is doing.

The emphasis was on the dark cloud passing away, giving way to the sun shining over Burundi. But that would take a miracle.

On October 21, 1993, the Hutu president of Burundi was murdered by Tutsi soldiers, sparking a horrific genocide that swept the nation. Students and staff were ordered to remain at the school where Freddy was working. No one came or left. Students heard of family and friends being murdered in the villages. Soon even the school became unsafe.

"The fighting came so close that the headmaster of the school had to run away, as well as a number of the Hutu teachers. Classes stopped completely." His eyes narrowed at the memory. "At 23, I was responsible for taking care of the lives of others. Frightened children needed encouragement, comfort, and words to carry them through this trying time. We could hear the sounds of babies and children crying beyond the school walls. They had been abandoned, left unattended and vulnerable. Some of the students were killed. There was no medical care so we had to rely on the Great Physician. In spite of everything, we saw miracle after miracle.

"There is one night that still haunts me." Freddy's voice wavered. "It was a Tuesday. I had just finished speaking to a group of students. That night, someone came and threw a grenade into the room where eight boys were sleeping, taking all their lives. Several others were injured. I went to their dorm in the morning and found them there. Dead."

What good could come of this mayhem? What could he do? Nothing. Or so he felt.

But this guy had a crazy kind of hope. See, he had a vision from God. In his belief that He could make it come to pass, he decided to leave his teaching job and go into full-time ministry with Scripture Union.

From paid to volunteer, he walked away with nothing to pursue God's call on his life. No money for food or rent. Nothing.

Nothing except hope.

"There are two things a man should not live without," he said. "Food and hope. The latter is most important. You can survive days without food, but you'd kiss the world goodbye in an instant without hope."

And there were many days he didn't eat at all. In fact, the leader of Scripture Union didn't want him to volunteer because they knew he had no source of income.

Freddy's reply shocked him.

"Sir, I am convinced that God has called me at this particular time to serve His people, especially the young people. If He does not provide, then I am ready and willing to die in His hands, and that will be His fault." Even Freddy was scared by his own confidence.

They allowed him to continue serving—how could they not? Amid poverty and starvation, he met and fell in love with his best friend, Marie Josée.

"She was way out of my league socially and economically, but I wanted to marry her and I pursued her, even in my malnourishment and poverty."

Her family was less than impressed; they had much higher dreams for their little girl. Four years and 11 months after meeting Marie Josée, he mustered all his courage, marched boldly to her door, and declared his intentions.

"After four months and 12 days, she confirmed that she had prayed and felt peace about accepting my proposal. Touchdown! I had won." His grin stretched wide as his wife shook her head.

They married in 1997 and had three sons, but the adventure was far from over. In fact, it was just getting started.

Freddy met a crazy *mzungu* (white) missionary and ended up biking across the country as his translator. In a time when security was low and instability was high, they knew they weren't promised tomorrow.

"We called ourselves 'the immortals.' That's how audacious we were. It was crazy faith!" He laughed.

Freddy traveled to Rwanda to meet Jean Baptiste.

"Hearing him talk about his dreams for Youth for Christ Rwanda got me excited. I knew my assignment was about to be handed to me."

It was.

A constitution for Youth for Christ Burundi was established at the end of 1999. Only 12 people attended the first meeting, and even fewer people caught his vision. They had no money, no support, nothing. Just faith in the One who had called them.

"My motto in life is simple, but few live it: 'For we walk by faith, not by sight (2 Corinthians 5:7, New American Standard Version).'"

The government gave them 10 acres of land. When asked if they had money to build on the land, he confidently said yes, even though there was none. But he believed there would be. Someone gave them the equivalent of US$50, which wasn't enough, but as Freddy said, "Big things grow from small seeds."

They pitched a tent on the land and started caring for five orphaned children, all the children they could afford to care for. With the little money left over, they planted cow grass, fields and fields of cow grass, which fed the cows, which provided milk for these five malnourished children.

That's how it all began.

"When I look back over the years, my heart swells with gratitude. I'm amazed by the things God can do with nothing." Freddy gripped the microphone and scanned the crowd of thousands.

"On that land where the cow grass once grew now stands Homes of Hope Orphanage, Shammah Health Centre, and Future Hope School, where 600 children attend, including the orphaned children in our care. This same model, including sustainability projects, has been started in three other locations, with dreams of many more.

BURUNDI: SOMETHING FROM NOTHING

THESE BEAUTIFUL PEOPLE

"Where we stand today, Gitega International Academy is now recognized as the best school in the country. Today we celebrate the first graduation and all that God has done."

The crowd burst into applause. He gripped the mic, waiting to continue.

"Who would have thought that God would transform a 10-acre plot of cow grass into a lighthouse for a city and beyond? Being classified as one of the top five poorest countries in the world in 2016 was a grieving statement to hear. Knowing the great potential of this country, I refuse to believe we are poor. We have untapped wealth. That does not make us poor."

The applause was deafening. There wasn't a dry eye in the room.

"I have learned that pursuing dreams can be done by anyone; however, staying consistent, diligent, and persevering through hindrances is done by few. To achieve a dream, one must be willing to face adversity."

He made eye contact with the graduates and urged them to chase after their dreams with reckless abandon.

"If God can use a village boy like me, then He can certainly use you."

When you come with empty hands, He fills them. When you bring what you have, He multiplies it. When you do what you can with what you have, He entrusts you with more.

A humble village start might have felt like nothing; surrendered, it is everything.
A season of genocide and bloodshed might have felt hopeless; survived, it brings hope to many.
And a tiny seed of cow grass might have felt futile; planted in faith, it yields something.

On that warm, sunny Burundian afternoon, this was more than a graduation. This was a reason to celebrate something from nothing.

———

That same day, Freddy released his first book, *Where the Cow Grass Grows: Planting Faith and Hope in Burundi* (Tuyizere 2017). Many of the quotes in this story were used with permission from his book.

≪ *Top: Homes of Hope*
≪ *Bottom: Gitega International Academy graduation, 2018; Shammah Health Centre; sunrise where the cow grass once grew*

BURUNDI: SOMETHING FROM NOTHING

THESE BEAUTIFUL PEOPLE

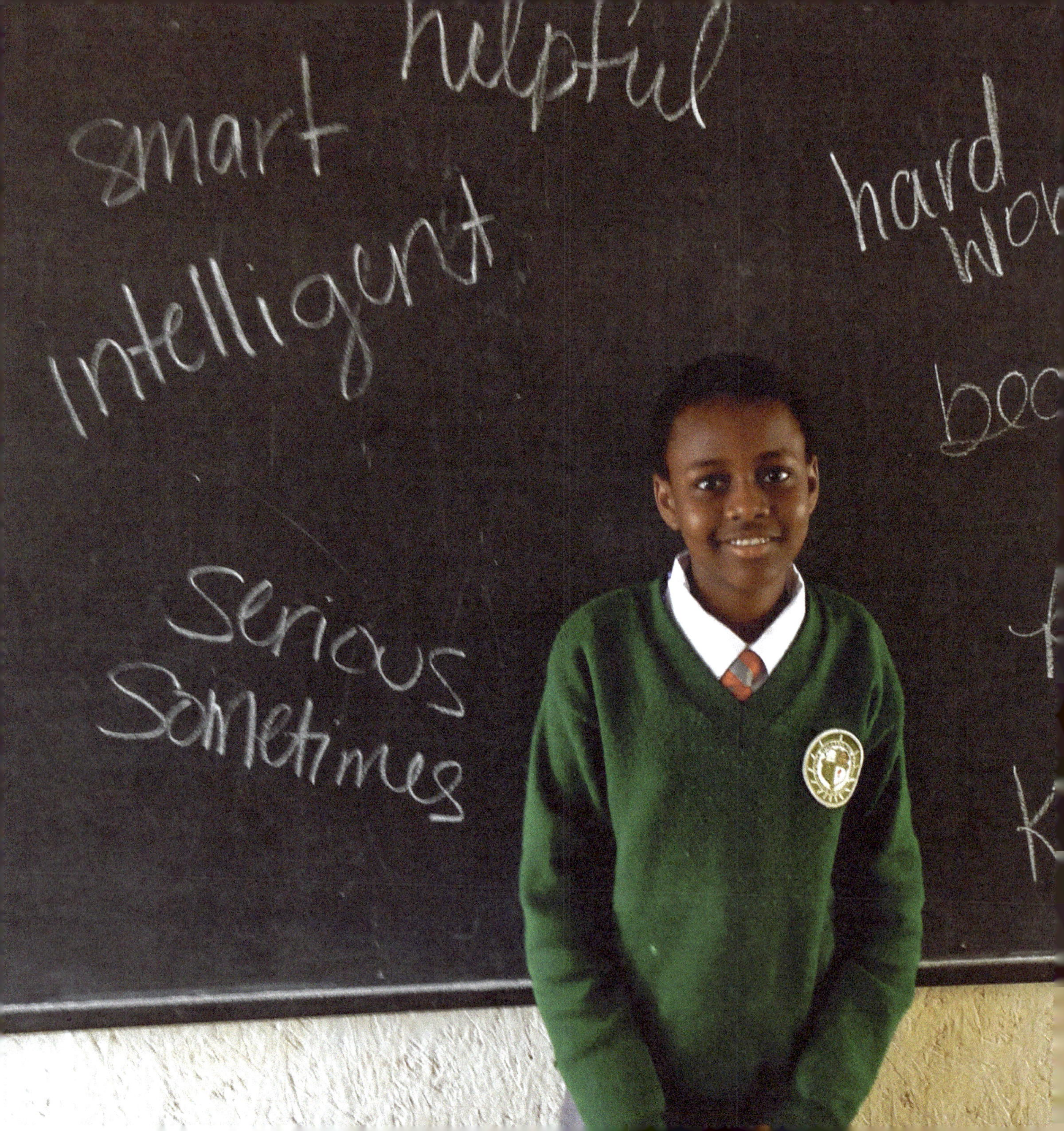
helpful
smart
intelligent
hard
serious sometimes

WE ARE AFRAID OF EACH OTHER

≤ Grade 7 Students' Story
Gitega International Academy, Gitega, Burundi

I was in Burundi teaching two Grade 7 English classes.

By the end of my month there, we were having a blast playing games and improving their conversational English—not to mention being serenaded by students who came to class late. Needless to say, most were only late once.

At the beginning, however, they were all silent. I would ask a question... nothing. I would try to get involvement... nothing.

Finally, I set my book down on the table and asked them what was going on.

"I know you guys are not all shy and I also know you all know how to make noise, but once I'm in here you don't want to talk or move or do anything. Are you afraid of me? Do you hate English? Can you understand me?"

To all of these questions, they shook their heads. Some mumbled a quiet no.

"Well, what is it, then? What are you afraid of?"

Their answer shook me to my core. Their answer was the reason for the exercise you see in this photo.

Their answer was, "We are afraid of each other."

PRODIGAL HOPE

≤ Doina's Story | Bujumbura, Burundi

prod·i·gal
Spending freely and recklessly.
Wastefully, extravagantly.
Having or giving something on a lavish scale.

We all know the story of the prodigal son, don't we? The one in Luke 15. The one where the son has everything at his fingertips.

Yeah, you know this son. The one on whom the father has spared no expense. The one who takes what's his and runs off, wasting his inheritance. The one who returns with his tail between his legs, begging for mercy.

And you know how it ends, right? The father, instead of serving up a heaping of "serves you right," serves up grace.

Well, this story is kind of like that.

A man had two sons.

—LUKE 15:11

Or, in this case, many sons and daughters. One of those daughters was named Doina.

Doina was born in 1987 in a small province in the south of Burundi. She and one younger sister lived with their parents in Gihofi for five years before moving to Bujumbura, the capital.

"My childhood was quiet," she recalled. A stable family, two parents with steady jobs, constant provision. Everything she could have needed.

"I remember playing with my sister a lot! We would build houses out of tree branches and then pretend to be a family, cooking as we saw our cooks do by putting soil in tomato cans. It was so much fun! I cannot forget it."

Mischief danced in her eyes as she reminisced.

"One time we were playing hide-and-seek and my sister decided to close herself in a corridor. Then we realized that we could not get the door open again. We had to wait 30 minutes for dad to come home to open it. I remember sitting by the door passing snacks under it while we waited. We were in big trouble, but now we look back and laugh. We get along so well! The thing we fought most about was over who got to hold our younger brothers when they were born. She was stronger than me, so she always won!"

Her family was nothing but pleasant memories. School was another story.

"There were two boys who would wait for me at the end of class so they could beat me. I was always afraid to go home because I knew they would be waiting. The solution was to get out of class early or pray that my parents would be at the gate of the school on time. Sometimes I would hide myself in different classrooms so that they couldn't find me."

**The younger son told his father,
'I want my share of your estate now.'**

—LUKE 15:12

He was likely too young... too entitled. He was lost and searching... searching for himself.

Doina had similar struggles. Being bullied is a sucker punch to your self-esteem: it manifests itself in many ways. Overconfidence became a mask for her insecurity.

"When I was in high school, I used to think I was the prettiest girl in the whole school. I even missed class one day because my dad would not let me leave the house in what I was wearing. My self-esteem was so low that all I wanted was for all the boys' eyes to be on me. To see my shape and know that I was the best and most beautiful in the class."

She had no idea who she was. She was lost and searching, looking for her value in the approval of others. And it led to pain.

"I had my first boyfriend in Grade 8. When he went abroad to study, we continued dating for three years but I left him when I came to know Christ in 2005."

His father...

—LUKE 15:11

We don't know for sure, but by saying "his father" we see a hint of relationship. Perhaps the son took this relationship for granted, or perhaps they had moments of closeness, where the conversation was real and honest.

Doina had those moments of closeness, too.

"I knew nothing about what it meant to be a child of God. I didn't even know it was in the Bible."

Let's back up a little. As a child, Doina had loved to pray. So much so that she designated a room in her house as a chapel. She was determined to become a nun.

"I always had a heart that longed for God, but I must admit that reading the Bible was hard and, honestly, boring. It didn't make any sense to me. I was practicing religion but nothing was changing in me. It was not a life—it was a one-way street, a religious practice to gain eternal life by acting like a good Christian."

When she met a born-again neighbour, she began to understand how salvation worked.

"It was so deep and so true that I immediately said, 'Yes, I do!' Then my new life began."

She joined groups of other believers who would encourage and strengthen her. No longer a chore to read the Bible, she began enjoying her quiet time with Him.

"It became so easy to talk with God. He felt so real and my thirst for Him was overwhelming. I had always struggled with self-esteem, but I learned that my Jesus was there for me as an intimate friend. My view of myself changed. I knew He would understand me and care for me more than anyone in the world. I developed a relationship of trust, and my habits of lying, fighting, anxiety, and verbally abusive behaviours slowly disappeared."

Doina had suffered from asthma from a young age. Jesus healed her of that, too.
"Since 2008 until now, I have seen no symptoms of my asthma. Nothing!"

The Father put a heart of evangelism in her and she began reaching out to the unsaved, speaking and sharing the Good News with anyone who would listen. She was already in the family and already prodigal. Living freely and recklessly for her Father.

"Everything was going so well. Until the day that I failed."

Failed her last year of high school.

"I couldn't understand how God could let this happen. I was embarrassed. After all, I was serving Him. My heart was in shock."

She locked herself in her room for a week, refusing to eat or talk to anyone.

"I felt deceived by God and utterly humiliated in front of the people I was preaching and sharing the gospel with."

Doina spent much of her time crying and begging God for an explanation.

"My only words to God were, 'Why are You doing this to me? What have I done? Talk to me. Tell me! How can You humiliate me like this?'"

I want my share of your estate now.

—LUKE 15:12

What caused the son to ask this? Did he not have everything at his fingertips? Provision, the very presence of his father? Perhaps it was a series of events that didn't make sense, a series of things that felt unfair.

These were the first of many questions Doina had.

"Surprisingly, God gave me a picture of Jesus on the cross. He told me, 'Jesus died for you, too. He did it for you, too, so He loves you no matter the situation. His love is in you.' For some reason, that gave me the strength, courage, and joy to continue."

Life went on and she repeated her last year of high school, graduating with higher marks than she had expected.

"Having been put down a lot in my childhood, hearing my own parents tell me I was useless, believing my siblings were all smarter and better than me, caused me to look down on myself. That's where my poor self-esteem came from and it birthed in me a desire to help others who feel the same way."

Doina has a deep heart for emotionally disturbed people.

"I wanted to develop that gift inside me so I decided to study psychology."

Shortly after, she believed God was telling her to study in England. She began to pursue it. International school fees were ridiculous, though, and her parents weren't able to afford it.

"I heard my dad saying that he wanted me to go to Kenya to learn English while searching for a university in the United Kingdom. I was so happy and I thought that it was God's answer as there was no British embassy in Burundi, but in Kenya there was one."

When she arrived in Kenya, she contacted an organization that helped people find schools and obtain visas for the United Kingdom.

"I got a school, did the English test, and everything was ready except the money."

She was still confident God would perform a miracle.

"It didn't change my faith in God. As time went on, I kept trusting in God that I would be able to start school on January 7, 2010. I just had to! We were in December and I was late with the finances but I said to myself that My God is always on time. But even beyond time, He can still do miracles."

It didn't happen.

"Again, there was another deep wound in me."

Another event that didn't make sense. Another event that felt unfair. Another event that caused distrust and disappointment in the Father.

"I was feeling humiliated again and I couldn't understand how someone could have faith to that point and be wrong. It felt like another deception from God."

A few days later this younger son packed all his belongings and moved to a distant land, and there he wasted all his money on wild living.

—LUKE 15:13

Doina went to the University of Nairobi in Kenya, defeated, disappointed, and angry.

"I stopped praying and reading the Bible. I had no communication with God and I fell. I got into a relationship with a guy who did not have a heart for God and I spent four years in a deep darkness. I was enjoying life without any limitations. Everything I had never done before, I was doing."

BURUNDI: PRODIGAL HOPE

THESE BEAUTIFUL PEOPLE

Living prodigally. Freely and recklessly. Wastefully and extravagantly.

About the time his money ran out, a great famine swept over the land, and he began to starve. He persuaded a local farmer to hire him, and the man sent him into his fields to feed the pigs. The young man became so hungry that even the pods he was feeding the pigs looked good to him. But no one gave him anything.

—LUKE 15:14–16

Desperation. The realization that his attempt to be free had enslaved him further.

"I felt like I was in prison, living a life that I did not understand. Then about a month before my graduation, I was informed there was a course I did not finish so I would not be graduating with my friends. Oh, how wounded I became again," she reminisced, the hurt of the moment still fresh in her eyes.

When he finally came to his senses, he said to himself, 'At home even the hired servants have food enough to spare, and here I am dying of hunger! I will go home to my father.'

—LUKE 15:17–18

Doina was crushed by the news and went straight to her room.

"Really, God? Are you starting this again? Is my life only for failing? Have you created me just to cry? What have I done now, Lord? Are You revenging me for having stopped praying?"

That's what she prayed. Or maybe just cried aloud to herself because sometimes we have to get it out before we can get it right.

"After that I began to weep. I decided that I was going to start living just one day at a time. Everything had been taken from me. Everything that I had drawn close to my heart had been removed. Everything except my boyfriend."

And she was afraid God would take him, too. Afraid He would punish her for her behaviour.

"For a year after I graduated, I partied and got drunk and did, well, everything. It was the worst year ever. Many of the people I used to preach to saw me fall. Some prayed. Some followed. In 2014 I became so tired in my heart. I needed God. I needed Him to talk to me once again. I needed Him to tell me something. Anything. There was a deep cry in my heart. I began the long journey back to God."

Slowly. Slowly. Slowly.

> So he returned home to his father. And while he was still a long way
> off, his father saw him coming. Filled with love and compassion, he
> ran to his son, embraced him, and kissed him. His son said to him,
> "Father, I have sinned against both heaven and you, and I am no
> longer worthy of being called your son."
>
> —LUKE 15:20–21

"I knelt down before God and asked forgiveness for everything I did. I asked forgiveness for being so angry. I understood that even if He showed me my future, He did not tell me when it would all happen. And even if He did not answer my prayers in the way or time I wanted, there was probably a good reason for that."

> But his father said to the servants...
>
> —LUKE 15:22

The father would have none of it. None of the begging. None of the grovelling.

> "Quick! Bring the finest robe in the house and put it on him.
> Get a ring for his finger and sandals for his feet. And kill the calf
> we have been fattening. We must celebrate with a feast,
> for this son of mine was dead and has now returned to life.
> He was lost, but now he is found."
>
> —LUKE 15:22–24

The father immediately restored his son's inheritance. Clothed him in a robe of righteousness. Gave him the family ring. Killed the calf. Celebrated the son who was dead in his heart but was now back in His life.

God reminded Doïna of the day she gave Him her life—to take control of it, to trust Him with it. He didn't bring up everything she did wrong or scold her. Instead, He spread His arms wide and said, "Welcome home, child."

BURUNDI: PRODIGAL HOPE

THESE BEAUTIFUL PEOPLE

<h1 style="text-align:center">So the party began.</h1>

—LUKE 15:24

The father was prodigal, spending freely and recklessly. The older brother thought his father was wasteful in his generosity, careless with his grace. He loved extravagantly. He served abundantly. He lavished hope without holding back.

Prodigal hope.

"My Father started building me again. My passion came back and my desires for earthly things disappeared. I grew apart from my boyfriend. The one thing that had not yet been 'taken' from me, I was now willing to give up."

The thing she loved so dearly was being outweighed by a greater, stronger love.

"In July of 2015, I finally let him go. My heart burned but my spirit was free."

She was being restored.

"The Doina I once knew was coming back with a refreshed passion."

And guess what? She still lives prodigally.

"I am using my testimony to help others through difficult times. We should trust Him in every situation, good or bad, and remember the promises we have made to Him. God is good *all* the time and what He allows to happen in our lives is good and important for our growth."

Doina is assistant to the national director of Youth for Christ Burundi and a sponsor coordinator in the communications department.

"My dream is to start my own counselling centre where I can help marginalized individuals, especially victims of abuse or low self-esteem. My life word is 'hope.' I want everyone to have hope in God. To never give up and to know that they are capable, special, and unique."

Doina already has the building for the counselling centre; she's just waiting for the timing and courage to start. She also feels called to be a pastor. God has repeatedly given her these verses:

≤ Top: Fofo (Doina's sister), Doina, and me at her bridal shower, 2017
≤ Bottom: Bridesmaid at the introduction ceremony, 2017; twins; welcoming the couple to their new home the day after the wedding, 2017

Wedding day, 2017

"You also will command nations you do not know, and peoples unknown to you will come running to obey, because I, the Lord your God, the Holy One of Israel, have made you glorious."

—ISAIAH 55:5

Arise, Jerusalem! Let your light shine for all to see. For the glory of the Lord rises to shine on you. Darkness as black as night covers all the nations of the earth, but the glory of the Lord rises and appears over you. All nations will come to your light; mighty kings will come to see your radiance. Look and see, for everyone is coming home! Your sons are coming from distant lands; your little daughters will be carried home.

—ISAIAH 60:1–4

"God is teaching me to be patient and acquire His wisdom instead of making decisions with my emotions. I am so thankful for the place that I am and I can't wait to see what else He has for me to do on this earth!"

I can attest to this newfound light and this wisdom. See, I was in Burundi while she was wrestling with leaving her boyfriend. I know it was a dark time in a dark place. I know how difficult it was to let go. And now I get to see peace, joy, and life overflowing in Doina.

Doina got married in July 2017 to an incredible man, miraculously hand-picked

BURUNDI: PRODIGAL HOPE

THESE BEAUTIFUL PEOPLE

by her Father—but that's a story for another time.

And she very well could be the most beautiful woman in the school or at Youth for Christ. Heck, in the whole city. Not just because she is beautiful, but because she is prodigal.

She spends herself freely on behalf of the hurting. She shares recklessly her passionate love for the Father. She is wasteful in her generosity and careless with her grace. She loves extravagantly and serves diligently.

All because He extended to her hope, a hope she now extends to others.

Free.
Reckless.
Prodigal hope.

WORLD CHANGER

≪ **Gaga's Story** | Gitega, Burundi

I met her at Gitega International Academy in Gitega, Burundi. The school Freddy Tuyizere started through Youth for Christ has quickly become the top school in the country.

She was tall and confident, athletic and tomboyish. She had eyes full of life and, I would later discover, a heart full of gold.

I saw right away she was strong and determined. A born leader. A born influencer. But most of all, a catalyst of change.

Gaga loved to learn.

"At school I am more of a C+ student. Sometimes I get a B. I never work hard to be an A student, and I think that's a weakness I have."

Sure, school wasn't her favourite place to be, and sometimes she struggled to apply herself, yet she was a top student. Not because of her studiousness—but her willingness to learn. Not because of her high grades—but her hunger for change.

I know this because I taught her Grade 10 leadership class. She was so earnest, always taking notes, always answering questions, always putting her heart and soul into every activity.

She wasn't afraid; she was an embracer of change.

Gaga grew up in a family of privilege.

"It's not like I was a princess or anything, but my parents were well known where we lived. We were like a noble family."

Her father lost his father at a young age and had to quit school to help his mother pay for his younger brother's education. He managed to study business and became financially successful.

BURUNDI: WORLD CHANGER

THESE BEAUTIFUL PEOPLE

Gitega soccer field where Gaga spent much of her time

"I grew up alone with my parents because there are 12 years between me and the youngest of my five older siblings. By the time I reached Grade 5, all my siblings had moved to other places."

Even after three miscarriages, her mother was convinced she would bear another child. That's why it took 12 years.

"When I was finally born in February 1999, everyone was so excited to meet me. I was the miracle child."

Everyone expected her to be spoiled. To have everything handed to her. She came from a life of privilege; she probably got everything she wanted, right?

"But it's not like that at all. My parents are humble people and my life is just like everyone else's. They work hard and they taught me to work hard."

I could sense Gaga's humility right away. She didn't flaunt her privilege. Gaga realized everything was a gift, so being thankful was the best response.

"My parents could afford to go anywhere in the world but they never even moved to the big city."

They taught her the value of contentment, the value of appreciating what you have while you have it.

"I lost my dad to diabetes on July 14, 2012, but we are so grateful for the years we had with him."

Gaga's leadership skills haven't gone unnoticed. She was selected to attend the Pan-African Youth Leadership

BURUNDI: WORLD CHANGER

THESE BEAUTIFUL PEOPLE

Program in the United States. She has also been able to travel to Ethiopia with her basketball team.

She doesn't allow her loss to dictate her attitude. She doesn't allow herself to stay the same.

"It's been six years since I became a Christian and started to seek God for myself. I have not regretted it for one single day!" The joy on her face was indescribable. "I look back on how I used to be and I get so excited about my future because I believe what God said, that there is a bright future ahead for each of us!"

Gaga's dream is to study abroad then return home to Burundi. Jesus has given her a heart that aches for her own people.

"I want to serve my people and make an impact in my country and on my continent."

She is content but she won't settle. She is not only a humble embracer of change, but also an fierce ambassador of it.

"I want to help people discover their potential, talents, and gifts. I want to see my country rise above poverty and stand tall—without fear, without dependence on anyone."

And if she could tell the world one thing?

"I would tell them that whatever you are facing, whether good or bad, it is only for a short moment."

Don't cower—run forward.
Don't quit—take another step.
Don't resist and complain—embrace and change.

That's what Gaga does. And that's how Gaga is going to change the world.

Not because she was born into a family of privilege. Not because her family is well known.
Not because of her grades or her IQ.

No, those things don't make a world changer.

She doesn't shy away from the difficult; she faces it head on. She doesn't quit when the path becomes rough; she takes one more step.

She is an embracer of change today. She will be a world changer tomorrow.

BE KIND

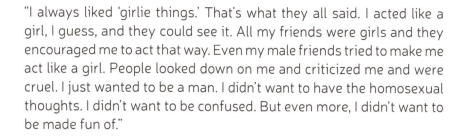

⩽ Jessy's Story | Bujumbura, Burundi

"I always liked 'girlie things.' That's what they all said. I acted like a girl, I guess, and they could see it. All my friends were girls and they encouraged me to act that way. Even my male friends tried to make me act like a girl. People looked down on me and criticized me and were cruel. I just wanted to be a man. I didn't want to have the homosexual thoughts. I didn't want to be confused. But even more, I didn't want to be made fun of."

There's nothing worse than being teased for just figuring it out. As if the rest of the world has it together and you're the only one struggling.

"The only reason I made it through the beginning of high school was because my older brother had gone there and everyone loved him. He told everyone that I was strong and that I could beat them up. It wasn't true, but they were afraid of me and they left me alone."

Too alone.

"I used to just say to myself, 'Just hold on—it's all going to be OK.'"

A brave thing to wish for.

"Then I met the most incredible group of people. There were eight of us—Gaga and myself started it. We would organize events around the school. But the thing is, they accepted me. Just like I was, they let me in. With all my struggles and fears, they didn't leave me out."

Kindness. Isn't that all any of us wants?

BURUNDI: BE KIND

THESE BEAUTIFUL PEOPLE

"We all met Jesus on the same day—October 24, 2014. I know it sounds ridiculous, and it's not like I don't still struggle, but that day I gave my homosexual thoughts and feelings to God. And I celebrate that day."

It's not so much about those things being taken as it is about being overwhelmed by someone's love. By someone's presence.

When you realize you're accepted. When you realize you're valued. When you realize you're not so broken that wholeness is out of reach.

That is transformational.

"We grew strong together as a group because we encouraged each other. Yeah, it was hard, but our unity comes from that patient struggle."

He was right. I met with this group several times during my stay in Burundi and witnessed firsthand their genuine care and commitment for one another. And guess what—it spills out all over their school.

"We have something we call 'Love in Action,' where we organize donations of food, clothes, and toys for the needy in our community. We all need each other. Until we realize that, nothing will ever change."

I asked Jessy how he wished he would have been treated from the beginning, through the struggle.

He replied, "My mom was supportive of me and I am so grateful. She just loved me and prayed for me. But my eight siblings all made fun and ran away from me. It would have been better if they cared for me, asked me how I felt, and then tried to find solutions without insulting me. Do it kindly and humbly."

Be kind, for everyone you meet is fighting a hard battle.

—PLATO

What we're fighting isn't who we are. What makes us feel "less" doesn't determine our true worth. What isolates us can be what brings us together.

If we can be kind. If we can hold people while they ache.

So if you're hurting… Hold on, it's gonna be OK. And if you're broken… Hold on, it's gonna be OK. Hold on to us, the other broken ones.

We're sorry for the times we haven't been kind. We're sorry for the times we fought against you instead of for you. We're sorry for the times we weren't careful with your heart.

Jessy will be graduating high school in 2018. He wants to study medicine and work in the government so he can bring positive change to his country. He has made a commitment to reach back, even to a society that once caused him pain.

And we want to take a pledge to be kind. Will you take it, too?

Be kind—he's hurting.
Be kind—she's broken.
Be kind—they're fighting battles you know nothing about.

You're not asked to understand it. You're not required to have all the answers. You're not expected to agree or give up what you believe.

Just promise you'll be kind.

BURUNDI: BE KIND

THESE BEAUTIFUL PEOPLE

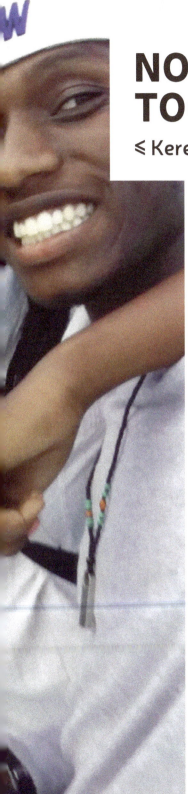

NO THING IS TOO SMALL

≪ **Keren, Lily, and Patience's Story** | Bujumbura, Burundi

I'd had a rough day—make that a rough half year—and I was looking forward to hitting the beach alone for the day. Doina's wedding was in a few days and I was done sitting in hot cars and tailor shops while the sun beamed down around me. I just wanted to go to the beach, lie in the sun, and withdraw. That was what I needed, right?

I was a bridesmaid in Doina's wedding. Between dress fittings and parties, time was flying. This was the last day at the beach to catch up with an old friend. Sun, sand, and a one on one. Perfect!

Or not. It was the only day during my three-week visit that was cloudy, cold, and rainy. My friend did come to see me at the beach, but she also brought along three of her friends.

"Great, a crowd," I thought to myself, but I threw a smile on my face and was genuinely glad to see her. It was cloudy anyway so I might as well just roll with the punches.

We sat and shared our stories. Who could have guessed it would have been exactly what I needed?

Doina's three friends—kids, really—were amazing. Two were graduates of Gitega International Academy, where I had taught two years earlier. Neither had been there at the time, so we hadn't met. The third volunteered at Youth for Christ and worked closely with Doina. All three had outstanding stories and even more outstanding

≪ *Left to right: Me, Gaga, Keren, Lily, and Patience*

BURUNDI: NO THING IS TOO SMALL

THESE BEAUTIFUL PEOPLE

hearts. Although I had never intended for them to be in my book, the more I listened, the more I wanted to include them.

So with great pleasure, I introduce Keren, Lily, and Patience.

Keren.

Humble warrior. Poet. The sweet, gentle, kind, and quietly passionate one who endured the painful taunting of kids telling her she was "too ugly to be their friend." She questioned why God would make her this way if she was only going to end up alone. From primary school to Grade 8, she was friendless. When she switched schools to attend Gitega International Academy, she became friends with Gaga, Jessy, and their group.

Keren was an A student, the best in her class. Compassionate to a fault, even when she did something wrong it was in the spirit of helping someone else. Feeling sorry for students earning Cs and Ds, she would help them cheat to get better grades.

When she realized this was the right motive but the wrong action, she sat them down and explained that she would help them in their studies but not cheat. They became angry and hostile toward her, spreading rumours and threatening to beat her.

The whole time she loved them, even though it was like grade school all over again. Everyone hated her, but she continued to reach out in love and help whenever she could.

"Jesus had put this love in me and I couldn't help it. I just loved them!"

Her eyes shone as she adjusted herself on the ocean-blue couch overlooking the beach.

She had no desire to see those who taunted her suffer—she was called to something higher. From an early age, she had an acute awareness of her purpose on Earth. God had given her a vision years earlier during one of the nights she was awake with insomnia: she was called to enrich Burundi by fighting for the poor and marginalized. She didn't take this call lightly. In fact, when she became severely ill and her grades dropped, when she couldn't even get out of bed, she kept smiling.

"Everyone was worried about me, including the students who hated me, but God had given me a vision and I knew I that I would not die until I saw the development of my country. I just *knew* it!"

Her eyes beamed and her soft voice resounded with intensity.

"The rules were broken so that I could be here today," she said, to the giggles of her classmates.

"My grandfather was a priest and my grandmother was a nun," she said. "Obviously, if they had remained celibate, if they had followed the rules, I would not be here."

In the same way, I know she'll work outside the box for the development of her country, creating change that wouldn't be possible without her. Keren is going to study economics after graduating in 2018.

"It's your turn, Lily."

Keren flashed a sly smile in Lily's direction as she pulled a pillow tightly around her waist. Lily feigned shyness with a dramatic wave of her hand, sending her long black braids swirling around her neck and shoulders.

"Really? Me next?" Lily teased, bouncing in her seat, tucking her legs under her, and resting her elbow on the back of the couch. She hardly noticed Patience, who had been sitting right beside her, slip quietly off toward the water.

Lily was bright, lively, passionate, bold, and colourful. Fiery like a spark. There was nothing shy or timid about her.

Like many Christians, Lily grew up in the church, knowing all the right things to say and do, a pro at going through the motions. But one night at a meeting, there was an altar call.

"I told myself that I'd done that already. I mean, I've grown up in church so I'm sure that I've already done this, haven't I? I sat back in my seat and relaxed. Not even a minute later, the entire congregation got up and went forward!"

Her arms were outstretched and animated, her eyes wide with disbelief.

"I later realized that I had never asked Christ into my life and so I did. I had a peace that I had never experienced before," Lily said.

Contrary to the person sitting before me, she hadn't always been the nicest person, which Gaga confirmed. But people weren't always the nicest to her either.

When she was young, her family would tell her that she was too tall, too fat. They insisted no man would ever want to marry her. She would return from family functions in tears, questioning why God had made her so undesirable. She would never forget, nor would I, how God answered.

"You cannot be beautiful to everyone. I made you beautiful for Me. Not everyone will find you beautiful, but I did not make you for everyone. There is a specific person who is looking for your kind of beautiful, and I made you that kind of beautiful. That's it."

Eyes sparkling, Lily popped straight up in her seat, waving her arms as she exclaimed, "Now I look in the mirror and I'm like, 'Yeah! I love all this! *All* of this is beautiful!'"

Not only that, but God had given her a vision that every person in Burundi would have access to health care. It was a big dream, a God-sized dream.

"I am hoping to study psychiatry so I can hear people's stories and know how to help them better. This will also keep me working closely with medical professionals. I'm volunteering with Youth for Christ because I don't want to be idle!" she said.

It made perfect sense that such a spark would start a wildfire—a wildfire of change in Burundi. This girl loved Jesus and she loved herself. I know no better way to equip yourself to love others.

"Now, where is Patience?" Lily asked.

She whipped her head around to see his tall, slender frame meandering up the boardwalk, notebook in hand.

"I'm sorry, guys," Patience said, as he slouched down on the couch with a sombre face. "I felt bad walking away during the stories, but God was telling me to go out on the beach and pray."

That's Patience for you.

He used to be addicted to drugs, but now he was addicted to thinking and dreaming and learning. He wanted to study philosophy and law.

"But I want to start with Bible school so that I have a solid foundation," he said. He leafed through his notepad, where he had written everything God had been speaking to him on the beach.

God spoke so clearly to him, and he listened so profoundly. What he shared with us spoke directly to my heart, a testament to his attentiveness to the Spirit.

"I am a leader and I will always be a leader," he stated confidently.

I believed him. I believed all of them.

These kids were not much more than half my age, yet they had the maturity and wisdom of some twice my senior. But what really struck me was what happened on the way home.

We were walking to the bus stop in the dark. We heard a loud thud behind us and turned to see a woman carrying bundle of clothing on her head and three buckets in her hands. Some of her buckets had come crashing to the ground.

Before I knew what was happening, Lily was rushing to help her, Patience not far behind. Gaga explained what was going on. They gathered the woman's things and helped her find her bus. She was lost and likely overwhelmed by the bustling sea of people.

"This is how we will change Burundi," Gag said, smiling at me as we made our way through the crowded park to our own bus.

She was right. For these kids, no "thing" is beneath them. No thing is too humiliating, too insignificant. No thing is too small for them to risk making a difference.

This is how they will change Burundi.

Because the small things are actually the big things.

AFRICAN WOMAN

by Keren

African woman!
Who can describe you
hard-working
committed and productive
A hoe in your hands
children around you
A husband to care for
a home to maintain
A blessing to your society
but no one feels your pain

Tears like make-up on your face
scars like tattoos on your body
You remain courageous
ready to carry your cross
You beat them all
African woman!

African woman!
Who can define you
An adorable heart
Forgiving to a judgmental society
A piece of gold never losing its value
Selfless to a selfish neighbourhood

Exposed to ugly experiences
A slave to your nation
expected to be nothing
Yet unknowingly you are everything to them
Hope to the hopeless
The genesis of love
The foundation of peace
African woman!

BURUNDI: AFRICAN WOMAN

THESE BEAUTIFUL PEOPLE

TO BREAK EVERY CHAIN

≤ David's Story | Burundi, Africa

"My life is now a free life!"

We all have chains.

Some we have bound ourselves.
Some others have tied for us.
Some have already been removed.
Some we can't seem to shake.

We all have chains.

Sometimes we think we're the only ones.
Sometimes we think others are the only ones.
Sometimes they're visible.
Sometimes they're hidden.

We all have chains.

Some are short and easy to undo.
Some are longer and need untangling.

Our chains might look different. They might even be made of different things. But one thing is for sure: we all desire freedom, but our chains keep us in bondage. And we don't always believe that freedom is possible.

———

I met David at the Gitega International Academy, where I was teaching a Grade 9 leadership class for a month in 2015. Something about him stood out right away.

BURUNDI: TO BREAK EVERY CHAIN

THESE BEAUTIFUL PEOPLE

Each day he sauntered into class with thick-framed square black glasses perched on his nose and a crooked grin on his lips. A free spirit, his contagious energy brought the class to life.

Yeah, that was it. Life. David was full of life. But just as you should never judge a book by its cover, so you should never assume a carefree existence from a carefree disposition.

I had no idea what those sparkling eyes had seen, what thoughts had once darkened that bright mind, what words had entered those sensitive ears.

It's not like David didn't have a "good" Christian upbringing. His father is a pastor and his mother is the coordinator for the Tearfund Organization. Both parents were present; both had stable jobs. Surely no chains could take hold in such an ideal situation.

"But I had no older brother. I so desperately needed an older brother. He passed away when I was two."

It was just David and his sisters. He soon realized the girls were favoured. They were always right, so he was beaten instead of them.

"Not one day would go by that I didn't have a fight with my family. I was so stubborn. When I was five years old, I began to hate my sisters."

His mom gave birth to two more boys, but he wouldn't hang out with them because they were always with his older sisters. Whom he hated. A chain had taken hold.

"When I was 13, my mom brought a girl who was older than me to live with us and be like a maid or caregiver for us."

She slept in the same bed as them because David's younger brother was afraid of the dark.

"One night, she came in our room and she asked me if I have ever had sex and she made me do it. I didn't have a choice. She was stronger than me and no one would understand if I said that she raped me." Another link was added to the chain, tightening its grip.

"The next week I told my mom and she told me it was my fault."

His body shook as he relived it. His eyes changed. His voice broke.

The chain lurched.
The links snapped shut.
The coils tightened.

At 13, he set his jaw, determined to fight back. Bound by the anger in his soul, he set out on a path of destruction. Destruction of himself. Destruction of others.

"I was so angry. I started sleeping with every girl I could find to get my revenge. I didn't care. Nobody else cared. Why should I?

"I started smoking and drinking. Trying everything to revenge the chains. To drown the thoughts. To numb the pain. And when I was 15, I tried to kill my sister."

As if one act could erase the faults of women. As if one life could free him of his chains.

His hatred had grown stronger than his reason. His anger had driven away self-control. His chains had choked out his life.

"Then my dad came and told me about Jesus."

See, David wasn't so far gone. One life *could* free him from all of his chains. One act *could* erase the faults of mankind. But he wasn't ready to give up his chains. Not yet.

"When I went to Gitega International Academy, my friends there helped me come to know God."

He met the Man who sacrificed His own life for not only David's life, but also the lives of the women who had wronged him. He met the Man who could snap his chains.

And snap they did. Maybe not right away, or all at once. Without audible sound or fanfare. Just the gradual but profound warmth of life returning to numb places.

"I got my purpose in Jesus and I came to know who I am by reading the Bible."

BURUNDI: TO BREAK EVERY CHAIN

THESE BEAUTIFUL PEOPLE

The sparkle began to return to his eyes. The light began to chase the dark from his mind. The truth began to erase the lies his mind had believed.

And those merciless chains? The ones wrapped tight around his spirit? Well, they loosened and fell like scales. Slowly that heart began to heal and that spirit came back to life.

"He chose me from nowhere. He called me. He redeemed me. He gave me another chance at being loved and accepted. He gave me a chance to have life and have it to the full. My life is now a *free* life!"

Free indeed!

Even as I write this, I want to jump up and down and cry for joy. In the words of this Chris Tomlin song,

My chains are gone; I've been set free.
My God, my Saviour has ransomed me.
And like a flood, His mercy brings,
Unending love, amazing grace.
This is indeed amazing grace.

"From the time I received Jesus, I started to notice how many people don't have the money to reach their full potential. I am becoming a businessman so I can build a school for vulnerable children. I want to give them a chance to show the world what they've been given, and do it with a smile on their face."

Before you judge the book by its cover, before you assume someone's past by their present, remember, someone might not always have been free—or might not be completely.
We all have chains.

Some we have bound ourselves.
Some others have tied for us.
Some have already been removed.
Some we can't seem to shake.

Our chains might look different. They might even be made of different things. But one thing is for sure: we all desire freedom. The question is, do we have the faith to believe it's possible?

Though our chains feel unrelenting, there's a love that is relentless.
A love that exists to break every chain.

ZIMBABWE

Innovative. Industrious. Resilient.

All words I would use to describe the Zimbabwean people.

When asked, "What do you do?" a Zimbabwean will have a difficult time answering because he or she rarely does just one thing. They have multiple sources of income, and just listening to their list of jobs makes my head spin. It also makes my one-word answer to the same question sound fairly lame. But it's not busyness for pleasure; it's busyness for survival. They have many jobs because they have to.

Zimbabwe means "great house of stones." Since independence in 1980 until the peak of a nationwide crisis in 2008, Zimbabwe's foundation has been shaken and this house of stones has crumbled. President Robert Mugabe's election in 1987 ushered in a long series of events: A land redistribution campaign sent foreign farmers out of the country and caused commodity shortages. An urban rationalization program destroyed the homes and businesses of more than 700,000 opposing party supporters. Price controls resulted in panic-buying and empty store shelves. Several rigged and internationally condemned elections have kept Mugabe in power to this day. And overprinting money to decrease the nation's deficit has crashed the economy and sent hyperinflation rates soaring at 79.6 billion percent.

At one point, Zimbabweans had monetary notes valuing millions and trillions of Zimbabwean dollars. The largest note in circulation was a 100-trillion-dollar bank note. A running joke is that Zimbabweans have to carry a paper bag full of money to the store to buy milk and bread. Well, they used to.

In 2009 the Zimbabwean currency was changed from the Zimbabwean dollar to the United States dollar. This did not equally reflect the cost of living and wages. Now commodities cost more, but wages remain the same.

Hence why you'll rarely meet a Zimbabwean who does just one thing.

With a population of more than 14.5 million, in 2012 it was estimated that 72.3 percent of Zimbabweans were living below the poverty line.

≪ *Walking with lions*

ZIMBABWE

THESE BEAUTIFUL PEOPLE

MWARI VAKANAKA, ASI
USA TOMBE NE SHUMBA

**GOD IS GOOD,
BUT NEVER DANCE
WITH A LION.**

—ZIMBABWEAN PROVERB

The last recorded unemployment rate in 2009 was at a shocking 95 percent. Since then it has lowered slightly to a still high 70 percent.

The 30 percent of Zimbabweans who are employed earn an average of $253.00 per month, making their gross domestic product the third lowest in the world.

In 2015 it was estimated that more than 1.4 million people were living with HIV/AIDS in Zimbabwe, ranking it fifth in the world for prevalence.

All these factors contribute to a high representation of human trafficking and exploitation, especially along Zimbabwe's borders with South Africa, Zambia, and Mozambique.

It's easy to become overwhelmed and discouraged when you hear such statistics, but that's not the first thing you'll notice about Zimbabwe or her people.

You'll notice they are innovative, industrious, and resilient. They are a people who do not make excuses. Day after day, they find a way. And I believe Zimbabwe will one day be a great house of stones again because her people have learned the importance of rebuilding, no matter how many times they crumble.

Every time they get knocked down, they come up stronger, wiser, more determined.

Zimbabwe is three times the size of England, with 99.4 percent of her population from African descent. The largest proportion are Shona, and the second largest ethnic group is Ndebele. She has three national languages—Shona, Ndebele, and English, successively—and 13 minority languages.

Once a rich country, the ruins of Great Zimbabwe speak to her past as a medieval trading hub.

Zimbabwe is home to Victoria Falls, the largest waterfall in the world, also known as the "Smoke that Thunders" *(Mosi-oa-Tunya)*. I've visited the falls several times in my travels and can't help but stand in awe.

Astonishing, powerful, the falls are a force to be reckoned with.

And I don't believe the falls are part of Zimbabwe by mistake. I believe they're symbolic. Symbolic of her future. Symbolic of her people.

They, too, are astonishing. They, too, are powerful. They, too, are a force to be reckoned with.

So lean over the edge. Look deep into the eyes of these people. These astonishing, powerful, beautiful people.

≤ *Top: Part of Victoria Falls*
≤ *Middle: Possibly the same monkeys that broke into our house—twice; famous Baobab tree*

ZIMBABWE

THESE BEAUTIFUL PEOPLE

THROUGH IT ALL

≤ Sheunesu and Susan's Story | Bulawayo, Zimbabwe

It was one thing after another from the moment we entered Zimbabwe until the moment we left.

The airline attendants didn't believe we had the correct visas. Our baggage was overweight and we had to convince them to allow us to take it for a minimal fee. My shoulder was out of commission from a bad accident two weeks earlier so, despite my eagerness to help, I couldn't even carry my own bags.

We were questioned at one of the many roadblocks, only to realize I had brought the wrong passport. The car battery died. Our house was broken into and destroyed twice—by monkeys. The camp where we were supposed to help was canceled at the last minute…

The list went on and on.

It was one thing after another, a whirlwind of events at whose centre was a hidden treasure. A quiet calm. An undeniable lesson.

———

I had met Sheunesu several years earlier at a training centre in South Africa. Now my friend and I were staying with him, his wife, Susan, and his son, Micha, for a month, to serve in whatever way we could.

He was just as I remembered him: full of life and energy and more passion than many experience in a lifetime. He's a mover and a shaker with only two modes of operating: laughing and causing mischief, or learning, teaching, and initiating something. He's the embodiment of "young at heart."

Left to right: Sheunesu, Susan, and Micah

Susan is also a force to be reckoned with. Slightly more reserved, she's one of the hardest working, most self-sacrificing, and most driven people I've encountered. She always has something on the go, an idea brewing in her eyes.

Perfectly matched, they're innovative and dedicated to their Father and their faith.

Micha is as mischievous as his father, as intuitive and sincere as his mother, and as confident and fun-loving as the two of them combined.

Sheunesu is the director of Youth for Christ Zimbabwe. Susan is the manager of Willow Park campsite, a Youth for Christ project. Between their jobs and caring for Micha, their plates are full.

The youngest of six children, Susan's mother was a nurse and her father worked for the Zimbabwe railroad. At 16, Susan accepted Christ into her life. After graduating high school, she moved to the capital, Harare, to live with her sister and find a better job.

"I was attending a women's group at my church when I was invited to my friend's house, whose mom was the head of our group. While I was there, I entered a room full of native carvings and animal skins used for ancestor worship. Apparently, this woman was also a traditional healer. It confused me. I couldn't figure out how she could be a Christian and a traditional healer at the same time."

Inquisitive, Susan bought books about traditional healing to understand it better.

"But when I opened the first book, I saw a vision of flames before me and I was gripped with terrible fear. I dropped the book and never attempted to read any of them again. I knew I needed to leave that church!"

Her mind was made up. She found another church, and she found Sheunesu.

Sheunesu is the middle child of five children. His father was a policeman and his mother was a devout Christian, making sure they were in church every time its doors were open.

"I enjoyed church. I was the best churchgoer you've ever seen. When my youth leader invited me to go to a Youth for Christ crusade, I was excited, but what happened that night I never saw coming. The speaker was talking about a relationship with Jesus and not with the church. I was arguing vehemently under my breath until I heard him say, 'Going to church doesn't make you a Christian any more than going to a hamburger take-away makes you a hamburger.' I got it. Just because my mom had a relationship with Jesus didn't mean that I did. I made my commitment that night and it changed my life more than I could have ever imagined!"

He spent the next six years sharing Jesus with everyone he knew and becoming a computer engineer. In that order.

"My schooling took most of my time and I found myself spending less time at church."

But he did manage to make it to a friend's birthday party, where he saw Susan for the first time. And as only Sheunesu could do, he grinned wide, strutted up to her, tapped her on the shoulder, and said, "One day you'll make a man a good wife."

That she did. On December 21, 1996, she became his wife. Susan quit her job in Harare with the United Nations and moved to Bulawayo, where Sheunesu was working for an information technology company.

Two years later, Samantha was born. The economy was beginning to go downhill and Susan's brother sent her a ticket to join him and his family in the United Kingdom. She would be able to attend university and work.

"This meant I would have to leave Sheunesu and Samantha behind to live in the safety and comfort of the United Kingdom." Susan's eyes were determined. "But I just couldn't leave them. Two weeks before I was supposed to fly, we canceled the ticket and I stayed."

The following year, Micha was born. The economy was hitting an all-time low. Banks were closing and people were losing any bit of money they had. Several times, Sheunesu and his family lost everything. Time

The whole family before Samantha passed away

Michah and his big sister

after time, they started over, and time after time, they were overwhelmed by obstacles beyond their power.

Inflation was out of control. During my stay in Zimbabwe, Sheunesu and Susan pulled out old bills in denominations of millions, billions, and trillions.

"How do you begin to do that kind of math when you have to count change?" I asked. They shook their heads and laughed.

To leave would have been tempting. To leave would have been considered wise.

"But as a family we were committed to do the best we could in Zimbabwe. We struggled like all the other families and, with the help of the Lord, we got by."

In 2005 Susan was given another opportunity to go to the United Kingdom. She was attending a conference there and hoping that she could find a job and stay.

"Two days into the conference, I was praying with a couple when the husband said he had a message for me from the Lord." Susan grinned. "It was that I was to go back home to Zimbabwe and God would make a way for our family to walk through. I was stubborn, however, and continued enrolling in college. Two months in, I got a call from Sheunesu saying Micha was sick in the hospital. I knew immediately that I needed to go home."

ZIMBABWE: THROUGH IT ALL

THESE BEAUTIFUL PEOPLE

They couldn't have guessed what His bigger purpose was in her return. Four years later, they would be hit with the most devastating loss a parent can face.

"On September 28, 2009, Samantha passed away from liver failure. We were heartbroken but so thankful for the time we had. I cannot compare the degree I would have gotten in the United Kingdom to the gift of being with my daughter in her last four years." Susan's eyes were misty.

"Samantha had given her heart to Jesus in 2007. She loved the Lord passionately," Susan said.

"She taught me so much about the youth," Sheunesu added, his eyes with a faraway look. "She joined the field hockey team but instead of playing she was on the sidelines interacting with the kids. I asked her why she did not play and her answer stunned me. 'Dad, I'm here to share Jesus with everyone.' And she did. Sharing Jesus with young people became our passion."

Sheunesu beamed with pride. Clearly she was a girl after her fathers' hearts, earthly and heavenly.

"Her passing left a large hole in my heart," Sheunesu confided.

Two weeks after burying their daughter, Susan was diagnosed with stage 2 cervical cancer.

"My faith was now at its lowest and, to make it worse, we did not have health insurance because of the high inflation," Susan said.

They faced enormous doctors' bills that they couldn't pay.

"The doctor suggested we contact our previous health insurance and ask for reinstatement. We prayed. The health insurance man laughed at me and threw me out of his office. Then, as if an angel of the Lord took control of him, he rushed back out to me and asked me to give him my documents to pass on to the proper people. Two hours later, we were approved with a fee of only $400 instead of $5,000!" She raised her hands to heaven in celebration.

Susan underwent surgery in November 2009. Six months after the surgery, they learned she was pregnant. They were shocked but excited, until three months later, when she lost the baby. The miscarriage caused her to spiral into depression.

"I looked good on the outside, but my heart was crushed. I had lost two children in nine months. A dark cloud of depression settled over me and I didn't know how to shake it off."

It took two young girls' heartbreak over the loss of Susan's baby to speak life back into her soul.

Youth for Christ camp, where they live and work

"One of the girls said to me, 'Never mind, Auntie. God's plans are not to harm us.' Her words were like an ice-cold bucket of water under a hot Zimbabwean sun. They washed over my soul and the dark cloud was lifted. The cloud was gone but Jesus was not finished with me yet."

A year later in Namibia for a youth training, they watched the film, *The Father Heart of God*.

"As soon as the father's son died, I broke down and the pain of my loss overwhelmed me again. In that moment, I heard God say to me, 'Susan, I understand what it is to lose a child. I understand completely.' I had been trying to bandage my broken heart without giving it to the Healer. I left the session and spent the next two hours in my room crying out for God to heal the brokenness in my heart. When I left my room, one of my classmates approached me with a paper where she had written a message she felt God had given her for me. It read, 'I understand.'"

Not long after, they had an opportunity to come full circle in their healing journey.

"We were driving down the road when we came upon an accident that had just occurred. A small boy had bolted into traffic, dying instantly as he was struck by a car. In the past, Sheunesu and I would have driven on, fearful of what to do and say. But not this time. We knew what the Lord would have us do. We comforted the driver, as well as the matron and other children who were with that child when he died. We then worked with the police to find the parents of the dead boy. The Lord enabled us to offer comfort as they received this devastating news."

It was time to ease out of their season of grieving and move on with their calling of reaching out to others in a world of hurt.

Sheunesu was part of the board for Youth for Christ Zimbabwe while working as a computer engineer. He felt a strong call toward working with youth. They both did.

"Susan and I were praying about what we should do: stay in computing or move forward with more involvement with the youth. The confirmation did not take long. Four different people who did not know each other came one by one saying exactly the same thing, 'Sheunesu, you are in the wrong place. You should be doing God's work.'"

He met with the international director of Youth for Christ, who invited him into full-time ministry as the director of Youth for Christ Zimbabwe. Sheunesu and Susan have been a blessing ever since. Their testimony and wisdom, tenacity and energy, undying faith and quiet confidence in a good Father—all were learned in the middle of a whirlwind.

"The Lord has been good through it all," they said with confidence.

What a statement to make after everything they've endured.

You might have trouble reading those words after everything you've endured. When it's been one thing after another, a whirlwind of heartache and pain, grief and loss, unwanted change and unfulfilled promises.

But at the centre of the whirlwind is a hidden treasure, a quiet calm, an undeniable lesson.

There is something you can hold on to. There is Someone you can trust. There is a purpose and a plan for greatness on the other side, for none of your pain will be wasted and every teardrop will be turned into a sea of hope and healing for others.

You can lean in and press on when life is falling apart.
You can experience peace and calm in the middle of the storm.
You can laugh and have joy because there is One who is forever faithful.

Through it all.

ZIMBABWE: THROUGH IT ALL

THESE BEAUTIFUL PEOPLE

KEEPING THE SPARKLE

⩽ Benjamin's Story | Bulawayo, Zimbabwe

We sipped coffee and talked about life in the cool Zimbabwe evening.

I'd been begging to hear his story. Finally, the moment had come.

Steam swirled up from our mugs. I leaned in closer as he began to speak. I took a long, slow sip of coffee and couldn't help but think, "The struggle is real, and so is this young man."

This is part of Benjamin's story.

———

Benjamin was born into a complicated but loving family in Harare, the capital of Zimbabwe.

"My dad's business was growing and life was good. I was even able to go to private school and not many kids can afford that. I mean, things were good!"

I was captivated by his honesty and the sparkle in his eye. Excitement filled his voice as he recalled this happy time.

But when Benjamin turned 11, life threw a curveball... a curveball that could have dimmed the twinkle. The death of his father.

"We lost everything: the family business, the cars. Things got hard.

Much to my surprise, his eyes haven't lost any of their shine, even as he recounted this difficult time.

ZIMBABWE: KEEPING THE SPARKLE

THESE BEAUTIFUL PEOPLE

"I watched my mom struggle to provide. She used to walk to work so that we would have tuck money to buy snacks from the tuck shop at school. I watched her work so hard for us. I think that's why I have that same drive to work as hard as I do today."

Work hard he did. And still does. Benjamin is an innovator, entrepreneur, gifted musician, and poet. He has a million ideas in his mind and works hard to bring them to fruition. In Zimbabwe's unreliable economic state, however, this has proved to be challenging.

Benjamin was a teenager when he met Jesus.

A valiant prayer warrior, his mother led him and his brother to Christ as a solution to their vicious quarrelling. The impact proved to be so much greater than brotherly reconciliation.

"I remember I used to have these dreams where I would feel like something had its hands around my neck, choking me. It was terrifying. But my mom came to pray over me and it left! I was delivered! God delivered me and I remember thinking, 'Wow, is this really happening?' I had never experienced Him like that before and I knew this was for real."

Many other experiences would follow this one as he learned to hear and follow the voice of the Spirit. He remembered praying for a young girl with a chronic heart problem.

"As I prayed, I felt her relax, and she told me the pain was gone!" he said, his face re-enacting the joy and surprise of the moment.

"And then one night, I heard screaming as I lay in bed. I was scared but I had to see what it was. I made my way towards the sound. The closer I got to the gate, the louder and shriller the scream became and I knew it was a young girl. I opened the gate to find her screaming and convulsing. The closer I got, the worse it became. I prayed for her in the name of Jesus and she was delivered. Jesus delivered her right then and there and I began to think, 'God, what is this? Why children? What is the devil doing with these children?' It disturbed me so much."

But it also stirred something within him.

"I was sold out!" he exclaimed, eyes twinkling. "I got involved in everything I could: Bible studies, church programs, children's ministry, hospital ministry. You name it, I was doing it. My friends and I would meet constantly to pray. Our house became a house of prayer."

Then life threw another curveball, one that caused him to leave his country for a season. He ended up being away for several years at the University in Namibia.

"I was running away," he admitted. "I just couldn't be in Zimbabwe anymore."

For a moment, it looked as if the sparkle had left, but then a grin spread across his face as he started the next part of his story.

"There was this girl…" The sparkle was even brighter. "I mean, I have always had a fascination with girls since I was young, but this one… This one was the most beautiful girl I had ever seen in my life!"

His enthusiasm was contagious and I couldn't help but laugh out loud. Whoever this girl was, she made his eyes shine and his heart skip a beat.

"I would see her around campus and think, 'God! Just *wow*. Seriously, well done!' Then one day I got a tap on my shoulder. When I turned around, it was her. Her! And she wanted to talk to *me!*"

I'm confident the look of sheer joy on his face now was nothing compared to that day.

God had given her a word for him. He listened intently to every word. Whether he liked the words or not, he found himself falling for the messenger.

"I finally got the courage to ask her out and she turned me down. Both times."

The third time, she accepted.

"I was ecstatic. She was everything that I've ever wanted in a wife and I was determined that this was it. The relationship was just so good!"

Just around the corner, another series of curveballs threatened to extinguish any glimmer of light left in his eyes.

ZIMBABWE: KEEPING THE SPARKLE

THESE BEAUTIFUL PEOPLE

The night Benjamin told us his story

"She came to me and said, 'We need to talk.' We all know what that means. Her news: 'God wants us to break up.' I was devastated. To make things worse, soon after that I lost my best friend and my cousin in separate car accidents."

By now Benjamin was living alone with his younger brother in Bulawayo because his mother had moved to Australia for work. It's a lot to deal with at any age, let alone at 24, when you're under the stress of providing for your household.

"I lost my best friend, my cousin, and the girl I was going to marry in a matter of months. My life was falling apart and I thought, 'God, what is this? What are you doing?'"

The pain was evident in his eyes, the events fresh. I noticed that, although the sparkle had dimmed, it hadn't disappeared.

"I'll be honest; I still struggle a lot. Sometimes I find it hard to even open my Bible. I don't love God in an emotional sense. At this point, I love God because I have to. I just have to."

I had only met Benjamin a few weeks before at a training camp in South Africa. I'd watched him teach and encourage and pour himself into those kids. I never could have guessed his struggle.

The struggle is real. And so is Benjamin. But his story is also not over. He is walking this path, step by step. One day at a time—which is all we can do anyway.

Using his business mind and creative gifts, he recently started his own clothing line and is working on his first demo rap album. He spent a year in Germany, leading a dance and drama team on tour. After starting a dance and drama team in Zimbabwe, he is now in New Jersey, United States, studying at a Bible college. Serving the God who gives and takes away.

The road is hard, but he won't quit. And despite the way he feels, he's an inspiration to everyone around him.

I'm captivated by his honesty, yes, but even more amazing than that, no matter how difficult the struggle... he hasn't lost the sparkle in his eye.

 BOTSWANA

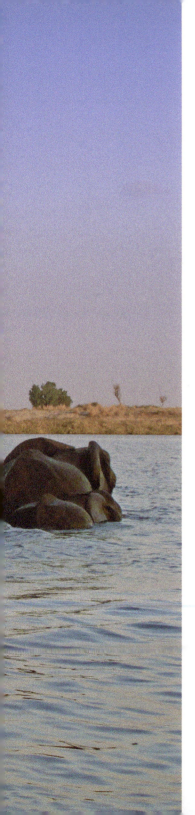

"Twila, your pace!"

I felt a hand on my arm and realized I had gotten far ahead of my friend, Philip. I thought I had been barely moving.

I'd run into him on my way to the shops. He was going the opposite direction, but he stopped, turned, and said, "I'll take you halfway." Then he walked with me all the way there and back.

No agenda. No hurry. No problem.

Because in Botswana, tomorrow is another day. If it doesn't get done today, tomorrow is another day. And that is Botswana and her people. Relaxed. Gentle. Peaceful.

There has never been war. It's more likely you'll find people dancing instead of fighting. Singing rather than shouting. Greeting and welcoming each person in the room rather than ignoring them.

In the beginning, Botswana was one of the poorest countries in the world. After her independence in 1966, things started to turn around. Today she is considered a middle-class country with the highest gross domestic product in Africa.

She is the longest running successful democracy on the continent. Although she's among the highest in the world for HIV/AIDS prevalence, those numbers have been rapidly decreasing, proving Botswana's comprehensive treatment plans are effective.

Education is funded by the government. Even university is subsidized and students are given an allowance for living expenses. Although unemployment rates remain high, Botswana boasts one of the fastest growing economies on the continent, making the future bright for 60 percent of the 2.2 million population that's of working age. The Batswana used to have to go to South Africa and Zimbabwe to find

≤ *Herd of elephants crossing the Chobe River at dusk*

BOTSWANA

THESE BEAUTIFUL PEOPLE

work before independence, but the economy improved after the discovery of diamonds. Now, with a decrease in international hiring, more and more jobs are available in their own country.

The Batswana love this because they prefer to stay home. Proud of their beautiful, dusty, landlocked country, they're content to stay within Botswana's borders, despite the recent four-year drought that has devastated the agricultural sector and despite the alarming increase of crime and armed robbery sweeping the nation.

Pula means both "rain" and "money" in Setswana, emphasizing the value placed on the two commodities. If you've ever been in Botswana when the rain finally does come, you understand. When it has been upwards of 40 degrees Celsius and thick with humidity, when the clouds have been gathering for days, threatening rain but holding back, and you feel that first drop, then the second, you know you'd better get inside because it's coming. And when the rain comes—oh, when it comes—it makes a North American thunderstorm look like a light drizzle. *Pula* brings sweet relief after the excessive heat and lack of rain in October, aka "suicide month."

Botswana places great value on her women. Women are seen much more as equals in education and the workforce than in surrounding countries.

Botswana has an "every child has a home" mentality. You won't find street children or many homeless people in Botswana. Although many children have been orphaned due to the HIV/AIDS pandemic of the 90s, they'll never be called orphans. Instead, they'll be placed into a family's care, usually a relative's. In Botswana everyone is your brother or sister, or aunt or uncle, or mom or dad. It's difficult to determine who's biological family because the Batswana use these words interchangeably. This speaks to their strong sense of community.

Botswana is also a hot spot for tourists. With the highest concentration of elephants in Africa, and parks like Chobe National and the *Nxai Pan,* there's no shortage of sights to take in. In fact, 40 percent of her land is protected as game reserves and parks.

All her safari lodges are locally owned and operated, a business model to which Botswana attributes part of her economic success.

Lesedi la rona, which means "our light," is the name of the largest diamond discovered in the last century. The size of a tennis ball, this precious rock is valued at more than US$70 million. Jwaneng diamond mine, where this gem was found in 2016 in southern Botswana, is the richest mine in the world.

≤ *Mochudi sunrise*

BOTSWANA

THESE BEAUTIFUL PEOPLE

KE TLA GO BONA
FA MPHONA
**I'LL SEE YOU
WHEN YOU SEE ME.**

—BOTSWANA PROVERB

The Batswana love their football and their freedom, their fat cakes and their *pap*. They're proud of their language and culture. They're relaxed and easygoing, even the way they walk. I've never met people who walk so slowly in all my life.

There's no sense of urgency among the Batswana people. They're at peace and they're content. And though their lifestyle might cause those of us from the fast-paced world to tear our hair out, we have much to learn.

For the Batswana, people come before plans. Relationships come before agendas.

So leave the dishes in the sink. The toys will be fine where they are. The yard work can wait and the laundry isn't going anywhere, unfortunately.

Sit and rest and take the time to stroll slowly down the dusty paths of Botswana.

Because it's in the slow and relaxed moments that we are present. It's in the breathing deep and the opening of the eyes and the mind. That's where we see them. That's where we meet them.

These beautiful people.

≪ *Top: Ivory elephant sculpture, Gaborone International Airport; sunset over the Chobe River*
≪ *Bottom: Dust settling on the football field at sunset*

NALEDI: TRULY A STAR

≤ **Moses' Story** | Mochudi, Botswana

Naledi. Star. A fixed, luminous point in the night sky. Or, in this case, my Setswana name.

I met Moses in 2010. It was my first time in Botswana—my first time in Africa, actually—and from the moment I stepped out the plane, I knew this continent was home.

I had travelled from Canada with a Youth for Christ Project Serve team and we were staying for two-and-a-half weeks. I stayed a little longer… Ten months longer.

One night, we were hanging out at the drop-in centre amid a slew of youth. Kids huddled around the foosball tables, eyes peeled, shoulders tense, jumping and shouting when someone scored. Kids played board games and soccer. Some just sat on the porch talking.

That's when Moses meandered in.

He knew many of the young people, as well as the staff. Making his way from table to table, he greeted almost everyone by name. I thought to myself, "He must be a regular." Something about him caught my attention, besides the fact that he was tall. Instead of loud or obnoxious, his was a gentle presence not easily ignored.

I would later learn he was a volunteer with Youth for Christ and was fondly known as Tall Moses, as opposed to Short Moses, another volunteer.

≤ *Meeting Moses, 2010*

BOTSWANA: NALEDI: TRULY A STAR

THESE BEAUTIFUL PEOPLE

Playing with the goat that would become our supper

Tall Moses and I quickly became good friends. He had an openness and sincerity about him, a hunger for the things of God, and a deep desire to serve Him.

His name soon changed from Tall Moses to My Little Brother Moses. The same age as my younger brother at home, I unofficially adopted him. He gave me the Setswana name Naledi, which means "star," because it was his sister's name and he thought it suited me.

Over the next 10 months, we did almost everything together: chatting at the office, taking walks, laughing, crying. I'll never forget the time he took me to see "the lands," a Botswana term for the fields almost every family owns for livestock and agriculture.

After we arrived, he gave me the grand tour. I could tell his heart and soul were in this land. Just before we let the goats out to graze, he told me to pick a goat that I liked. I chose a big brown one and we rode it around and played with it. Then he laid it down on the ground and asked me to hold it there a minute.

He asked, "Have you ever seen a goat being butchered?"

Confused, I replied, "No."

"Do you want to?"

He grinned at me. Before I knew it, blood was pooling around the throat of the goat I was holding. I was horrified. I would never have picked a goat if I knew he was going to kill it. And just for me? I was overwhelmed at such a generous act of hospitality.

I was taught how to prepare the goat's insides with *posho,* a staple starch in Botswana, and we enjoyed a meal together. When it was getting dark, he looked at me and said, "It's time to go get the goats."

"OK, where did they go?" I asked.

"I don't know," he said casually.

"Well then, how are we going to find them?" I asked, half mocking.

He gave me a less-than-assuring glance as he replied, "We'll find them."

We walked for a short while. Sure enough, I saw some goats through the trees. Excited, I grabbed him and pointed in that direction.

"Over there!" I squealed.

He looked a bit closer.

"No, those are not mine," he said and continued walking.

"What? How do you know? Are they marked?" I asked.

"No, they are not marked. I just know." He started walking quickly in another direction.

Flabbergasted, I caught up to him. Eventually, we found the goats and led them back to the pen. Moses shut the gate behind them and gazed thoughtfully over the herd. Dark now, the sun was sinking fast.

"They are not all here," he said.

BOTSWANA: NALEDI: TRULY A STAR

THESE BEAUTIFUL PEOPLE

Moses' lands and goats

I gave him a look that said, "You're kidding, right? Did you just count them? There are so many goats in here! How can you be sure?"

He looked at me and chuckled.

"I just know. You'll see."

Off we went. Sure enough, we found more goats. After getting them safely inside, he took one more look across the hundreds of goats stumbling over each other. Slowly, he climbed inside and grabbed one small one from the middle of the group, walked to the side, and set it down outside the fence.

"That one isn't mine," he said, matter of fact.

He looked at me and laughed, then answered the question burning in my wide eyes.

"When you work with the same goats for so many years, you just know them."

That phrase has stuck with me over the years: "You just know them... When you spend that much time, you just know."

I thought about all the time we had spent together over the past 10 months. And I thought about how Moses had lost his mom when he was 10 years old. How his father had never married his mother and wasn't around much. How he and his sister were raised by their grandmother. How he watched his father go to prison for beating and hospitalizing the woman he lived with. Apparently, she'd been emotionally and physically abusing him for years and he'd had enough. He spent nine years in prison, and Moses would often visit.

Moses spent some of his years struggling in school, rebelling, fighting, getting into trouble with the law, and nearly going to prison himself. That was the moment he started to turn his life around. By now every single boy he used to hang out with had been in prison at least once.

Except Moses.

Somewhere along the way, Moses met Jesus. He knew there was a void inside him that needed filling. That's when he started getting involving in the Youth for Christ programs at his church.

Desperate to learn more about this life of faith, he threw himself into every opportunity he could get his hands on. Not a high performer in school, he started university at a lower level, studying plaster technology, a course that specializes in cast and splints for limbs. His work visa for the Netherlands has just been approved, where he will move to be with his "other half," as he fondly calls his fiancée.

I can't even count the number of times I've sat back and asked myself, "How the heck did he turn out so good? What made the difference? Why the change?"

The answer came from the young man himself.

"When you work with the same goats for so many years, you just know them."

I guess it's true for people, too. When you spend enough time with someone, you get to know them. But unlike the goats, you also get to be like them.

BOTSWANA: NALEDI: TRULY A STAR

THESE BEAUTIFUL PEOPLE

Moses' fiancée, Moses, and me at a last–minute rendezvous, Paris, 2014

Moses threw himself into getting to know his Jesus, the same way he has thrown himself into every other task. He has spent enough time with his Heavenly Father that he has become like Him. He has worked with the same God for so many years that now he just knows Him.

Moses gave me the name Naledi because he thought it suited me. I'd never been able to figure out what my name, Twila, meant until the day my friend told me, "Your name means 'star.'" I nearly collapsed on the spot.

BOTSWANA: NALEDI: TRULY A STAR

THESE BEAUTIFUL PEOPLE

Rushing home, I sent Moses a message with the news. He could hardly believe it.

"I swear, I didn't know that when I gave you that name! I didn't know!"

I'm beginning to think someone should have given him the name Star instead. Because that's Moses: A star. A fixed, luminous point. A steady, constant light. A person you can count on. A star.

"A star is *born* when atoms of light elements are *squeezed under enough pressure* for their nuclei to undergo fusion (Brill n.d., emphasis mine)."

A person born under pressure. A person squeezed by the elements of life into something that shines bright. A star.

When stars accumulate new material, they generate sound. The stars might be singing but, because sound cannot travel far through space, no one hears them.

A person who doesn't make a loud ruckus. A person without fuss or flaunt. A person whose impact is felt without noise, who silently gives himself away.

Moses does that. He has spent a lot of time with the One who is a perfect example of silent sacrifice. And I know that, no matter where life takes him, some things will never change. He will always be someone who stands out without shouting out.

I might bear the name Star, but my little brother Moses truly is one.

STRINGERE: THE BINDING FOR THE BROKEN

≤ Tefo's Story | Mochudi, Botswana

Uh-huh, you know what it is.
Black and yellow, black and yellow, black and yellow…

This song rings in my head every time I think of Tefo.

It was July 2010. I was on the first 25-person team with Project Serve to travel to Mochudi, Botswana, on a two-and-a-half–week mission trip.

And it was *freezing.* Yes, you heard me. Freezing! We woke up shivering (and hungry) at 4 a.m., thanks to jet lag. I distinctly remember wondering if we were on the wrong continent.

That's how little I knew. Probably wouldn't have hurt to consult Google or crack a book before boarding the plane.

June is the coldest month of the year in Botswana and it can get down to zero degrees Celsius at night. Doesn't sound so bad? Imagine no heaters. You learn to sleep in your clothes and shower during the day—and only if you're the reason for "that smell."

When the drop-in centre was open, which was every evening while we were there, you played basketball or football to feel some kind of warmth.

This is where I met Tefo. On a cold "winter" night at drop-in.

He sauntered in, tall and lanky. Headphones hanging from his ears, phone in hand. He was quiet and stayed to himself, but as I hunkered down next to him on the porch that evening, one thing I noticed right away: his eyes were kind.

I tried to strike up a conversation out of thin air. He was listening to the song "Black and Yellow" and he politely answered my questions, but that was it. Pretty one-sided conversation—all on my side. Luckily for me, and likely much to his dismay, I could probably talk the bark off a tree.

I grabbed a basketball and convinced him to play. And that's how I came to know Tefo.

Even after the rest of my team went home every Saturday night, we would sweat it out on the basketball court. And believe me, winter doesn't last long in Botswana, so the sweat was never lacking.

Tefo and I would always be on the same team. When one of us would get a basket, the other would say, "Uh-huh, you know what it is," and the other would reply, "Black and yellow, black and yellow, black and yellow."

You could say we bonded over our shared inner gangster. And when we could barely breathe anymore—because these were no ordinary games of half-court basketball—we would sit on the ground and talk and laugh and carry on. He would smile and I knew there was something special about this kid.

So he became like a younger brother to me. Quiet and shy, he still refused to dance even though I knew he liked to. Kind to those around him and deeply caring toward his family, he carried himself with a maturity rarely found in boys his age.

Little by little, I learned more about him. And the more I learned, the more space he took up in my heart.

———

Tefo was born in Kanye, Botswana, in 1993. When he was five years old, they moved to Mochudi, a large village located 45 minutes from the capital, so he could start preschool. At that time, his father was working in South Africa.

"He came home to visit for three months and I was so excited to see him. But when he left again for South Africa, he never came back."

Gone. Just like that.

His mother raised him and his brother the best she could.
"She was so strong," he said, pride in his voice. "I know it wasn't easy, but I thank God for the strength He gave her. I'm here because of her. She taught us to love and trust in God. I love my mom so, so much."

At school, he was even teased for spending so much time with her.

"They called me a girl. Told me I spend so much time with my mamma that I am obviously not a boy."

And my heart broke because something like that can cause a heart to freeze over. To become hard and unyielding. Bitter. Unforgiving.

But there's none of that in Tefo.

———

Five years later, I returned to Botswana. I didn't tell anyone I was coming; I wanted it to be a surprise.

One day, I was walking that old familiar road from my house to the office. All of a sudden, I saw him.

He was sauntering down the street, tall and lanky. Even taller than I remembered. Headphones hanging from his ears, phone in hand. When he realized it was me, he yelled my name and bounded down the street, sweeping me up into the biggest, best hug.

"Surprise!" I yelled, and we walked the rest of the way together.

He talked my ear off. I could hardly believe what I was witnessing. The growth. The maturity. The drive and ambition for life. The courage. The outgoing personality.

I wanted to scream. I probably did.

My heart overflowed with pride as I listened to him talk about his ideas and dreams and plans. About his friendships and his desire to follow God and his commitment to serve.

His eyes were still kind. And his ways were still gentle. And his laugh was still contagious.

I realized in that moment what was so special about Tefo: his strength. No, not his physical state—he could use a hamburger or two!—but his strength.

strength
The ability to resist being moved or broken by force.
The quality that allows someone to deal with problems
in a determined and effective way.

—Merriam-Webster dictionary

Tefo had all the reasons in the world to be broken. He had enough disappointment to keep him down. Enough lack of positive male influence to make him a deadbeat. Enough pressure to push him over. Enough pain to close off his heart. And enough problems to cost him his peace.

But he managed to find strength.

Where? Where does one find the antidote for disappointment? Or learn what it means to become a man? Can you just wake up one day and decide to stand? Can you force a heart to open up when it feels like it might bleed out?

The word "strength" comes from the Old English word *strang,* akin to the Old High German *strengi* and Latin *stringere,* meaning "to bind tight."

BOTSWANA: *STRINGERE:* THE BINDING FOR THE BROKEN

To bind tight.

Strength comes from being held. We can't expect to remain whole when we're not being held tightly together. We can't expect to be marked by strength when we've allowed gaping wounds to fester, instead of binding them for healing.

It's not something we can manage on our own. And I think Tefo must have grasped that truth younger than most.

We can dig all day within ourselves but we'll never be able to banish disappointment on our own, teach ourselves to grow, pick ourselves up, pour anti-freeze on our hearts, or fill our bank accounts enough. We must end this search within ourselves. We must find *Him,* as Tefo did, the keeper of strength, the giver of *stringere,* the binder of the broken.

He heals the broken-hearted and binds up their wounds.

—PSALM 147:3

SOUTH AFRICA

South Africa, the rainbow nation.

South Africa's racial diversity is something you notice right away, something that takes tourists by surprise: "There are white people in Africa?" But who can blame them, if all they know is what they see on television.

So yes, there are *many* white people on the continent of Africa, especially in South Africa. Born and raised in Africa, these white Africans are mostly Dutch and British descendants. Dutch Afrikaners speak Afrikaans; British South Africans, English.

Equally as many coloured people live in South Africa. The first time I heard the "c" word, I gasped. I could hardly bring myself to say it because of its connotations in Western society. In South African culture, it's simply the term used to describe a mixed-race person, not offensive or degrading in any way. The rest of South Africa's nearly 54.5 million population is known as Black Africans.

Even South Africa's landscape is diverse, from industrial, landlocked Johannesburg to coastal Cape Town to the Drakensburg mountains to rolling wine country. And let's not forget the two nations engulfed within South Africa's borders: Lesotho and Swaziland.

Not only does South Africa have a rainbow of ethnicities, but also a rainbow of languages: 11 national languages, to be precise, and countless dialects. If you ask a South African—or any African, for that matter—how many languages they speak, the number would average five or six.

Although this diversity is now celebrated in the country, it wasn't always that way. In fact, it used to be the exact opposite.

The Dutch (Afrikaners) landed on the southern tip of South Africa in 1652 and founded Cape Town, one of this nation's three capital cities: Cape Town, legislative capital; Pretoria, administrative capital; Bloemfontein, judicial capital.

≤ *Drummers*

SOUTH AFRICA

THESE BEAUTIFUL PEOPLE

Vineyards

They moved north and claimed land from the indigenous black inhabitants. When diamonds and gold were discovered several years later, immigration and wealth grew, as did the enslavement of the natives. When the British came, the Afrikaners fought and lost. After the second South African War (1899–1902), the Dutch and British began ruling together in 1910. South Africa became a republic in 1961 but not before apartheid was instituted by the Afrikaner-dominated National Party, which came into power in 1948. This policy favoured the white minority and discriminated against the black majority.

Translated, *apartheid* means "apartness." And it accomplished just that. Races were no longer allowed to mix socially or relationally. Mixed-race families were torn apart and mixed-race children didn't fit into either category. Stores, streets, and whole sections of cities bore signs reading "Whites only." Whites were incredibly favoured, whereas blacks and coloureds were severely disadvantaged in everything, from land to food rations to education. Only a small amount of land was given to blacks, even though they were the majority. "Black spots" were removed from white communities by segregating blacks in townships outside the city. They couldn't own land, only rent. Many people lost land that had been in their families for generations.

Leaders of the African National Congress (ANC) opposed this movement, but many—most notably Nelson Mandela—spent decades in prison for their efforts. The ANC was made up of several organizations and Christian movements committed to fighting this institutionalized bias. They intentionally broke the laws of apartheid, willingly offering themselves up for arrest. As the minority, Afrikaners were afraid of losing their jobs, culture, and language. It was a movement fuelled by fear.

SOUTH AFRICA

THESE BEAUTIFUL PEOPLE

The end result was anger, bitterness, and an intense resentment that lingers to this day. Now growing up is a generation that has never experienced apartheid but that can still be influenced by earlier generations and their biases. Even their main sports—rugby, football, and cricket—remain largely ethnically divided.

Today the unemployment rate is at 26.8 percent, mostly in the townships. In 2015 a total of 19.2 percent of adults and almost 7 million people were living with HIV/AIDS, putting this nation at number four in the world for prevalence. The country's lower end minimum wage is $1.85/hour and the average salary is 7,443 South African rand (CAD$756.66). Extreme wage inequity means the more "privileged" employees receive 40 percent of wages.

But South Africa, like everyone and everywhere, is more than her mistakes. She's so much more than her hardships and hurdles.

In 1967 the first heart transplant was performed in South Africa by Dr. Chris Barnard ("First Human Heart Transplant" 2010).

Twelve percent of the world's gold is mined in South Africa.

The world's longest wine route is here (Howard and Howard 2012), as is one of the world's longest ultra-marathons, the Comrades Marathon (Brown 2017).

The automatic pool cleaner (Bruton 2011) was invented in South Africa, which is also the only producer of Mercedes Benz C-class right-hand-drive vehicles.

Colourful beads hold great significance, especially in black African culture. Nelson Mandela wore the beads across his chest instead of a suit to his sentencing to send a message of African identity.

The *braii* is my favourite part of South African culture. A barbecue-style event, several kinds of meat will be roasted over a fire or charcoal barbecue. South Africans love their meat so much that chicken is almost considered a salad.

Like the *braii,* it's this spirit of celebration, of common ground, where amends are made and peace is planted. Now is the time for a generation to rise up and practice peace and reconciliation. This is the generation who will grow up to bring every colour of that nation back into the rainbow it was meant to be.

I invite you to dive in. Search for lessons like buried treasure.

Perhaps you'll find ancient wisdom, or new promises, through these beautiful people.

WHEN TWO ELEPHANTS MEET ON A NARROW BRIDGE, **THEY GET NOWHERE UNTIL ONE OF THEM BACKS DOWN** OR LIES DOWN.

—SOUTH AFRICAN PROVERB

THERE'S ALWAYS THAT ONE

≤ Edwin's Story | Porchestroom, South Africa

I grew up kinda sad, with no mom and no dad.
Thinkin' bout it, the Bible was the only thing that I really had.

"I was six years old. My parents fought a lot. A lot. And that's where I got my picture of love.

"As a young kid looking up to your dad, you wanna be like him and do everything he does. I thought that was how you should treat a woman. By fighting her and always arguing.

"Yeah, so technically I had parents, but the way I was raised I sometimes wondered if I would have been better off... you know, without them.

"I grew up with a heart of stone. I didn't care about people's feelings. Didn't know what love was. I held grudges and I put myself in a box."

Distracted, didn't know the good from the bad.
And all this pain affected my future and now it's my past.

"In Grade 6, I started smoking cigarettes. How did I get them? I stole them from my role model: my dad.

"I failed that grade. I hung around older guys and started smoking weed, sniffing cocaine. By Grade 7, I was selling. Twelve years old and selling drugs.

"I'm sure my mom must have known something was wrong. I always came home late, always had money. I was never at school. But every time she'd ask me, I'd tell her, 'No, of course. No, I'm not smoking anything.'

SOUTH AFRICA: THERE'S ALWAYS THAT ONE
THESE BEAUTIFUL PEOPLE

"I thought it would help. I thought it would fix things, especially between my parents. But it made it worse—so much worse. It tore them farther apart. It still eats me up inside."

Never had a father figure to guide me to be strong.
Went out on a streets by myself to smoke strong.

"June 16. I remember that day, a South African holiday. That day, I started doing crystal meth.

"It makes you feel strong. It makes you feel beautiful. It makes you feel like you're better than other people when you're not. I became addicted.

"That's when everything began to change. My mom chased me away to live with my grandma. I was 13 years old. That lady, my grandma, she was pure gold. She prayed for me every day. Every. Single. Day.

"But now I knew the streets. I knew how to sell. I knew all the suppliers. Things got hectic. I didn't sleep at 'home' anymore. I'd go away for weekends and not tell my grandma where I was. I'd do whatever pleased me in that moment.

"I dropped out of school in Grade 10. I had no time for school—I just wanted to smoke. I started stealing stuff from my grandma's house, doing anything I could, to get money for more drugs."

Errbody wanna be at the top.
To get there, gotta work real hard like a slave.
Don't get no days off—take a breather, sip of water, then get back on it.

"'Focus on your school or I'll have no choice but to chase you away, too.' My grandma was serious.

"I'm the only grandson she has, so if she loses me… that's it. I went back to school after seven months. They didn't accept me. I had to work so hard for my points. I was still smoking weed but less crystal meth. Just sniffing more.

"But then there was this one. This one teacher.

"'Each day you must come to my class and work on your marks.' She singled me out.

"I would go every day, but when the pressure got to be too much, I bailed. Because that's always easier isn't it? I didn't need this, did I?

"I failed again, so I had to go back the next year. Still, my grandma prayed. And when my grandma prays for me, she doesn't pray for me to be successful. She prays for me to be a good person. For me to have a beautiful heart.

"Because 'a beautiful heart can reach for success and make other people happy. Dreams without movement are still just visions.' I'll never forget her words.

"In 2011 she sent me to Cape Town to live with my aunt and uncle. My uncle worked all the time. My auntie didn't like me much. The feeling was mutual. She would lock me outside, make me sleep on the porch. I didn't go home for holidays because I wanted to make my grandma proud and I knew what would happen if I went back.

"I got sick. Someone had used witchcraft to put a curse on me—someone in the family. We went to see the witch doctor and he gave me something to drink but I refused. It was creepy. The guy lived with a mouse and was blind, but he said he'd been expecting us."

So I went on my knees and started to pray
but I was like, "God, I don't even know what to say.

"From that week on, I started praying. I had been born into a church-going family and baptized as a kid, but I had rebelled. I was just smoking weed now, no other drugs. Every time I wanted to do them, I thought about my grandma and I just couldn't do it. I tried reading books and writing music. None of it worked.

"I prayed. I really, really prayed.

"The next time I went home to see my grandma, she could tell I was still smoking weed, but she was so, so proud of me. She told me that God was working and doing something. I didn't believe her. She told me she had a dream where I stopped smoking and my friends were looking up to me. I didn't believe her.

"I was praying, but I didn't have faith. I didn't believe that He could make a way for me. I just wanted Him to fix everything in an instant. Sure, my mom had changed a lot since my dad left, but she never visited. Just tried to buy me by sending me stuff. And my dad was all empty promises.

"'It's fine to make your mom proud, but most of all, make yourself proud,' my grandma said. She was a wise woman.

"When I went back to Cape Town after that visit, the weight was gone. I felt like she took the weight off my shoulders. That's when the bond between us grew. We had such amazing conversations. She became my number one woman.

"When I got back, my uncle sent me to live at a hostel because of my aunt. But I ran away. I didn't like it at all. The principal complained to my uncle that I wasn't following the rules, so I had to go. That night, I walked away from the hostel with my stuff. Barefoot. When I got to my uncle's house, the lights were all off and it was dark. I was locked out.

"Then there was this one. This one old granny.

"She lived on the same street as my uncle, but she wasn't part of our family. The first time she saw me, she didn't know my name so she called me 'Pakistani.' Mostly 'cos I always had a shirt tied around my head while I did yard work. She told me I looked like her son who had passed away years ago.

"Her lights were still on. When I passed her house, I greeted her. She asked me what was wrong. I told her I got chased away from the hostel because I was naughty. I couldn't lie to her. She was too forward, too straight! The way she treated me was on a different level—a level that demanded respect and honesty.

"That night she took me in. She became my second granny. And it was just as well. My uncle would no longer greet me or this granny. He would keep the things my mom would send for me. I had trusted my uncle and this made me feel bad.

"My new granny wouldn't let me hang out with my bad friends anymore. She would make me sit with my books day and night.

"'If you don't get this right, you don't eat,' she would tell me. And I like food, so…

"Then there was this one. This one teacher at my school.

"She told me that I could get the highest marks in the class if I wanted to. That I wasn't stupid. That I wasn't a fool.

"She put me in the front of the class and she would always call on me for everything: to read aloud, to do anything. I usually got it wrong, but she kept picking me. She would even tell guest speakers and other teachers to choose me for stuff.

"And I always thought, 'Why me? There are so many other brilliant kids in this class!'

"Then there was this other one. This other teacher from the same school.

"She was related to that old granny who took me in. When she found out, she would always get me to help her with things, too. She took an interest in me.

"I started thinking, 'What's wrong with these people? There are so many other kids here!'"

Wake up in the morning, feel like I don't deserve this.
Tears fell on the ground, feel like I be drowned.
Poverty is killin' me, what am I gonna do now?

"When it came time to go on a class trip to the Western Cape, of course I didn't have enough money. I didn't have *any* money. But these people… these crazy people. They told me if I got good enough grades, they would pay for everything.

"'We believe in you, Edwin. We know you can do this!' they told me.

"So I did my best. It wasn't great, but I was trying and they saw that. They paid the 7,000 rand (CAD$686.00). Between the four of them, they bought me everything I needed. They even gave me 1,600 rand (CAD$165.00) for spending money.

"I still wondered, 'Why me? There are so many kids who are struggling at this school.'

"But I did it. I graduated. And I went on that trip. By the time I got home, I wasn't smoking anything anymore. But I still didn't go to church.

"The next year, I entered my final year of high school… in a white school. I was the first of my friends to go to a white school. I got into a lot of fights. I didn't like white people; I was racist.

"But there was always this one. This one teacher. This one person trying to help me. And of course, he was white.

"He liked me a lot. He saw potential in my music and in my athletics. I started liking him because I felt like he was black even though he looked white."

He said He knows my needs and all is OK.
Whether the darkest hour or the sky is grey.
The Father, the Son, the beginning, and the end.
The first and the last, a father and a friend.

"I just wanted to feel loved. I didn't know how to give it, I didn't know what it looked like, but I wanted it.

"Finally, in 2014 things came to a head.

"By now I had moved back to Porchestroom. That old granny in Cape Town had passed away. She had played such a huge role in my life, and I wasn't even there when she passed. I didn't get to tell her my last goodbyes. I know she would be so proud of me right now.

SOUTH AFRICA: THERE'S ALWAYS THAT ONE

THESE BEAUTIFUL PEOPLE

"One Saturday night, I was walking home and I saw this drunk man lying in the grass. I felt like I should pick him up and take him home. As I bent down, I saw some money sticking out of his pocket. How tempting is that?

"I told myself, 'I'll just take the 10 rand and leave him on the corner right here.' But I didn't.

"'Tappi down. Tappi up. Tappi… tappi.' That's all this drunk idiot was saying and I was so frustrated! I wanted to yell at him to wake up and tell me where he lived so I could take him home. When I finally got him home, he took that money out of his pocket and tried to give it to me.

"I was amazed. As I walked home, I had a feeling I should go to church the next day. When I woke up in the morning, I was full of joy. Just knowing I didn't steal that 10 rand.

"Church started at 10 a.m. I woke up at 6 a.m. I was so excited to go to church and I had no idea why.

"I only had one pair of old, broken sneakers. I put them on and walked to my friend's house. He took so long to get ready that we missed half the service, but that's the day I gave my life to Christ. When they asked if anyone needed prayer, I felt like someone pulled me out of my chair and took me down the aisle. Like when someone yells, 'Freeze!' and your hands just automatically go up.

"It was like someone broke a glass in me—all the tears fell down. That's the Holy Spirit. I was saved in September and baptized on October 5."

That's the reason why His love for us will never end.
He has favour on us, He can't pretend.

"I began to realize why people helped me so much. Why there was always that one: that one person, that one granny, that one teacher. It's because many are called, but few are chosen. And I'm one of the chosen ones.

"It was God… God putting people here to help me. I kept asking where God was and why He wasn't speaking. But He is right here!"

On birthdays, Christmas, put my Father on that wish list.
I'm focused on my Father, forget 'bout Father Christmas.
Turn my back against sin and that is my last twist.
I'm hard-twisted like my dreadlocks, holding on to God and I'll never stop.

SOUTH AFRICA: THERE'S ALWAYS THAT ONE
THESE BEAUTIFUL PEOPLE

"I told God, 'You know I love music, so lead me into this.'

"Then bam—out of nowhere—this guy comes. Years ago, he'd been part of iThemba, a dance team that tours Germany once a year, proclaiming peace and reconciliation. He had seen me dance in the past and knew that I was talented in the arts, so he told me I should join iThemba. I told him to quit giving me these Zulu words.

"'What kind of coloured are you?' I asked him.

"He asked me if I'd like to go to Germany. And I was like, 'Hmm, Germany? Say what?'

"He showed me pictures and I told him to hook me up. Thinking I wasn't serious, he never got back to me. But I was serious and I hunted him down. If this was what God wanted, then I wanted it, too.

"But there was a problem. The training fees were too much. I prayed, day and night. Sat with a Bible in front of me. Didn't even know what to do with it!

"People told me I should see a pastor. I did. He helped me fill out all the paperwork. To this day, I have no idea if anyone ever paid the money, but I got an interview.

"The interview was the next day. I didn't have any money. I didn't have any way of getting there and it was pretty far away. I guess this is how God intended to show me He was God.

"I woke up the next day: it was the morning of my interview and I was stressed! I went to the church at 8 a.m. The guy I needed to see didn't come until 10. He gave me some money and I called my cousin to ask if he could take me to Florida, Johannesburg. He said we'd get a taxi, no problem. He came late. When we got downtown, all the taxis were on strike.

"Finally, a guy picked us up, but he dropped us off in the middle of Soweto—*not* where we wanted to go. We had to search everywhere for a train station. When we bought our tickets, we had four minutes to get to our train.

"We ran and made it just in time. We still had seven stops before we would get to Florida and I was totally freaking out. *I'm going to be late. I'm going to miss my interview.*

"I flipped open my phone and found this picture that read 'God's timing is perfect.' I made it my screensaver and I told God, 'I'm not stressing anymore. You've got this.'

Surprising the team at their final banquet and concert, Germany, 2015

"We got off the train and started walking with no idea where we were. We asked someone and he said, 'Florida.' We asked him where 10th street was. To our surprise, he said, 'Just two streets over.' We were there.

"I walked into the church late. Like, two hours and 30 minutes late. But they told me another girl still had to go before me, so I waited another hour and a half for my audition. I was two hours late and God gave me another hour and a half!

"I did my audition. I was accepted on the spot. I saw the 7,000 rand (CAD$730.00) fee again and I panicked.

"They told me, 'Don't let money take you away from God's work. Just come.' I never heard about that money again."

I wanna change my 'hood to reach the nation,
Hope what I'm spittin' really makes a difference.

"And here I am today, at the end of my eight-month tour with iThemba in Germany. That journey is ending, but a new one is starting.

"As of 2015, I'm three years clean by the grace of God. My grandma is so proud of me! And I'll be home in time for her heart operation in a few weeks.

"I'm only one year old in Christ, still a baby. I don't understand the Bible because I haven't taken the baby steps yet. But I feel like God has given me this special ability to connect with people.

"I've learned He doesn't write in the clouds. You don't hear a big voice or anything like that. We ask God for something and He sends it but we miss it because we don't like it or we expect it to look a certain way. We're looking for answers when the answer is right in front of us.

"I rap about life. Real life. My life. I want to focus on my music. I won't stop. I'll just keep writing. And I'll always put God first."

———————

I met Edwin at the training camp for iThemba in February 2015. He caught my attention right away.

He was raw and real, witty and talented. He was also insecure and I remember him trying to run away at least once. He expressed his fear of sharing his story with others and I suggested he turn his story into a rap.

Nearly 10 months later, a friend and I shocked the iThemba team with a surprise visit to their final banquet and concert in Germany.

When Edwin took the stage and rapped out his story, I could hardly keep back the tears. That rap is now woven into the story you've just read.

So yes, Edwin. You will change your 'hood. And your words do make a difference.

We *all* can. And our words *all* do.

Because of that one. That one who believes in you. That one who sees in you what you can't yet see. That one unrelenting, unchanging current that pulls you in, pulls you toward the One.

In Edwin's words:

There is a heaven and a hell
Tell me where you see yourself
You got two choices and both require pain
Make a move and not excuses
Don't live your life in vain.

There's always that one. It might as well be you.

SOUTH AFRICA: THERE'S ALWAYS THAT ONE
THESE BEAUTIFUL PEOPLE

SPOILED PLEASANT

 **Ant and Nellie's Story** | Kleinmond, South Africa

"They are simply the best!"

"They take us out for a meal on our birthdays."

"They have a pool where they live and we have a key to the house. Anytime we want we can just go in and make ourselves at home!"

"Yeah, and eat anything we want. And she is a *crazy* good cook!"

"They are just so generous."

"And kind. And fun-loving."

The girls all talked at once, trying to describe the phenomenon of Ant and Nellie. We were eight girls living in one house from several countries across the globe. Each of us there as volunteers with Youth for Christ Botswana. Each of us travelling on our own. Each of us away from home.

All I'd done was ask a simple question, "Who are they?" Before long, I was so excited to meet them. As it turned out, every word about them was true.

I watched over the next 10 months as they cared for us, prayed for and with us, and found out about our lives and families. I swam in their pool and ate their food. Even after I left the country, they stayed in touch with me.

SOUTH AFRICA: SPOILED PLEASANT

THESE BEAUTIFUL PEOPLE

In 2015 I was able to visit them in Cape Town. Again, they were exceedingly generous in their hospitality toward me and my friend. We never could figure out why. Why take such an interest in us? Why spend so much time and energy and resources on a bunch of foreigners?

We felt blessed, but some would say spoiled. Then shake their heads at Ant and Nellie and say, "You've spoiled them rotten."

They aren't all wrong. But I would say that perhaps we were not spoiled rotten. Perhaps we were spoiled pleasant.

———

Ant and Nellie were born and raised in South Africa.

They met at university through a mutual friend. Let me tell you, some of the stories they told about their courting years had us in stitches.

Ant was an introverted loner and Nellie was full of mischief, gradually pulling him out of his shell in her heeled boots and little skirts. They're the kind of couple who has a lot of fun together and genuinely enjoys each other's company. It's rare and beautiful.

They got married, even though Ant wasn't a believer. His parents had divorced and he had been badly burned by the church in the process. He wanted to be as far away from it as possible.

Nellie grew up in the church with a strong faith and a heart for serving.

"A couple of years into our marriage, I awoke one night to an intense feeling of evil in the room and a voice that urged me to make a choice," said Ant. "That was a turning point in my life."

Now Nellie and he could fully live out their faith together for the first time.

"I started working for the Botswana Harvard AIDS Institute Partnership on November 1, 2005. I love working with health data, and this was such a unique opportunity. It was also supposed to be a short-term contract, so we decided I should take it while Nellie continued with her teaching job in Cape Town. My contract ended up getting renewed every year, so we decided Nellie should join me in Botswana.

She moved up in 2009 after our girls completed their studies."

Before going to Botswana, Ant had felt the nudging toward mission work but not evangelism. One day at a seminar for missionary support, it all hit home.

"I knew that's what I was supposed to do," he said.

Nellie's gifts of service and hospitality fit right in with that calling. They made it their personal mission to be a support to missionaries in Botswana—some through their church, and some from Youth for Christ Botswana. That was us!

That was where the spoiling began.

But they would say, "It's nothing." And they would say, "In comparison to others, we have not done much."

Ant once said, "It is not about doing great things for God, but rather getting your relationship with God right. Everything else is of secondary importance."

Get your relationship with God right first. Because everything flows out of that.

What they do pours out of them because they're connected to the Father. It comes as naturally as breathing. It's no daunting task or heavy responsibility. It's not something they *must* do, but something they're compelled to do out of love for God and His people.

Their "nothing," however, has impacted all who crossed their path. Their "not much" has inspired and touched us.

It might not seem like a lot of work to stretch out a hand, but that touch can revive a lonely heart.

It might not seem like a lot of work to cook a meal, but that home-cooked dish smells of family and belonging

It might be second nature for you to pray for someone, pay for their meal, or lend a helping hand, but those are expressions of genuine love.

SOUTH AFRICA: SPOILED PLEASANT

THESE BEAUTIFUL PEOPLE

Ant and Nellie have a way of instantly making you feel part of the family. They have a way of making you feel at home, no matter who you are, or how long or short they've known you. Doesn't that sound a lot like the Father's house? Doesn't that sound a lot like the way His family should treat each other?

It's the mark of one changed life changing another. The stamp of a Saviour. The natural result of a relationship with a Heavenly Father.

Because weren't we first spoiled by Him? Haven't we been graced with gifts we could never deserve? Haven't we been pardoned at the expense of Him freely offering His life?

After all that, shouldn't we end up spoiled rotten? Shouldn't we all be greedy, entitled children who never grew up? I suppose we could be, and sometimes we probably act like it, but this kind of spoiling is different. We've had everything handed to us. All that's left to do is accept it and then let it spill over onto everyone we meet.

This kind of spoiling makes you more pleasant. It makes life more pleasant. Like Nellie said, "We cannot claim glory for anything on our own. All the glory goes back to Him."

Yeah, they spoiled us. But He started it. They're just passing it along. And the blessing keeps going around and around.

"The young volunteers we met from around the world that donated a portion of their time to come to Botswana for Youth for Christ became a constant source of joy and a highlight of our time there. Contact with missionaries, whether young short-term volunteers or older long-time missionaries, is like a life-blood and essential to my spiritual growth," said Ant.

"Meeting Youth for Christ volunteers was such a blessing and still is today. I was touched by each one of them, no matter how short or long their stay in Botswana. Their zest for life, love and trust in Jesus Christ, and courage to come alone to Africa inspired me so much. This younger generation showed me, as an older person, another kind of faith in our Lord that I shall always cherish! And till today I give glory to Him, the One who puts the intricate puzzles of our different lives together in such amazing ways," added Nellie.

And they're the same to this day: living testaments that you can make a difference just by being who you are, where you are, with what you have, simply by trusting in Jesus.

Two years later, when I asked Ant what they're doing now, I couldn't keep from grinning at his response.

"We moved to Kleinmond, South Africa, where I work mostly from home supporting the District Health Information System databases. I work under contract from Health Information System Programme. Nellie is full-time spoiling me and is also involved with missionary support through our local church."

They couldn't stop being a blessing if they tried.

Maybe it wouldn't hurt to spoil each other a little more. Show a little more grace. Give a little extra time and attention.

Not because you feel you should "do something." Not because you want to check it off your list. But because it pours out of you, from a place first filled to overflowing by your Father. From a place of relationship.

You can't give what you don't have. So let the Father spoil you. Soak it up; don't resist. But also don't sit on it. Pass it around. Spoil someone else.

I think we could all stand to be spoiled every now and again. Because there's nothing wrong with being spoiled pleasant.

MADAGASCAR

It's unlike any other African country and nothing like the Dreamworks film.

That was my first thought when I arrived. I was taken aback by the diversity of her people. "It looks like an Indian, an Asian, and an African had a bunch of babies," I said to a local. He smiled and said, "Well, it's true."

Madagascar was one of the last land masses to be populated by humans. Once attached to the continent of Africa, she gradually detached and drifted to her present location off the coast of Mozambique. Between 35 and 550 A.D., settlers from present-day Indonesia landed on the island, followed by Arab and Persian traders around the seventh century. African migrants arrived in 100 A.D., contributing to the multi-ethnicity and joining what would become a centre for slave trading in the nineteenth century. In 1896 the French colonized the island, which wouldn't regain independence until 1960.

This sub-tropical island is now home to more than 24.4 million people who speak French and Malagasy, with more than 60 percent under 25 years of age.

Most of the population is poor and rural. Girls are often taken out of school and forced to marry young. Combined with a lack of medical professionals, early maternity causes severe complications during childbirth. More than 50 percent of Malagasy children under the age of five are malnourished. In 2013 more than 40 percent of women aged 20–24 were married, and one third of them had given birth by 18. Despite the legal age for marriage being 18, parents often give early consent.

Surprisingly, less than 0.5 percent of the population is living with HIV/AIDS. What makes Madagascar one of the poorest countries in the world is the hourly wage, which keeps 70 percent of the population below the poverty line despite an incredibly low unemployment rate of 2.6 percent.

≪ *Fields in Amparafaravola, Madagascar*

MADAGASCAR

THESE BEAUTIFUL PEOPLE

NY OLOMBELONA HOATRA NY
LANDIM-BOATAVO, KA RAHA
FOTORANA, IRAY IHANY.
**HUMANS ARE LIKE THE
BRANCHING OF A SQUASH PLANT.
AT THE BOTTOM, THERE IS ONLY
ONE STEM.**

—MALAGASY PROVERB

Madagascar's main export is vanilla. You can smell it in the air at the market and in the parts of the country where it's cultivated. Its perfume is pervasive.

Because of her favourable climate, Madagascar can produce almost any fruit or vegetable you can think of. Although there's no shortage of delicious food to eat, the Malagasy people's main dish is fondly known as the "Malagasy mountain." Rice.

The Malagasy people eat rice at every meal, along with a drink called rice water. Traditionally, they prepare *romazava* to go with the rice, a meat dish of cubed beef, pork, or chicken coated with chopped onions, spinach, tomatoes, and garlic.

A total of 75 percent of the flora, fauna, and wildlife are endemic to Madagascar, meaning they don't exist anywhere else in the world unless imported.

Madagascar used to be home to the elephant bird, which became extinct in the seventeenth century. It was the largest bird in the world, believed to have been more than 10 feet tall.

Not only is she home to some of the most beautiful beach vacation destinations, but she also hosts some of the world's largest remaining rainforests.

She's a rare find, internationally forgotten but waiting to be discovered. Waiting for her time to shine.

So dig deep. You won't be disappointed, I promise.
You're about to discover Madagascar's greatest and most unique treasure.

Her people.

≤ Top: Fianaratsoa, Madagascar
≤ Middle: Antananarivo, Madagascar
≤ Bottom: Amparataravola, Madagascar

MADAGASCAR
THESE BEAUTIFUL PEOPLE

THERE'S NO STOPPING HIM

 ≤ Clement's Story | Antananarivo, Madagascar

Perseverance.

The word rang in my mind as I sat across from him. His office was small but organized, with a simple cement floor, some filing cabinets, and the desk between us. I glanced around the room, taking in the light that streamed through the windows and splashed across the papers neatly stacked next to the closed laptop, wishing it was as warm as it appeared.

"Things are not as they appear," I thought to myself, pulling my sweater a little tighter and turning my attention back to him.

Turns out the phrase described him, too.

At a glance, he appeared to have had it good. Easy even. His ministry was thriving. He had a law degree. His smile was broad and genuine, his family strong and healthy. He showed no signs of stress or struggle, pain or frustration, loss or grief.

Yet as I sat there, absorbing every detail of his story, I wondered how this could be.

———

Clement grew up in a town about 170 kilometres from Antananarivo, the capital of Madagascar. He was raised in a loving, Christian home; however, after the death of his mother in 1991, his father was left with the responsibility of raising five children alone. Knowing this, Clement decided to study in a public school to reduce the burden of school fees. After completing his secondary education, he knew his father could never pay for his dream of studying law. He simply had to wait.

Fortunately, a friend offered to pay for him to take a computer class. It wasn't exactly law school, but it was something. After volunteering with Youth for Christ during secondary school, he had acquired the skills necessary to land a gig as a part-time radio presenter. This job paid the way for Clement to be the inaugural student of a small, private Youth for Christ university. Due to his previous experience, he studied communication. Not the dream, but a step in the right direction.

Near the end of his studies, with a thesis to write and final exams to fund, Clement lost his job. Discouragement threatened to set in until he got a phone call from the mayor of Antananirivo, asking him to be his personal assistant. His salary as an intern covered the cost of his thesis and final exams.

But Clement's dream to study law hadn't died.

He had been volunteering with Youth for Christ for several years when they asked him to cover the administrator's three-month maternity leave.

"I knew I had to work to pay for my schooling, but at the same time I had been taken care of spiritually by Youth for Christ for many years. I wanted to give back, so I accepted even though it was not a paid position, and even though I had no idea where the school fees would come from."

A grin tugged at the corners of his mouth as he continued.

"So many miracles! One friend came, wanting to give me money and she didn't even know why. It was the exact amount of one of my books. The Youth for Christ administrator had studied law and I could borrow her two books. I went to the university office to negotiate paying later; they accepted. They said I just had to pay the exam fees.

"One day, David Kadalie, the pioneer of Youth for Christ Madagascar, was praying in his office when he called me in. 'Clement, I'm struggling here,' he said. 'Though I am broke, the Lord is telling me to give you the rest of the money I have. He's saying that I *must* give you this money.' It was the exact amount of my exam fees."

His face was radiant.

"Then I got a job in a new garment factory because I knew how to speak English. I didn't have any experience sewing, which was the nature of the company. They hired me for translation and the little bit of human resources experience I had. I worked there for three months doing the job of three people. I started work at 6 a.m. and finished at 10 p.m. Nonstop. They had promised to hire people to help me but they never kept their word."

I don't remember blinking once as he recounted his work situation. I'm willing to bet my eyes were bulging, along with a vein in my neck. This is *preposterous!* How can they do that?

"How are you not angry and bitter about that?" I probed.

His response undid me.

"I simply did it with love in my heart for Christ. I took the money I earned there to use towards my fees and then I left because there was no time for school. I'm thankful for that job because it came at the right time. In 2003 I was able to start my first year of law school."

Clement had passed his previous exams at the end of his three-month administrator position with Youth for Christ, but now he had law school to pay for. That's when he was asked to take on the ministry administrator position full time. He accepted and began the process of becoming a staff member, though he didn't yet feel the call of God for the position.

"It is hard. When people here see missionaries, we think of foreigners coming to Madagascar. We never think that we can be missionaries. You have to raise your own support—the money for the ministry—and mobilize the people. I thought that would be too hard for me."

He folded his hands on the desk in front of him and sat up straighter. His grin was contagious and I found myself smiling, too, although I had no idea what was coming next.

"That's how I met my wife, Mialy. She was working with Youth for Christ in another city and came to Antsirabe, where I lived, to take a survey of youth."

Just over one year later, they were married.

In Malagasy culture, usually the woman moves to where the man lives or works. Instead, Clement moved to Antananarivo and immediately began looking for a job.

"I resigned from Youth for Christ as a staff member, intending to volunteer in Antananarivo (Tana) instead. I had studied law and I wanted a job in that field."

Once again, David Kadalie asked him to work for Youth for Christ Tana. He accepted, although Clement made it clear that he wouldn't work there forever without the call of God.

"But then one of the staff left and I automatically took over his position."

Again, not even a hint of disappointment in his voice that life was not going as planned. But he didn't give up on his dream.

MADAGASCAR: THERE'S NO STOPPING HIM

"I kept trying to get another job. Out of the 80 people who applied, I was one of the few to be accepted by the economic development board. I would start the job on Tuesday. The Saturday before, David came to do training. He blessed me and said, 'Clement, you have always made it clear that you don't have the call. Go and do it. Do the work you applied for. But if one day you find it is not the right thing for you, then come back. The door is always open.' No one told me 'No, no, no, you can't leave.' They loved me and made sure I knew that I was always welcome."

Things were shaping up nicely until he went to church the following day.

"I had to make a decision about the job on Monday, and here I am in church on Sunday, and it is as if the sermon was addressed specifically to me."

The priest spoke about the good shepherd and Jesus' example of serving the sheep. His love for the sheep. His willingness to even die for the sheep.

"Yeah, *that* love. Even Jesus did it, even unto the cross. I asked myself, 'Clement, are you trying to learn from Christ? Or when there is something hard, you want to give up and find a better thing?'"

The Sunday message touched Clement and Mialy. They knew it was time to give their lives to serving Christ in Youth for Christ.

"It's important to be sure you are not doing it because you feel forced, but that you are doing it from your heart," he explained.

The next day, Clement apologized to his employer and declined the job—yes, the good job. The excellent job. He turned it down to stay at Youth for Christ for free.

His wife, on the other hand, had known she would work for Youth for Christ since her youth, but her parents forbade it. Out of respect for them, she had taken a job at a bank.

"From that time up till now, it has all been confirmed."

He smiled and I relaxed into my chair. Now everything could fall into place.

"In June 2013, God spoke to me and Mialy that we should serve full time with Youth for Christ. My wife would have to leave her good job at an American NGO and we would lose the only source of income we had."

People talked. They said to Mialy, "Clement is already struggling as a missionary. You have two children. How can you quit your job?"

"So we told God that we have six months until we officially make the decision and there are six things that need to be taken care of in that time. We have bank loans, the children need to be able to go to school... Lord, if You called us then we will take those things as confirmation."

If nothing happened in six months, they would conclude that being missionaries was their idea and not God's.

"Within a few months everything was sorted out. After tithing, the money I made from translating was the exact amount of our bank loan."

The headmaster of the children's school allowed them to study for free. And it was a good school! On and on went the list of miracles, until everything on their list was checked off.

In 2014 Clement and Mialy became full-time staff at Youth for Christ Madagascar. They had a distinct call but not a clue about the hurdles around the bend.

"Sometimes you believe God will provide, but you already know at the end of the month there will be some money coming from somewhere."

Now Mialy had no salary. There was no reserve, nothing to fall back on. Clement's face showed nothing but absolute trust and confidence.

"We had to put back all our faith and trust totally, 100 percent, in believing that God will provide for us." He smiled. "And He did."

Volunteers would bring them vegetables and food.

"The Lord touched many people. He had to teach us humility."

Looking into his eyes, I cannot picture this man without humility: it oozed from his innermost being. The thought of him having to *learn* this made me wonder about myself.

"Every day there was a miracle. We didn't have any money, but every day we lived with joy. The rent got paid. There was work to do. The children were fed. It was amazing!"

I blinked back tears, thinking how incredible your faith and how desperate your need must be to see miracles every day.

MADAGASCAR: THERE'S NO STOPPING HIM
THESE BEAUTIFUL PEOPLE

And to live with joy in such circumstances. All of us have circumstances, but do we stick it out long enough to see the miracle?

"In 2014 I was selected to attend a Young African Leaders Initiative in Washington in the United States, followed by a presidential summit. President Obama designed the program for sub-Saharan Africa. Five hundred young leaders from 50 countries were to be selected from the 50,000 who applied. Five hundred of the applicants were from Madagascar and I was one of the six who were chosen.

"When I returned from that two-month adventure, Mialy and I were busy planning our strategy for Youth for Christ Antananarivo in 2015."

Taking a break for Christmas, they travelled to see their families in Antsirabe. Clement was exhausted from the struggle to bring a vision into reality. Mialy, too, was sick.

On January 2, 2015, they received a call that would change everything.

"Our place had flooded."

Their house and office building were on the same lot. The lot where we were seated.

"The fence behind the house collapsed from heavy rainfall on December 29. This had never happened before and the family did not want to upset our vacation, so they waited to call us until the new year."

My jaw dropped. I could sense their weariness, then the shock of receiving the call. I would have been absolutely discouraged. But not Clement and Mialy.

"Luckily, we had spent quality time with God on December 31, telling Him that we were ready for *anything* He wants us to do. So when we heard about the flood, we had peace immediately."
Everything in the house was destroyed.

"But we still had peace. We told ourselves, 'It's a new start, so let's change anything we wanted to change since we have to fix it up anyway.'"

So they did.

"We were told the fence had been fixed and so we didn't need to worry about that happening again. There was nothing to be afraid of anymore."

By January 11, they were ready. Their first planning meeting was in session from 2 p.m. to 6 p.m. that day. Right here on this land. In this room where I now sat, all ears.

"It started to rain hard. We had been praying and just after we said 'Amen,' we heard someone shouting outside. The fence that was rebuilt had collapsed again. Within 15 minutes, our house and office were flooded a second time."

This time my jaw did hit the floor. I covered my mouth with my hands, not believing what I was hearing.

"Oh, Lord. It was dangerous. We were stuck inside the house and couldn't get out. The neighbours could hear our children crying and they came to help. It was already getting dark outside so it would have been impossible for someone to see us. When they arrived, they tried to open the door but they could not; the water was already up to our chests. The neighbour ran home to get something to break down the door and then we were able to get out. We left everything behind."

My heart was pounding as I listened. This would be the point at which I would give up: "Enough is enough. What do you think You're doing, God? What kind of good plan is this?" Not exactly a warm welcome to the ministry.

As I leaned back in my chair, I knew what I would have done: I would have quit. But not Clement.

"Now we didn't know where to go. The school our children attended was next to the house. They have one room upstairs where people can sometimes stay, so we lived there right next to the students. We would have to finish bathing, eating, everything by 6:30 in the morning before the students arrived."

You would think a complaint would be appropriate, but instead...

"Lord, thank you. We were affected by the flood, but You still take care of us."

An emergency meeting was held with the Youth for Christ board, a fantastic group of dedicated and generous individuals, to make arrangements for living and food.

"God has a plan and we must accept to be moulded by God. We don't know the reason for all of this, but we know God allows us to face this so there must be a lesson and we must be willing to accept this."

This is what they explained to their two children: Miangali, five years old, and Naltina, three years old.

MADAGASCAR: THERE'S NO STOPPING HIM

Flooding outside the Youth for Christ office

Flooding inside their home

"We lived in that one small room at the school for three months while trying to find a place to rent, but it's difficult to find something you can afford."

So they had to stay: two adults and two children in one room for sleeping, eating, living. No kitchen. Clement was 33 and Mialy was 34.

Clement leaned forward and raised his hands. His face brightened and he smiled at me intently.

"But, it was also time to implement the changes we had planned the year before. The work must go on and so we continued to pray."

Perseverance.

It wasn't the first time the word had popped into my mind during our conversation, but this time it exploded in my heart, leaving its mark on any part of me that felt like giving up was an option.

"By the end of April, all our stuff was still in the house that had flooded. There was nowhere else for us to go with it."

The land was owned by nuns, so they are able to rent it for a cheaper price; however, the nuns told them they had to come back and live in the flooded house, or get rid of all their belongings because they wanted to clean up the building and use it.

MADAGASCAR: THERE'S NO STOPPING HIM

THESE BEAUTIFUL PEOPLE

"We didn't have peace to live in that house again, but where will we put the rest of the furniture that survived the flood? So again we prayed to the Lord. We didn't know what to do."

The day before Clement and his wife had to decide whether to stay or leave, the nuns visited the house. When they arrived, they discovered that during the three months it had been closed up someone had broken in and stolen all the interior doors!

"The people who were going to move in decided they didn't want to live in a house that had been broken into, so the nuns offered the house to us again and that became our answer. We cleaned it up again and moved back in. We said, 'If this is the house, Lord, we accept it.'"

They moved in April. Soon after, Clement left to attend the closing of Young African Leaders Initiative in South Africa, with hopes of receiving one of the US$25,000 grants they would be awarding.

"Back in 2008, Youth for Christ had a vision to have a centre for training and leadership development. Over the years, people would offer us land but it would never come through. Situations where people didn't keep their promises was discouraging but we believed that God was teaching us something. We learned patience and we learned to trust that He gives in His own time."

Again with the perseverance.

"In 2014 we heard of a grant that could assist in building the training centre and we felt that we should at least try."

After much prayer and many failed attempts to get land, a board member donated a piece of land to begin the application process.

"We were asking for US$53,000. Near the end of the application, we found out we had to pay 1 percent of that amount to apply. Now, where were we going to get that money?"

Hurdle number one.

"We mobilized volunteers and the board and were able to provide the required amount just in time. Months went by. We didn't hear anything so we asked, although without much hope. It was already past the date when we should have heard."

They received good news: they *might* get funding but there was no guarantee. Pray!

Hurdle number two.

"Just after that, we got an email requesting a 90-second video, and the deadline was in a week or two. Now we had to raise funds to do that video properly. We were able to get it made and edited, but when we wanted to send it, it wouldn't go! We managed to upload it to YouTube, but for some reason, it changed to 91 seconds. We tried everything but they accepted it as it was. We prayed they would be able to play the video at their meeting since it was not in the format they requested."

Perseverance.

I sat there thinking, "Wow, there's no guarantee you will get any of this money. What if you don't get it?"

I would have quit. But not Clement.

"So here we are in April 2015. We have not heard anything yet concerning our request. I am at the Young African Leaders Initiative in South Africa and they are handing out these US$25,000 grants. I didn't get one."

The grants were only for those who were in the business and entrepreneurship tracks. Clement was in civic leadership. He was discouraged, but one day before the closing ceremony he received an email from Foundation for the Nations. They were giving him US$25,000 for the training and leadership development centre—the grant they had worked so hard to apply for!

"It was a shock for me: The time. The amount. Everything. I said, 'Lord, Yeah. When I went to the United States, I thought it would open doors for me, but I was wrong. Today you have proven that you are taking care of your child. You are not late.' It was as if God bent down and said, 'Here is your $25,000. Not from the American government, but from Me.'

"'Thank you, Lord.' I was in tears the whole evening."

Hurdle number three.

"We had just finished planning everything for 2016 and were taking our two-week break when we got the call. The nuns told us we had to leave our house and office because they needed it for someone else."

At this point, I was determined that nothing could surprise me. Wrong again.

"Where are we going to go? We have already moved three times. God, where do you want us to go?"

Once again, they began looking for houses and, once again, nothing. It was already September 2015, and they needed to be out by the end of the month.

I was sitting in this office near the beginning of October 2015. We had just finished a huge Youth for Christ conference for all the Indian Ocean islands, hosting delegates from several countries of inland Africa, myself included. Clement and his team were in charge of all the logistics.

It hit me that this had been happening only weeks before the telling of this story.

"Because of the conference beginning on September 20, with delegates arriving even before then, we had only two weeks to find a place to live and to move all our belongings."

They looked and looked, but nothing. They were running out of time.

"We started thinking that maybe it was God's will that we move to where the training and leadership development centre is now being built, but we really didn't want to. It is far from the city and transport is difficult. It's in the middle of nowhere and we didn't want to leave our comfort zone."

I smiled, wondering if this guy even had a comfort zone.

September 17, 2015. Still no house.

"We didn't have a choice. We had to go to Ampitatatafika and find a good house, a good school, and a church. September 21 was the first chance I had to go and I only had until noon. I went at 10 a.m. and started walking through the village. I asked everyone I met if they knew of any places for rent."

Still nothing. Suddenly, a lady ran up to him and exclaimed how she had overheard him talking and felt sorry for him. She told him there was a house he might want to look at.

She said, "If I look at you, it's a good house for you. They just built it. It's nice."

Clement grinned and explained, "I had tried to look smart that day. I made sure I dressed nice so people would not be afraid of me. So they would trust me."

I grinned back, imagining him strutting through the village in his finest. And it worked! Kind of.

"We walked and walked and came to the house. It was a brand-new house! I was already thinking, 'Thank you, God, but let's find out the rent first.' The owner welcomed us, but to my surprise, he led me past the brand-new house around the corner to the back, where the old house was."

It was in *very* poor condition. No running water and no indoor toilet.

"Lord, what is this?" Clement asked, discouraged. "It had no comfort at all, I have to admit. If you looked at the house you would say, 'I would never live here,' but the other house was already rented out and this was all that was left. So we said, 'If this is the house You have chosen for us to live, Lord, then we have no choice but to accept it with a cheerful heart. At least there is a house.'"

The rent was cheap and he took photos to show his wife. The owner informed him there was a church around but they would have to go there on foot. Just one thing left on the list: a good school for the children.

They walked for more than an hour and finally came to a school. Clement was impressed. It was a good school—far away, but with transportation and lunch included.

It was nearly noon when Clement returned home to discuss the options with his wife.

"We accepted and moved the following day."

September 22. One day before the conference began.

I was dumbfounded. I had lost count of all the reasons to give up. And not bad reasons... *reasonable* reasons! Valid excuses to curl up and complain. Valid excuses to believe maybe this isn't where you're supposed to be.

But not Clement. For Clement and Mialy, these were just more ways for God to prove His faithfulness. "If I summarize it, we feel like babies being led by the Lord and learning day by day. He doesn't expect you to be a perfect person. He is moulding you constantly. He teaches us, and sometimes He disciplines us because that's not the way we should do it. He is understanding and we feel it every day, even in small things, right down to which taxi I should take in the morning."

When I asked Clement if he ever imagined this would be his life, he laughed and replied, "No, never. I studied law because I wanted to become a diplomat working in foreign affairs. It's the reason I learned English as well. I moved to Tana because of that dream. When the Lord called me, that desire changed. Everything that I have learned I now use with Youth for Christ!"

It's true. Youth for Christ Madagascar was the first organization to become part of the government's initiative to promote volunteerism throughout the country. This is due, in part, to Clement's knowledge of law. He was instrumental in the instigation of this opportunity not only for the Malagasy people, but also for foreigners.

"We believe that if God wants to do something, He will see it through until the end. It's only because of the Lord that we are where we are today. When you look at our story, you know that."

I don't think anyone could argue with that.

The training and learning development centre is approaching completion, as far as they can go with the US$25,000. They're still believing God for the remaining funds to complete the building and fulfill the vision.

"We prayed for this place for seven years, and now it has finally become real!"

The excitement in his voice is tangible, and rightly so. His perseverance has paid off in so many ways—this is simply one of them.

"The centre is to support young people. Many of the students stop school after primary because they can't afford to attend private schools and there are no high schools in the village where the centre is located. The dream is to open a good Christian high school that can host 180 students per year, to empower them with hands-on training as well as leadership skills."

They will begin programs in 2016 for young girls but must await the remaining funds to launch the high school.

"On November 21, 2015, we had a board meeting at our house. The members were shocked at our living conditions and suggested we move into the centre. They said someone must live there and be in charge of it. We never thought we would live there, but once again, on January 12, 2016, we moved, this time into the centre."

They're using one room for the four of them.

"This is what the Lord gave and that's fine for us. Our family has always been facing everything together. We explain everything to the children so they understand what is happening."

Their children are seven and four years old.

This is how they started 2016. Without missing a beat, they have a team of volunteers and ministries

New training and leadership development centre

The whole family

taking place: prison ministry; Operation Smile, where children receive free surgery for cleft lip and palate; school ministry; and girl's empowerment, to name a few. They also have a volunteer internship program, something I was privileged to be a part of in a small way.

"This year is doing things with quality in Youth for Christ Tana. Striving for excellence."

And get this: the Youth for Christ Antananarivo ministry is now the model they want to use across all Madagascar, among other countries.

If anyone had an excuse to lie down or quit or sprint in the opposite direction, it would be Clement and Mialy. If anyone had a right to complain or despair or curse or beat the ground, it would be Clement and Mialy. But if anyone would be most likely to push through and persevere, it would be Clement and Mialy.

"I'm thankful. When I look at my history, I see God."

I glanced once more around the room, taking in the light streaming through the windows and across the smiling face of this man who had been through so much. His eyes revealed a depth that can only come from a life marked by such perseverance and gratitude.

"Things are not as they appear," I thought to myself, as I stood to shake his hand.

MADAGASCAR: THERE'S NO STOPPING HIM
THESE BEAUTIFUL PEOPLE

And just as this tiny office, so neat and tidy to the naked eye, held such incredible stories, the same could be said for Clement.

He might not always have it good—but he has a good, good Father. His ministry is thriving—but it came at a great price. He has a law degree—but it didn't come without struggle. His smile is broad and genuine—but it has been tested in the fire. His family is strong and resilient—but that didn't happen by chance.

Perseverance.

The thing we talk about most but practice least. The thing we so desire but rarely possess. The thing we recommend to others, despite having given up long ago.

I can say this for myself. But for Clement? There's no stopping him.

Let us not lose heart in doing good, for in due time we will reap if we do not grow weary.

—GALATIANS 6:9, NEW AMERICAN STANDARD VERSION

THE SILENT GIVER

◁ Franck's Story | Antananarivo, Madagascar

It was a beautiful, sunny day in Madagascar. A little too chilly for the shorts and tank I was sporting, but all that was forgotten as we stood on a little plot of land surrounded by rolling hills of rice fields and foot paths.

That's where I met Franck.

We were there with several of the leaders of Youth for Christ Africa, witnessing the construction of the training centre, a long-hoped-for building miraculously coming to fruition before our eyes.

They introduced him as the one in charge of the completion of this project.

He stood tall, clipboard in hand, determination in his eyes. He looked young but I was instantly impressed with his English and his grace and poise.

I didn't see Franck much over the next two weeks. Toward the end, I got to spend a day with him and a few other young leaders.

I learned that Franck was 29 years old. He enjoyed sports like basketball and swimming, putting us to shame in the pool. Although few of us could communicate with each other, that day we sang and danced and played the guitar for hours. Then we went for pizza and ice cream. It was a day when I needed the warmth of friendship and family, when I needed the gift of "normal." Franck gave me that.

Not only was Franck able to communicate with me in English and translate for the others, but there was a genuine warmth about him, a quiet confidence. He was a bright, young adult with an inclusive heart and an infectious determination to succeed.

◁ *Dancing with Franck by the pool on the day he made me feel at home*

MADAGASCAR: THE SILENT GIVER

THESE BEAUTIFUL PEOPLE

And succeed he has. He acquired his diploma in civil engineering in 2013.

"My best memory is the day I received that diploma," he remembered. "We all celebrated because I am the first in my family to become an engineer."

His father was so proud that he even went to church that Sunday.

"My father had never been to church with us before. Ever. But that day he came, and he has been coming ever since!"

See, Franck understands something. Change doesn't have to be shouted from rooftops. Differences don't have to be announced or advertised. One simply has to be present. And that's enough.

Franck came to know Christ in 2007. Since then he has been a light to everyone around him. Not a big fluorescent spotlight that makes you cover your eyes or look away. More like a candle, a gentle flicker that beckons you in. Makes you wonder where it comes from. Before you know it, you're captivated. You can't look away.

He's in the second year of his PhD program, teaching civil engineering to students at the university and volunteering with Youth for Christ as project manager for the building of the training centre. He plans to finish his doctorate in 2017.

"I hope to have a job after that!" He grinned.

He's hopeful, as he should be. Because character takes you farther than charisma, and light outshines darkness. Successful people understand that blowing out someone else's candle won't make theirs shine any brighter; yelling louder won't increase the substance of their words.

Sometimes you'll be the one who needs that flicker of hope, the warmth of friends and family. Sometimes you'll be the one who needs the gift of feeling normal for a day, feeling like you have a voice.

But always, we must be that candle for others and light the way. Like Franck, we should be as loud as a candle, which makes no noise at all but quietly gives itself away.

≤ *The warmth of friends*

MADAGASCAR: THE SILENT GIVER

THESE BEAUTIFUL PEOPLE

BAREFOOT AND BRAVE

⩽ Jaona's Story | Moramanga, Madagascar

"Do *I* have to wear shoes?" I asked him, looking down at his bare feet.

"Of course not! This is the village!" He grinned at me. This was the best answer I'd received since arriving in Africa almost 21 months ago.

I took off my shoes and didn't put them on again for the next two days. *Freedom!* Besides, it was Moramanga. *No one* was wearing shoes.

We had just arrived and Jaona was giving me and Ravo a tour of the tiny village on foot—barefoot, as he often was. As we plodded down the dusty paths, greeting neighbours and shopkeeper and children and... everyone, he told us stories and made us laugh with his contagious smile and constant jokes.

In charge of Youth for Christ Moramanga, Jaona lives in the village with his family. He has six siblings, some of whom live overseas or elsewhere. Two of his sisters live at home, one of whom was a semi-professional athlete. Jaona spent many hours training her in running and football, until she was forced to stop due to injury. His mother is also there, but he lost his father a few months after I left.

The village they lived in from birth had only a public primary school, where his parents were teachers. During that time, his elder brother had several health issues and needed to be hospitalized for six months. Because his father was the teacher and needed to be at the hospital, Jaona missed an entire year of school. The children then moved to Moramanga on their own when Jaona was 11 to attend secondary school.

That's brave—when you have to take care of yourself and your siblings at age 11. But you do it anyway.

MADAGASCAR: BAREFOOT AND BRAVE

THESE BEAUTIFUL PEOPLE

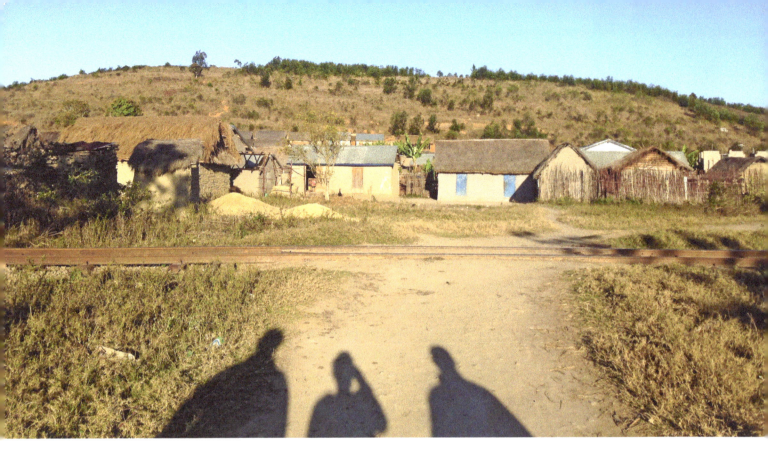

He struggled in secondary school.

"I spent three years in the last class of high school. I think it is because I spent too much time playing football and sports. I often missed school.

"But from childhood, we were all good at football. When we were young, my brothers and I played football at night from 7 p.m. to 9 p.m. with moon lighting because we did not have time in the day. When I was 11, my brothers and I joined a football club. Unfortunately, that club closed three months later, so we started to play Wednesday afternoons and all day Saturday. We often won and got a little money that we could buy bananas with. At the same time, we played on our school team.

"I started to play on the civil team at age 17. I was in second division and I was elected to be with the first division in my club at the age of 20. They called me David Beckham because I was good and I was a centre midfielder."

In his bare feet, too, I'd imagine.

He also admitted to struggling with time management, which contributed to his prolonged graduation.

"I am just not good at administration. I don't like it. That's why I am looking for someone to work with me in that area."

Communication is also a big struggle in Moramanga. Jaona, although conversational in English, struggles to truly express himself in the language. He's always looking for ways to practice and improve, even studying theology at a Baptist seminary in the United Kingdom.

That's brave—when school has been a struggle and you'd rather be kicking a ball in the dirt with your bare feet. But you go anyway.

"My parents were newly converted Christians when I was born. I went to church since childhood and I liked the Bible stories. I loved Sunday School. I enjoyed doing church work like sweeping the church building and clearing the courtyard. Since the age of seven, I was interested in spiritual things. I understood that hell was bad and paradise was good but only for those who accepted Jesus. Every Sunday, I wanted to stand up and tell the congregation that I accept Jesus as my Saviour and Lord. This is what we do in our church. But I did not dare. I was constantly afraid, thinking that if I died I am going to hell. I prayed every night to not be taken away before I got salvation. Finally, at age nine I declared in front of the church after a sermon that I accept Jesus."

That's brave—when you're faced with something that scares you. But you step out anyway.

"I was so relieved after because I had assurance I would not go to hell. I had peace. But after we moved to Moramanga, I became distracted by football. Me and my two brothers did not go to church often. At age 16, I found myself wanting to get more involved but it conflicted so much with my games. I knew I wanted to share the gospel with my schoolmates but I did not have the courage to do so. I found I was attracted to the non-Christian life and there were times I questioned my salvation. I committed many sins but at the same time I felt a call to share. I often asked God why my life became worse after I accepted Jesus. It was a big battle in my mind."

That's brave—when you're afraid to admit you're struggling. But you reach out anyway.

"My pastor was always asking me why I never accepted to be baptized. I felt like once I am baptized I will have all kinds of obligations. I wanted to be free. Free to just do whatever I wanted and baptism felt like too much commitment."

MADAGASCAR: BAREFOOT AND BRAVE

THESE BEAUTIFUL PEOPLE

But his pastor wouldn't let him off the hook so easily. He saw something in Jaona.

Yes, Jaona was restless—but he was also full of life. Yes, he was doubting—but his hunger to find out was greater. Yes, he was afraid of commitment—but deep down he had a heart to serve. Yes, he was always barefoot and a little unorthodox—but he wasn't afraid to get his hands (and feet) dirty.

"My pastor told my parents that he thought I had a call to be a pastor, and they should encourage me to study theology after high school. I wanted to be a farmer."

He has done and continues to do both. He studied theology for four years and was asked to work with African Inland Mission Madagascar. He taught pastors for two years, then left the organization when he felt the call to reach out to his relatives and the surrounding villages.

"We built two churches. I was grateful to God. He did it!"

Now he is leading a small church in his village. He is also coordinating the Youth for Christ centre in Moramanga.

"We have opened a secondary school, where I am the principal and the English teacher. And I do farming: I grow rice the traditional way.

"I would love to extend the Youth for Christ school up to high school and provide lunch for the students. Part of my dream is to open a centre for women to train them in making grass tents. I also want to have a health care centre in our village because I am getting busy now taking sick people to the hospital by motorcycle at night. We also have to take people who have mental health issues into the capital, which is far. Many people are dying because they cannot get treatment and they are coming to me for help. I also dream of having a Bible school in my region."

These are all good and big dreams, but it's difficult in Moramanga. As we walked barefoot through the streets, it was clear: although one of the most beautiful places I have ever seen, nothing comes easy here. Nothing comes without significant struggle.

Like health care, education is lacking. Before Jaona had even opened his school, hundreds of students wanted to enroll, more than they had the funds to accommodate. Electricity is also lacking. There is barely enough power to run two lightbulbs in the house for a few hours after dark, let alone charge electronics or have the internet. Even if your phone is charged, there's likely no network so communication is next to impossible.

"I'm just a small dreamer kicking up dust in a big needy country," Jaona said.

That's brave—when the things you want to do seem impossible. But you dream them anyway.

I was only in Moramanga for two days, so I had limited time to trek around barefoot with Jaona. But over the course of those two days, my feet ran down dusty paths and across train tracks and stones. They got caught on bushes and thorns, and stomped in the mud to soften it for bricks. They jumped in puddles. They felt the rough wood of the truck bed and the pain of a brick thrown from the top of the pile, the warmth of the sun and the 10-degree Celsius cool of night, nearly numb.

My feet were covered in dirt and mud, bumps and bruises. Just like his. And they taught me something: shoes do serve a purpose. They keep your feet clean and dry and, for the most part, free from injury.

But Jaona went barefoot anyway, as did I, despite bewildered looks from passersby and children pointing in amazement.

People wondered why. As I looked down at my filthy, worn, battered feet, I grinned and replied, "It makes me feel free."

Many people would look at Jaona and wonder why. Why do you go barefoot when you can wear shoes? Why do you dream when you could be disappointed? Why do you press on when it seems impossible? Why do you take risks when you could play it safe?

And I think he would look down at his filthy, worn, battered feet, flash a mischievous grin, and say, "Because it's just better this way. I'm free."

That's brave—when you decide that feeling pain is better than feeling nothing at all. That being free is better than being protected. That looking spent is better than looking beautiful because spending yourself on behalf of others *is* beautiful.

So what if it brings dirt and scrapes and bruises? So what if I risk it and fail? At least I have felt. At least I have tried. At least I am free.

As I slipped my feet back into my shoes at the end of those two glorious, barefoot days, I took with me a little more than the dirt from Jaona's property. I tucked away a little of his bravery, too.

Because I don't want to avoid dreaming for fear of being disappointed. I don't want to hold back because it seems impossible. I don't want to play it safe because the risk feels too great. And I definitely don't want to wear shoes when I could be barefoot.

Barefoot and brave.

MADAGASCAR: BAREFOOT AND BRAVE

THESE BEAUTIFUL PEOPLE

MALAGASY MANGO TREES

≤ **Ravo's Story** | Amparafaravola, Madagascar

"These are the mango trees my father planted. I remember standing here planting them by his side."

We were standing on the land owned by his mamma, looking at a bunch of Malagasy mango trees on 30 acres of the most beautiful farmland I'd ever seen.

Walking among rows of pineapples, rice, and other fruits and vegetables, our footsteps broke the silence. The view was breathtaking.

I had been in Madagascar a few days. I was staying with Ravo, his wife, Lalasoa, and his son, Mike. Ravo and his family welcomed me with open arms, immediately making me feel at home. Lalasoa was such a fabulous cook that I forgot what it was like to feel hungry.

But more than that, they had a rare love and respect for each other that shone most vividly when Ravo spoke to and about his mamma.

As soon as I met her, I was intrigued. I couldn't communicate or understand her stories—oh, how I wish I could!—but I could see how her son honoured her. Her face was always glowing.

The house they lived in now was Ravo's childhood home. He was born in the room where he and his wife now sleep. He had four brothers; his only sister had passed away several years ago. His parents had been teachers in a public school for 40 years, living in Antananarivo from 1971 until retirement. After retiring, they returned to Amparafaravola, where Ravo's father passed away in 2008.

≤ *Left to right: Mike's cousin, Ravo, Mike, Lalasoa*

MADAGASCAR: MALAGASY MANGO TREES
THESE BEAUTIFUL PEOPLE

Mango trees planted by Ravo and his daddy

Ravo grew up and did most of his schooling in Antananarivo and had the opportunity to go to university in Moscow.

"My dad got me a bursary for school in Russia. These opportunities are usually reserved for government children, not for simple people like my parents."

His parents had accepted Christ around the time he graduated high school. They kept encouraging him to join their cell group.

"I went once. It was strange and a little boring. But I told myself, 'It is just for one year, then I will leave them all and go to school.'"

He survived the year, and in 1989 he left to study mechanical engineering in Moscow for six years.

"But the Lord was waiting to meet me in a special way."

In 1992, in an underground Bible study that was forbidden under the communist regime, Ravo gave his heart to the Lord. He went from wanting nothing to do with a cell group bible study to leading it for his final years of school.

But a relationship with Jesus wasn't the only blessing awaiting Ravo in Moscow.

"I met Lalasoa in Moscow. She was studying hotel management and tourism."

MADAGASCAR: MALAGASY MANGO TREES

THESE BEAUTIFUL PEOPLE

This didn't surprise me at all, after having experienced her hospitality and culinary giftings firsthand.

They were married in Moscow and moved back to Madagascar.

"We had an opportunity to move to France or Switzerland, but we wanted to go back home first to see our families. After deciding to live in Antsirabe, we met a man named David Kadalie, who was the pioneer of Youth for Christ Madagascar."

"We have now worked for Youth for Christ for 17 years. We did not move to Europe."

In that time, Ravo's parents had returned to their home in Amparafaravola. Shortly after, his father passed away, leaving his mother to look after the home and the 30 acres of land she had bought when they first married.

A hard-working businesswoman, she was tough as nails but kind and generous. Meanwhile, all her sons lived and worked in other cities in Madagascar.

"She didn't tell us what was going on because she didn't want to worry us," Ravo said.

It wasn't until a family celebration that they realized something wasn't right.

"She could hardly get out of bed. She was sick. Her face was troubled and we could tell something was desperately wrong."

That's when they found out she wasn't physically sick; she was heartsick.

"People were stealing her land. They tore down the house my dad built on the land. They took advantage of her age and generosity. Everyone knew when her money arrived from the government. The next day, people would be lined up outside her door, asking for loans. Loans they never paid back."

She was losing her land, her livelihood—and in the process—her health.

"When I saw that, I didn't know what to do. Me and my wife prayed and prayed. We were so involved with the ministry of Youth for Christ but I also knew that my brothers could not leave their jobs to go and live with her in the village."

God gave them a vision to start Youth for Christ in Amparafaravola. As the national director of the organization, Ravo knew he could do his job from anywhere in the country.

"We didn't even tell mamma we were coming. One day we decided to move and the next day we packed

Standing with Ravo and his mom (left) after receiving a gift for speaking in a local church

everything up, arrived on her doorstep with the moving vans, and said, 'We are here to stay.'"

They moved in and began slowly working to get back what was taken from her. People spoke poorly of them, knowing they could no longer take advantage. They weren't welcomed in the village, which made it a difficult and discouraging time.

"But we now have all of the land back. Mamma has her health back. She is happy and smiling again."

They cultivated this land to grow rice, fruits, and vegetables to support themselves and the ministry. They also use their home and the little English they know to offer language classes. This has gained the trust of the community, where knowing English is highly valued but extremely rare.

"We moved here to say thank you to mamma. She is 82 years old and she deserves to be taken care of. I read the Word to her every evening and disciple her."

MADAGASCAR: MALAGASY MANGO TREES
THESE BEAUTIFUL PEOPLE

His wide grin and his bright eyes told the story: for him, it was an honour and privilege to look after his aging mother, to give back.

"She has done so much. She raised all of us and brought us all to Christ. Now it is my turn and I do this with great joy!"

In 2016 I got word from Ravo that his mamma had passed away. I can only imagine how painful that must have been. But I also rejoice in the full hearts they must have, knowing they honoured her while they had the chance.

I picture us standing on the most beautiful farmland I've ever seen. I see the pineapples poking their spiky heads out of the ground. I hear Ravo tell me how they are grown; I hear his passion for the land and its potential. I listen to his dreams of building a guesthouse on the land: somewhere they could stay when they work the fields; somewhere guests could stay for a peaceful getaway; somewhere to replace what his father had built that was torn down.

I sense the fondness of his memories and the joy of having reclaimed what was stolen. I see the mango trees and hear him saying, "These are the mango trees my father planted. I remember standing here planting them by his side."

The mango trees are full grown now, bearing fruit and casting shade. At one time they, too, were helpless—tiny seedlings needing to be watered and nurtured. But now they are grown, and it's their turn. Now they give back.

It's a beautiful picture because that's what Ravo and Lalasoa are doing, giving back. The joy on their faces is an example to us all.

It's what so much of Western culture has lost: A respect and an honour for the elderly. A desire rather than an obligation to give back.

More grateful for what we can give than what we've been given. More willing to give back than to get back.

May we be more like Ravo and Lalasoa, and their Malagasy mango trees.

MADAGASCAR: MALAGASY MANGO TREES
THESE BEAUTIFUL PEOPLE

THE HERE AND HOW

Just like that, here we are.

Not at the end, but at a beginning of sorts. So much has changed in the lives of these beautiful people, it's impossible to keep up. Their stories, like yours, are never finished.

These people aren't just characters in a book; they're my friends, my family, my heroes, and my hosts. I'm sure by now you understand these are but a few of the gems excavated from the debris of history. There are more, so many more, if we will only dig deeper. Maybe then we'll realize that we, too, are beautiful people with beautiful stories to tell.

I used to be ashamed of my brokenness. Like the pieces of abuse, addiction, and heartbreak couldn't possibly add up to something beautiful.

And when I brought that box of pieces to Jesus, I hated it. I hated my box full of pain, my disgraceful pieces. But years down the road, as I look back at that day and ahead at the cross, I realize something: It was never about the broken pieces. It was about the box.

The problem isn't our brokenness. The problem is holding on to it instead of bringing it to Jesus, keeping it inside a box, hiding behind a mask. We see ourselves and our stories through the eyes of our brokenness instead of the eyes of Jesus, who *is* wholeness.

THE HERE AND HOW

THESE BEAUTIFUL PEOPLE

"How you choose to see people (including yourself) matters more than what you say or do. I'm convinced that our problem is not that we need more evangelistic tools, methods, arguments, or missional strategies—in fact none of these things are worth anything if we don't first see ourselves and others through the eyes of Jesus. I truly believe people intuitively sense how we feel (think) about them and that makes the biggest difference (Burke 2013)."

Burke goes on to ask, "What do you see when you look at others? What do you see when you look in the mirror? Do you see the mud? Or do you see the masterpiece God wants to restore? (Burke 2013)."

If I'm honest, I see the mud. In myself and in others. In a fit of misguided compassion and an attempt to "be Jesus," I try to clean up the mess myself, to no avail. And the one I try to "fix" sees a muddy picture of the One who longs to lovingly restore His masterpiece.

My problem isn't that I'm not enough. It's that I don't see myself, or others, as Jesus does.

This is what keeps us locked in silence, stuck in ruts of shame. This is what isolates and denies us the power within. The power of our testimony.

Revelation 12:11 says, "Our brothers conquered [the devil] by the blood of the lamb and by the word of their testimony (International Standard Version)."

Claiming the blood of the lamb and sharing our testimony are dangerous because both make Satan shake in his boots. If he can keep you quiet, his work is done. But when you're brave enough to say the hard things, you threaten his plan for isolation and condemnation.

Darkness and light cannot coexist. One chases the other.

Testimony brings the hidden things into the light, where they find healing. Testimony sheds the light of truth on the darkness of the lies we believe. Testimony opens the door for real, authentic relationship and the all-encompassing warmth that comes from knowing we are never, ever alone.

Imagine what would happen if we used our stories to tear down the walls of shame and isolation and to restore hope. Imagine what would happen if we realized we had a story worth telling!

Because we all do. Yes, even you.

So what's your story? Someone, somewhere, needs to hear it.

Here's a couple of next steps to get you from the *here* to the *how*.

1. DOWNLOAD THE SONG "THESE BEAUTIFUL PEOPLE."

Let it speak to your soul and remind you that you, too, are a beautiful person. A beautiful soul.

Get it on any app. Artists: Dokta B and Vallen B, Young 50m Mc Ubamba

2. WERE YOU IMPACTED BY ANY OF THE STORIES YOU READ?

Did one of these beautiful people touch your heart, or teach you something new? Were you encouraged? Do you have a word of encouragement to share?

Drop them a note at www.thesebeautifulpeople.com/THEHOW

3. WANT TO TELL YOUR STORY BUT DON'T KNOW WHERE TO START?

Need some help preparing and knowing how, when, and where to share? Sometimes all it takes is knowing someone is in it with you. Send me an email and let's get in touch.

Go to www.thesebeautifulpeople.com/THEHOW. I'd love to walk this with you.

4. WANT TO KNOW MORE OR GET INVOLVED WITH AN ORGANIZATION OR INITIATIVE YOU LEARNED ABOUT IN THE BOOK?

Connect with us at www.thesebeautifulpeople.com/THEHOW

IF WE REMAIN SILENT ABOUT OUR EXPERIENCES, IF WE REFUSE TO EXERCISE OUR GIFTS, IF WE FAIL TO RECOGNIZE WE'VE BEEN BLESSED TO BE A BLESSING, **WE CAN'T CONTINUE TO BE SURPRISED THAT PEOPLE DON'T KNOW HIM.**

—TWILA

The point is not to have the least dramatic or most traumatic story. When we stand back to look at the big picture, the point is that it looks like Jesus.

Even He has scars. And with those nail-scarred hands and wounded side, he reaches out and draws us in and whispers, "We're in this together."

Together in the *here*. And how do we get there?
Together is the *how*.

≪ *Photograph from Unfrozen Photography*

THE HERE AND HOW

THESE BEAUTIFUL PEOPLE

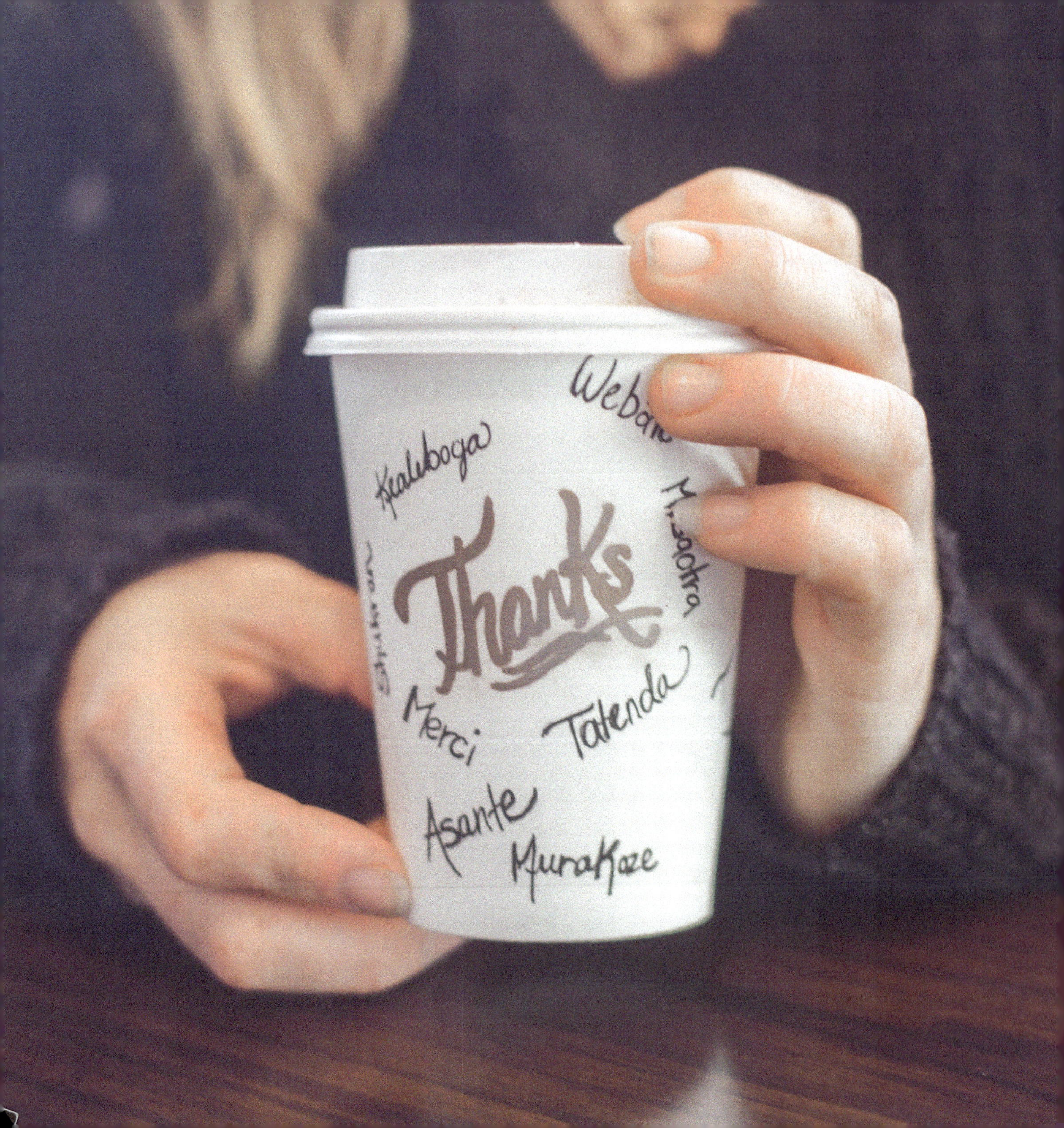
Thanks
Merci
Tatenda
Asante
MuraKoze

THE
HELP

I was not a writer.

As in, I had never written much of anything, ever. I hated blogs, mostly because I thought people only wrote about what they ate for lunch, or ranted about their pet peeves.

So you can imagine my reaction when I heard God say, "You should write a book."

My thought process was simple: "Um, no. Thanks, but no thanks. Hard pass," followed by fits of internal laughter and an immediate dismissal of the thought.

And again, when my Youth for Christ supervisor informed me I would need to write blogs instead of sending newsletters during my time in Africa, I laughed and said, "No, thanks."

He looked me straight in the eye.

"Yeah, you will," he said.

"I don't write." I rebutted, but he wasn't having any of my excuses.

"Just write one, Twila, and see how it goes," he insisted.

≤ *Photograph from Unfrozen Photography*

THE HELP

THESE BEAUTIFUL PEOPLE

I was preparing to leave for my two-year adventure, to share my story and inspire others to find their own. To be ready and willing to follow Him wherever and however. Apparently, I didn't want to start right away.

Yes, I wanted to keep people "in the know" while I was away, but a blog? Really? I *did* prefer the idea over the newsletters, so I did what he asked. I wrote one. And I fell in love with writing.

I'd forgotten all about that still, small voice that told me to write a book of stories until a friend said, "Twila, you need to write a book. Like, compile all the stories of the people you meet over there into a book!"

I'm not sure I was able to disguise my shock.

"Are you kidding me? I'm not a writer! I don't write books!"

Little did I know, that was just the beginning. From that day forward, countless people came to me on different occasions, all saying the same thing: "You should write a book."

Every time I would laugh it off and think of all the reasons I *shouldn't* write a book. But it happened so often that I made a list. I kept track of all the people, from nine countries, who had said those words: Joni, the lady at Williams Coffee Pub, Janine, Joanne, Marlene, Margaret, that random guy in Thailand, Maurice, Ant, Nellie, Pastor Carol, KTB, Benjamin, Sheunesu, Jess, Kayla, MJ, Koekoes, and David.

Finally, at a camp in South Africa in 2015, David Kadalie looked me in the eye and said those same words, but with such intensity that something in my spirit broke. I knew I couldn't resist any longer.

"You should write a book."

"Fine," I said. "I'll do it."

And now here it is. It's been an incredible journey, but I couldn't have done it without help.

Not without the ones who said those words. You didn't know the impact you had. You didn't know I'd already heard the whisper but was refusing to obey. You didn't know that without your words I might not have gained the courage to write this. A million times, thank you.

Not without the support of family and friends. You've been patient with me as I sacrificed my time with you to focus on the book. You encouraged me to take that time and cheered me on with your enthusiasm and excitement for the finished product. You helped me navigate this foreign path where all is new and unfamiliar. You're a part of the reason I made it. Thank you from my heart.

Not without the ones who spent countless hours reading and editing. Joanne, Jo-Ann, Jess, Leslie, Dan, Marcus, Micha, Willard and the rest of the "testing" team. You're a part of the reason this book was ever finished. You were the representation of the people now reading it and your time and insight have been invaluable to me. Thank you. Alexandra, I think we both know I would have drowned without you and your editing expertise. You are competent, creative, and an absolute joy to work with. Thank you for making this *passion project* the best it can be. I'm forever grateful.

Not without the ones who are technological geniuses. Karrie and Sherrie; Clint, Dan, and Susan (FistBump Media); Boaz, Baker, and Roger. You created design after design until the cover and logo were perfect. You worked diligently to organize my hundreds of video clips into a promotional video masterpiece. You offered your expertise in creating, in my opinion, the best website ever. You gave your time and talent to create a song that speaks straight to the soul. You captured these beautiful people through your lens. You found a way to recover all my stories when every single one was deleted from all my devices. You are my strength where I am weak. Thank you.

Not without the ones willing to share their stories. You're the brave ones. You're the bold ones. You entrusted me with your stories and I don't take that responsibility lightly. You allowed yourselves to be used to bring glory to God and hope and healing to others. My most sincere thanks to you, my heroes. Thank you for blessing me with your real stories and relentless hope.

And not without the One who planted the seed in my heart, watered it, and patiently waited for it to grow. You're the creator of these beautiful people and this book was Your idea. You're the One who wrote the original stories, and I'm humbled you would give me such an opportunity to write them down for the world to read. You're my greatest help. For all that You are, *asante Baba*.

Sure, the book has my name on it, but the truth is, I had help. So here's to the help. I couldn't have done it without you.

SELECTED BIBLIOGRAPHY

THE HEART

Adichie, Chimamanda. 2009. "The Danger of a Single Story." *TEDGlobal Talks 2009*. https://www.ted.com/talks/chimamanda_adichie_the_danger_of_a_single_story

UGANDA

"28 Mind-blowing Facts About Uganda." *One African Girl* (blog). January 11, 2016. https://oneafricangirl.com/2016/01/11/27-mind-blowing-facts-about-uganda/

"History of the War 1986 to Now." Invisible Children. 2014. https://invisiblechildren.com/challenge/history/

"Main Source of Household Earning." Uganda Bureau of Statistics. May 15, 2014. http://www.ubos.org/onlinefiles/uploads/ubos/UNHS_12_13/2012_13percent20UNHSpercent20Finalpercent20Report.pdf

"Social, Economic, and Political Context in Uganda." Interactions. April 5, 2010. http://interactions.eldis.org/unpaid-care-work/country-profiles/uganda/social-economic-and-political-context-uganda

"The 20 Most Beautiful Countries in the World." Buzzfeed. May 5, 2015. https://www.buzzfeed.com/travelguru/the-20-most-beautiful-countries-in-the-world-w9r0?utm_term=.lrJVK3Y8W#.wtWpBJMnQ

KENYA

Adharanand, Finn. 2012. "Kenya's Marathon Men." *The Guardian*, April 8, 2012. https://www.theguardian.com/sport/2012/apr/08/kenyas-marathon-men

"Culture of Kenya." Every Culture. March 25, 2006. http://www.everyculture.com/Ja-Ma/Kenya.html

Hodal, Kate. 2016. "Kenyan Creativity Broadens Employment Horizons for Disabled People." *The Guardian,* December 25, 2016. https://www.theguardian.com/global-development/2016/dec/25/kenya-creativity-broadens-employment-horizons-disabled-people-africa-prize-for-engingineering

"Kenya History, Language and Culture." World Travel Guide. 2017. http://www.worldtravelguide.net/kenya/history-language-culture.

"The World Factbook: Kenya." Central Intelligence Agency. Updated March 14, 2018. https://www.cia.gov/library/publications/the-world-factbook/geos/ke.html

"Wangari Maathai: Biography." The Green Belt Movement. September 25, 2011. http://www.greenbeltmovement.org/wangari-maathai/biography

Zimmerman, Kim Ann. 2013. "Olduvai Gorge: Oldest Evidence of Mankind's Evolution." *Live Science,* October 16, 2013. https://www.livescience.com/40455-olduvai-gorge.html

TANZANIA

"20 Fun Facts About Tanzania." Visit Tanzania Tours and Safaris. June 19, 2015. https://www.visittanzaniasafaris.com/20-fun-facts-about-tanzania/

"Culture of Tanzania." Every Culture. March 28, 2006. http://www.everyculture.com/Sa-Th/Tanzania.html

Dronacharya, Dave. 2015. "12 Interesting Facts About Tanzania You Did Not Know About." Linked In. October 19, 2015. https://www.linkedin.com/pulse/12-interesting-facts-tanzania-you-did-know-dronacharya-dave

Meades, Sian. 2016. "Hungry Hikers Get a Pizza Delivered... 19,341 Feet Above Sea Level." *Express,* May 12, 2016. https://www.express.co.uk/travel/articles/669585/pizza-hut-delivery-mount-kilamanjaro

"The World Factbook: Tanzania." Central Intelligence Agency. Updated March 14, 2018. https://www.cia.gov/library/publications/the-world-factbook/geos/tz.html

"Top 10 Facts About Tanzania." *Express,* December 9, 2016. http://www.express.co.uk/life-style/top10facts/741408/Top-10-facts-about-Tanzania

Ubwani, Zephania. 2017. "Why Tanzanian Engineer Impressed Top US Varsity." *The Citizen,* July 22, 2017. http://www.thecitizen.co.tz/News/Why-Tanzanian-engineer--impressed-top-US-varsity/1840340-4027262-format-xhtml-xek8knz/index.html

SOUTH SUDAN

"Sudan." Every Culture. September 14, 2005. http://www.everyculture.com/Sa-Th/Sudan.html

"South Sudan's warring parties agree ceasefire in bid to end four-year war." *The Guardian,* December 23, 2017. https://www.theguardian.com/world/2017/dec/23/south-sudans-warring-parties-agree-ceasefire-bid-end-four-year-war-machar-kiir

"The World Factbook: South Sudan." Central Intelligence Agency. Updated March 14, 2018. https://www.cia.gov/library/publications/the-world-factbook/geos/od.html

RWANDA

Annobil, Akosua. 2015. "10 Interesting Facts About Rwanda." Africa Business 2020. July 21, 2015. http://africabusiness2020.com/2015/07/21/10-interesting-facts-about-rwanda/

"Culture of Rwanda." Every Culture. March 26, 2006. http://www.everyculture.com/No-Sa/Rwanda.html

Southgate, Mandy. 2011. "Rwandan Genocide: The Hutu Ten Commandments." *Passion to Understand* (blog). August 13, 2011. http://passiontounderstand.blogspot.ca/2011/08/rwandan-genocide-hutu-ten-commandments.html

"The World Factbook: Rwanda." Central Intelligence Agency. Updated March 14, 2018. https://www.cia.gov/library/publications/the-world-factbook/geos/rw.html

BURUNDI

"Culture of Burundi." Every Culture. March 27, 2006. http://www.everyculture.com/Bo-Co/Burundi.html

"The World Factbook: Burundi." Central Intelligence Agency. Updated March 14, 2018. https://www.cia.gov/library/publications/the-world-factbook/geos/by.html

SOMETHING FROM NOTHING

Tuyizere, Freddy. 2017. *Where the Cow Grass Grows: Planting Faith and Hope in Burundi*. http://bbtmz.itpp.me/where_the_cow_grass_grows_planting_faith_and_hope_in_burundi_0692893822.aspx

ZIMBABWE

"48 Interesting Facts About Zimbabwe." The Fact File. Updated March 11, 2018. http://thefactfile.org/zimbabwe-facts/

"Culture of Zimbabwe." Every Culture. March 27, 2006. http://www.everyculture.com/To-Z/Zimbabwe.html

"The World Factbook: Zimbabwe." Central Intelligence Agency. Updated March 14, 2018. https://www.cia.gov/library/publications/the-world-factbook/geos/zi.html

BOTSWANA

"Botswana 50—50 Fun Facts About Botswana." Desert and Delta Safaris. September 29, 2016. http://www.desertdelta.com/blog/general-news/botswana-50-fun-facts/

"Culture of Botswana." Every Culture. September 14, 2005. http://www.everyculture.com/Bo-Co/Botswana.html

De Gaspari, Sabine. 2015. "13 Interesting Facts About Botswana." *The Travelling Chilli* (blog). August 17, 2015. https://www.thetravellingchilli.com/13-interesting-facts-about-botswana/

"The World Factbook: Botswana." Central Intelligence Agency. Updated March 14, 2018. https://www.cia.gov/library/publications/the-world-factbook/geos/bc.html

"World's Second-Largest Diamond Found in Botswana." *BBC News*, November 19, 2015. http://www.bbc.com/news/world-africa-34867929

AMAZING GRACE—FOR EVEN ME

Brill, Richard. n.d. "How Is a Star Born?" Scientific American. n.d. https://www.scientificamerican.com/article/how-is-a-star-born/

Nield, David. 2015. "Sound Can Travel Through Space After All—But We Can't Hear It." Science Alert. October 30, 2015. https://www.sciencealert.com/sound-can-travel-through-space-after-all-but-we-can-t-hear-it

SOUTH AFRICA

"7 Interesting Facts About Gold Mining in South Africa." Gold Bullion Pro. December 6, 2012. http://www.goldbullionpro.com/7-interesting-facts-about-gold-mining-in-south-africa/

"A History of Apartheid in South Africa." South African History Online. May 6, 2016. http://www.sahistory.org.za/article/history-apartheid-south-africa

Brown, Ryan Lenora. 2017. "56 Miles of Freedom." Runner's World. June 4, 2017. https://www.runnersworld.com/rw-selects/56-miles-of-freedom

Bruton, Mike. 2011. "SA Invention Cleans the World's Pools." *IOL,* 23 September, 2011. https://www.iol.co.za/lifestyle/home-garden/garden/sa-inventions-clean-the-worlds-pools-1143684

"Culture of South Africa." Every Culture. March 29, 2006. http://www.everyculture.com/Sa-Th/South-Africa.html

"First Human Heart Transplant." History. July 21, 2010. http://www.history.com/this-day-in-history/first-human-heart-transplant

Howard, Anne, and Mike Howard. 2012. *Honey Trek* (blog). August 29, 2012. "Longest Wine Route in the World." http://www.honeytrek.com/longest-wine-route-in-the-world/

"South Africa: Interesting Facts and Trivia." Why Go South Africa. n.d. https://www.southafricalogue.com/travel-tips/south-africa-interesting-facts-and-trivia.html

"The World Factbook: South Africa." Central Intelligence Agency. Updated March 14, 2018. https://www.cia.gov/library/publications/the-world-factbook/geos/sf.html

MADAGASCAR

"Culture of Madagscar." Every Culture. March 26, 2006. http://www.everyculture.com/Ja-Ma/Madagascar.html

"Elephant Birds." BBC. February 25, 2011. http://www.bbc.co.uk/nature/life/Elephant_bird

"Madagascar." The Observatory of Economic Complexity. October 9, 2017. https://atlas.media.mit.edu/en/profile/country/mdg/

"The Real Animals of Madagascar." Wild Madagascar. March 31, 2005. http://www.wildmadagascar.org/wildlife/animals.html

"The World Factbook: Madagascar." Central Intelligence Agency. Updated March 14, 2018. https://www.cia.gov/library/publications/the-world-factbook/geos/ma.html

THE HERE AND HOW

Burke, John. 2013. *Mud and the Masterpiece.* Grand Rapids: Baker Books.

CPSIA information can be obtained
at www.ICGtesting.com
Printed in the USA
LVHW07s1542280818
588154LV00002B/2/P

9 781525 528781